SOCIAL SECURITY IN THE UNITED STATES

A Da Capo Press Reprint Series

FRANKLIN D. ROOSEVELT
AND THE ERA OF THE NEW DEAL
GENERAL EDITOR: FRANK FREIDEL
Harvard University

SOCIAL SECURITY IN THE UNITED STATES

An Analysis and Appraisal of the Federal Social Security Act

BY

PAUL H. DOUGLAS

DA CAPO PRESS · NEW YORK · 1971

A Da Capo Press Reprint Edition

This Da Capo Press edition of
Social Security in the United States
is an unabridged republication of the
second edition published in New York in 1939.

Library of Congress Catalog Card Number 70-167847
SBN 306-70323-8

Published by Da Capo Press, Inc.
A Subsidiary of Plenum Publishing Corporation
227 West 17th Street, New York, N.Y. 10011

Manufactured in the United States of America

SOCIAL SECURITY
IN THE UNITED STATES

SOCIAL SECURITY IN THE UNITED STATES

An Analysis and Appraisal of the Federal Social Security Act

BY

PAUL H. DOUGLAS

Professor of Economics
The University of Chicago

New York WHITTLESEY HOUSE *London*

MCGRAW-HILL BOOK COMPANY, INC.

SECOND EDITION

PUBLISHED BY WHITTLESEY HOUSE
A division of the McGraw-Hill Book Company, Inc.

Printed in the United States of America by The Maple Press Co., York, Pa.

To

ROBERT F. WAGNER
ABRAHAM EPSTEIN
I. M. RUBINOW

Pioneers in the Movement for
Genuine Social Insurance

PREFACE TO THE SECOND EDITION

IN PREPARING a second edition of this book, I have somewhat altered the sequence of material which originally appeared in Part III and have made a few minor changes. I have also written additional chapters giving the progress of events in 1936, in 1937 and in the early part of 1938, respectively. In writing these last chapters, I have of necessity been compelled to use the present tense.

PAUL H. DOUGLAS.

CHICAGO, ILLINOIS,
December, 1938.

PREFACE TO THE FIRST EDITION

IN THIS book I have tried, not only to explain what the Federal Social Security Act provides, but also to trace the steps by which it came into being and to outline some of the problems in the field of social security which lie ahead. This act is, in my opinion, the most important which has thus far been passed under the present national administration. It is by no means perfect and, as the reader will see, I believe that it should be changed in certain vital respects. But it is a decided step forward and a worthy effort to protect better the lives of the wage-earners and salaried employees. One who for fifteen years has worked for such legislation may perhaps derive a pardonable sense of satisfaction in the fact that the American public has finally realized that it needs the greater protection against unemployment and old age which pooled social insurance gives.

In its larger aspects, the law is in the tradition which the Western European nations established during a period of expanding capitalism. Whether our newly established system can survive in its present form will depend not only upon the Supreme Court but also upon whether or not capitalism itself will continue in a substantially healthy state. If unemployment should maintain its present level for a long period, then it is quite clear that we shall have to use methods very different from those laid down in the present act.

Moreover, as I read the proof sheets in this strangely beautiful Italian city, I cannot but be haunted by the twin menaces of war and of the prolonged depression which overhang the world. Whatever the ultimate future may hold, it is certainly true that the prospects for the immediate years before us are not bright. In their social actions men are indeed curious, blundering and at times malevolent children. With one side of their nature they build up a flourishing material civilization embellished by beauty and by culture. With another side they seek to tear down and to befoul all that is fine. Perhaps there never was a time when the creative aspects of life were more widely menaced by these darker forces than now. Upon our generation is laid the heavy task of mastering these baser elements and of building a more secure and a more gracious life, not only for the few, but for the multitude as well.

From such somber thoughts, it is a pleasure to turn to the grateful duty of acknowledging the aid that I have received from numerous friends and associates. To I. M. Rubinow and Abraham Epstein I owe a great deal, not only in the way of specific suggestions, but also in the general stimulation that many years of association with them have brought. Dr. Joseph P. Harris, formerly Associate Director of the Committee on Economic Security, has helped me to understand some of the tangled issues connected with the so-called Clark Amendment. Mr. and Mrs. Richard W. Hogue were good enough to read the manuscript of the first four chapters and I have profited greatly by their suggestions and criticisms. To my friend and former student, Mr. Donald M. Smith, I owe much. He has helped to reduce the history of unemployment insurance legislation during the last five years in our forty-eight states to comparative order and during my absence from the country he has borne the major responsibility for seeing the manuscript through the press. My secretary, Miss Judith Lewis, has also been most helpful. But as in everything else, I owe most to my wife.

PAUL H. DOUGLAS.

SIENA, ITALY,
November, 1935.

CONTENTS

[xiii]

CONTENTS

PART FOUR

DEVELOPMENTS UNDER THE ACT

Part One

THE BACKGROUND

CHAPTER I

THE TIDE TURNS

The Opposition to Social Insurance

THE recent federal Security Act is the result of a very sharp change in public opinion. Prior to the great depression, the consensus of public opinion was that American citizens could in the main provide for their own old age by individual savings.[1] So far as unemployment was concerned, the articulate American public predominantly believed either that unemployment was being reduced to very narrow limits by "the stabilization of industry," or that unemployment insurance was a debasing "dole" which subsidized men for being idle and hence led them to shun work.[2]

This individualistic attitude toward the meeting of great social risks was of course characteristic of

---

[1] Yet see, of course earlier books such as Squier, *Old Age Dependency in the United States* (1912); Epstein, *Facing Old Age* (1922) and *The Challenge of the Aged* (1928), together with the investigations of the earlier commissions appointed in Massachusetts to investigate the subject.

[2] In the early part of the twenties, however, Professor John R. Commons and his group sponsored the individual responsibility plan which was presented to the Wisconsin legislature in the Huber bill. See Allen B. Forsberg, *Unemployment Insurance*, pp. 163–248; see also the pamphlets issued by the Wisconsin Association for the Prevention of Unemployment and Commons, "Unemployment Compensation and Prevention," *Survey*, Vol. XLVII (October 1, 1921), pp. 5–9.

the America of the twenties. The belief in rugged individualism, first created by the frontier but finding emotional support from the upward surge of the stock market, was a powerful force holding back all protective legislation while the rise in real wages lulled the majority of the working class into a condition of more or less acquiescent satisfaction. The struggle by organized labor to hold its own in the economic world against the attrition of prosperity and the vigorous opposition of powerful corporations left them with little energy to apply toward protective legislation for their members and their class. They were, moreover, hindered in making any such effort by the doctrine of collective self-help and anti-statism which Gompers had impressed upon the American labor movement for over forty years. Nor was there a strong political party of the left, as in Europe, to force the more conservative parties into passing social legislation in order to retain the working-class vote. For during the twenties the Socialist party almost literally withered away, and in 1928 polled less than 1 per cent of the votes cast in the Presidential election.

In addition, the presence of the forty-eight states, each supposedly sovereign in labor and industrial matters, made it difficult to get action even where there was a popular will. For commerce was in large part interstate, and if any one state imposed a tax or laid down a set of labor conditions which raised costs, it thereby placed many of the employers within its borders at a competitive disadvantage in the business struggle as compared with other firms in states which did not have such legislation. This pressure restrained the more progressive states from pioneering as they would have liked and kept the country as a whole closer to the legal conditions in the less progressive states. It is small wonder, therefore, that this country complacently drifted through the twenties with little effort to provide pooled protection against the great risks of indigent old age, unemployment and sickness which even in the boom years were playing havoc with the lives of so many.

The Change of Opinion about Old Age Pensions

But even prior to the depression, there were certain undercurrents of public opinion which were beginning to change on the subject of old age pensions. This was evidenced by the passage of optional acts on the part of eight states, which permitted the counties to pay old age pensions, and which in the case of Wisconsin and Minnesota provided for some state aid to any county which took such action.[1] This drift was caused by the increasing proportion of old people in the total population[2] and by the increasing inability of these old people to obtain gainful employment.[3] This latter development was

[1] These were Montana, Nevada, Colorado, Kentucky, Maryland, Wisconsin, Minnesota and Utah.

[2] In 1890 those sixty-five years and over formed 3.0 per cent of the total population. In 1930, they formed 5.4 per cent.

[3] In 1930, 41.7 per cent of those over sixty-five were not gainfully employed as compared with 26.2 per cent in 1890.

in turn created by the decrease in the proportion of persons who were self-employed as agriculture, the handicrafts and small trade gave way to large-scale industrialism and by the increasing speed of industry which made it more difficult for old people to be reemployed once they had lost their jobs. A growing dislike of county poor farms as proper institutions to care for the indigent aged also contributed to these undercurrents of sentiment. They were also fed by the propaganda work of the Fraternal Order of Eagles, which had embraced the cause of old age security, and by the intelligent activities of the American Association for Old Age Security under the able direction of Abraham Epstein.

But the depression made these somewhat submerged undercurrents far more dominant. The incidence of unemployment was especially severe upon the aged as well as upon the youths.[1] In addition, the failure of banks and the great declines in the values of real estate and of stocks and bonds completely swept away the savings of many persons and greatly impaired the reserves of even more. By the end of 1934 there were approximately three-quarters of a million aged persons who were on direct relief from the federal government, in addition to those receiving maintenance from other sources. The impact of all these forces increasingly

---

[1] Thus, the Massachusetts Census of Unemployment for 1934 which showed an average unemployment of 25.2 per cent also showed percentages of 27.2 and 29.8 for those from sixty to sixty-four and sixty-five to sixty-nine years respectively. See Report on Census of Unemployment in Massachusetts; January 2, 1934, *Massachusetts Labor Bulletin* 171, p. 8.

convinced the majority of the American people that individuals could not by themselves provide adequately for their old age and that some form of greater security should be provided by society.

As a result of all this, as the depression deepened, the states of the north and west began to pass old age pension laws. These almost universally tended to be mandatory acts instead of the optional laws of the twenties. California and Wyoming led off with this new type of legislation in 1929 and were followed by New York and Massachusetts in 1930.[1] Five more states passed such laws in 1931.[2] Then in 1933 there came a rapid flood of laws when no less than ten states[3] passed such measures. In 1934 one state, Iowa, passed a mandatory law. In addition, several of the optional states, notably Wisconsin and Minnesota, changed their laws to a mandatory basis. By the middle of 1934 there were, therefore, twenty-eight states and two territories (Hawaii and Alaska) which had old age pension acts, of which twenty-three were mandatory and five optional. By this time there were approximately 180,000 aged persons receiving such pensions, as compared with some 70,000 at the end of 1931 and 114,000 by the end of 1933. By the end of 1934, there were 231,000 aged persons on the pension rolls.

[1] See I. M. Rubinow, *The Care of the Aged* (1931).

[2] That is, Colorado, Delaware, Idaho, New Jersey and New Hampshire. The Colorado law replaced the previous optional law, which had been declared unconstitutional.

[3] That is, Arizona, Indiana, Maine, Michigan, Nebraska, North Dakota, Ohio, Oregon, Pennsylvania and Washington.

In addition to the movement towards mandatory legislation, the eligibility rules governing pensions were also liberalized. While the earlier laws had in general fixed seventy years as the pensionable age, the later acts tended instead to use sixty-five years. There was also a tendency to permit the pensioners to own several thousands of dollars of private property and to permit them to receive some personal income which would not be deducted dollar for dollar from the public pensions. Naturally also the mandatory pension laws almost invariably carried with them either exclusive financial support by the states or gave at least some state aid to the local governments in meeting them.

The American laws differed from the non-contributory pension systems abroad in requiring that the children and other immediate relatives of the aged persons must be unable to support them before such aid could be given. The personal responsibility of the family was, therefore, stressed far more under our American legislation than it has been in European pension systems.

The old age pension movement was, however, handicapped by two factors. (1) There were still twenty states without any pension laws, while if the ineflective optional laws were included, this total amounted to nearly twenty-five.[1] No pensions at all were being paid in the thirteen southern states. Illinois was still refusing to take action, while

[1] The optional laws always had greater coverage in the west than in the south.

Kansas, Oklahoma, New Mexico and South Dakota were still outside the fold. Similarly, three conservative New England states, Vermont, Rhode Island and Connecticut, had no laws. Maine, Kentucky and West Virginia had paid no pensions under their laws. It was probably no accident that the reluctance of the dominant race to provide pensions for aged Negroes, Mexicans and Indians accounted for a part at least of the slowness of the southern states, and for the failure of Oklahoma and New Mexico to take action. The counties where pensions were being paid included in fact only slightly over 40 per cent of the population. (2) The burdens of the depression and the growing financial difficulties of state and local governments prevented most of the states which had laws from paying adequate benefits. The average monthly pension for the earlier part of 1934 was about $19 or $20,[1] but by December of that year it had fallen to as low as $16.16.

Unless some form of federal aid were, therefore, extended the prospects were that many states would not adopt old age pensions at all, while the amounts granted would be grossly inadequate in many others.[2]

For some time Abraham Epstein and the American Association for Old Age Security had been trying to have Congress stimulate the states to take action by giving them federal grants-in-aid equal

---

[1] *Report to the President of the Committee on Economic Security*, p. 24.
[2] The actual status of old age pension payments by states is further shown

to one-third of their total expenditures for such pensions. Such a bill had been introduced in previous sessions by Senator Dill of Washington,[1] and

by the following table.

TABLE I

State	Number of pensioners, December, 1933	Number of pensioners, December, 1934	Pensions per 1,000 population in pension counties	Total expenditures 1934 in thousands of dollars
Arizona	1,629	2,010	4.61	518
California	14,604	19,619	3.46	4,289
Colorado	8,139	11,061	10.68	1,045
Delaware	1,586	1,583	6.65	193
Idaho	1,288	1,277	3.68	139
Indiana	......	23,289	7.44	1,434
Iowa	......	4,589	1.86	122
Maryland	131	262	.29	61
Massachusetts	18,516	20,517	4.82	5,750
Michigan	......	3,557	.84	103
Minnesota	2,566	4,753	2.41	611
Montana	1,034	1,309	3.45	180
Nebraska	107	1,115	2.48	20
New Hampshire	1,131	1,423	3.06	299
New Jersey	9,015	11,401	2.87	1,773
New York	51,106	51,834	4.12	12,651
North Dakota	......	3,914	5.75	24
Ohio	......	36,544	5.50	1,431
Oregon	......	6,484	6.82	600
Utah	944	1,122	2.87	117
Washington	7	2,464	2.41	250
Wisconsin	1,756	2,198	2.00	468
Wyoming	701	798	3.69	108
Grand total	114,260	213,123	3.98	32,186

Taken from *Social Security*, 1935, p. 237.

[1] See *Hearings before a Sub-committee of the Committee on Pensions*; United States Senate, 71st Congress, 3rd Session, on S. 3257 (1931); *Hearings, etc.*, 72nd Congress, 1st Session on S. 3037 (1932).

in 1933–1934 it was jointly sponsored by him and by Representative Connery.[1] This bill was not initiated by the administration nor actively supported by it, but it nevertheless met with the overwhelming approval of the legislators.

Those who were closely in touch with the sentiment of Congress during the closing months of the session of 1934 know how by that time legislative opinion had come enthusiastically to favor such federal action. The Labor Committee in the House and the Pensions Committee in the Senate both reported the Dill-Connery bill out with a favorable recommendation. Its authors apparently made repeated efforts to obtain the President's approval for it and to induce him to include it in his list of "must" legislation. But the President did not give the bill his sanction and this fact held it up in the Rules Committee of the House and prevented it from coming to a vote there. It would have passed the Senate during the closing hours of the session had it not been for a last-minute objection by one of the senators. The President's desire to combine old age pensions with a general program of social security and his belief that a unified program should be worked out were, therefore, powerful factors in preventing Congress from passing the Dill-Connery bill and also in impeding the passage of the Wagner-Lewis act, which will be mentioned later. This

---

[1] See *Hearings before the Committee on Labor*, House of Representatives, 73rd Congress, 2nd Session, on H.R. 1623; 7050; 7144; etc. (1934). *Hearings before the Committee on Pensions*, United States Senate, 73rd Congress, 2nd Session, on S. 493 (1934).

failure to act helped in turn to create the Townsend movement, which arose in the summer of 1934.

Unemployment Insurance

Let us now briefly review the situation as regards unemployment insurance. As it became apparent that recovery was not to be immediate, interest in this form of protection began to grow. Conferences were called in 1930 by the American Association for Labor Legislation and a plan was drawn up by this group which was modeled upon the Huber bill of Wisconsin, which had originally been drafted by Professor John R. Commons. This plan broke sharply with European precedents in that it made the employers the sole contributors in the belief that this would stimulate them to stabilize production and greatly reduce unemployment. This was said to be "the American plan" for handling industrial risks instead of the alleged European method of merely enduring them and then providing cash relief as a mitigation. By labeling it as "the American plan" the proponents of this measure also hoped to be able to head off demagogic criticism that it was "un-American." In its details, the plan called for the classification of industries into groups, each of which was to have a mutual insurance fund and which was to pay benefits only to the workers in those industries. These industrial funds were to be controlled by the employers. When the governing board of five was initially set up by a state, a majority were to be employers, and if the major

group of employers desired to elect a board composed completely of their representatives they
could do so and they could also set up employment
offices under their direction. The plan, moreover,
also permitted individual employers to "contract
out" from the industry funds and under certain
safeguards set up their own systems of plant
reserves.[1]

Certain advocates of the insurance principle,
however, of whom the present author was one,
came to believe that this plan contained great
dangers. Separate plant and industry funds were
opposed by this latter group because of the great
inequality of benefits which would necessarily
result from the wide differences between them in
the volume of unemployment. A state-wide pool
was, therefore, instead advocated to equalize and
ensure benefits. Control by the employers over the
funds and the employment offices was thought to
strengthen unduly the employers' associations and
the company "unions" and to reduce the possibility of effective organization on the part of
labor. This group was, moreover, decidedly skepti-
cal about the degree to which individual employers
or even an entire industry could stabilize employment, and did not believe that the proposed system

---

[1] See *An American Plan for Unemployment Reserve Funds*, issued by
American Association for Labor Legislation (1930); also Leo Wolman,
Unemployment Insurance for the United States, American Association for
Labor Legislation (1931). The report of Governor Pinchot's Pennsylvania
Committee on Unemployment, entitled *Alleviating Unemployment* (1931),
also reproduces the proposed draft of this bill, pp. 44–49.

of plant reserves would stimulate any very dynamic drive in this direction.[1] Finally, some of them felt that in order to obtain more adequate benefits, to ensure democratic control of the administration, and to obtain the cooperation of the workers in preventing malingering, a small contribution on the part of the employees would be desirable.

In Ohio, a group sponsored by the Cleveland Consumers League was studying the whole question. After it had compared these two conflicting points of view and had carried on independent investigations, it declared in favor of a state-wide pooled fund under public and not employer control, and with joint contributions by both the workers and the employers. It accordingly introduced a bill in the Ohio legislature which was drafted along these lines by Marvin C. Harrison. This bill was copied in Michigan and Illinois.[2]

More radical plans were drafted in the same year by the Conference for Progressive Labor Action and by the Socialist party. Both of these plans emphasized contributions by the government as

---

[1] See my article, "To What Degree Can Business Prevent Unemployment," *American Labor Legislation Review* (September, 1930), pp. 273–281, For a further criticism of the claims of the stabilizers see, I. M. Rubinow, "Stabilization versus Insurance," *Social Service Review*, Vol. V (June, 1931). pp. 199–213.

[2] For the main text of this bill with one or two modifications see *Alleviating Unemployment*, pp. 49–59; also Paul H. Douglas, "American Plans of Unemployment Insurance," *Survey Graphic*, Vol. LXV (February, 1931), pp. 484–486; Carter Goodrich, "American Plans for State Unemployment Insurance," *American Economic Review*, Vol. XXI (September, 1931), pp. 399–415.

well as by the employers, and advocated much longer benefit periods than those provided for in either of the other two drafts.[1] But while these proposals contributed to the ferment of ideas, their influence on actual legislation was slight.[2]

The first prominent political leader to advocate unemployment insurance had been Franklin D. Roosevelt, when he was governor of New York. This he did in the summer of 1930 at the conference of governors in Salt Lake City, and in January, 1931, he assembled the governors of seven eastern states in Albany to consider whether they could not jointly work out a program.[3] Out of this conference grew a continuing committee, which reported in the following year. The idea of unemployment insurance was, therefore, gaining ground; but the type which was being predominantly considered was the Wisconsin system of separate reserves. During the legislative sessions of 1931 the bills introduced were predominantly of the type advocated by the American Association for Labor Legislation. The movement for the system of separate employer liability was still further stimulated by the passage of the pioneer Wisconsin act in the early part of

[1] For a description of these plans see my article in *Survey Graphic* previously listed. Also Dale Yoder, "Some Economic Implications of Unemployment Insurance," *Quarterly Journal of Economics*, Vol. XLV (1931), pp. 622–639.

[2] The Socialist bill was, however, introduced into a number of state legislatures, including those of Pennsylvania, Illinois, New York, New Jersey, Connecticut, California, Vermont and Wisconsin.

[3] See *Proceedings of the Conference on Unemployment and Interstate Industrial Problems* (1931).

1932.[1] This bill carried the movement for employer responsibility and the separateness of the reserve funds still further by setting up isolated company reserves instead of the industry funds which previously had been proposed. The Wisconsin act was then substantially adopted as the model advocated by the Association for Labor Legislation. Incidentally it should be noted that the Wisconsin act was not to go into effect until July 1, 1933, and then only if voluntary plans conforming to approved standards had not been extended to cover at least 175,000 employees throughout the state. As a matter of fact, due to a further extension of time the collection of premiums did not start until July, 1934, while the payment of benefits has not yet commenced.

The movement toward separate plant reserves was further strengthened in the early part of 1932 by the endorsement given to it by the continuing committee set up by the Albany conference which had been called a year earlier by Governor Roosevelt.[2] Toward the end of 1932, however, the plan of a pooled fund began rapidly to gain ground. The original Ohio bill of 1931 had of course not been passed, but out of it had come a state commission

[1] For the text of this act, see Douglas, *Standards of Unemployment Insurance*, pp. 200–218. The text is also given with accompanying discussion in Hoar, *Unemployment Insurance in Wisconsin* (1932), and *Handbook on the Wisconsin Unemployment Compensation Act*, issued by Wisconsin Industrial Commission (1932). See also Paul Raushenbush, "The Wisconsin Idea: Unemployment Reserves," *Annals*, November, 1933, pp. 65–76.

[2] For this document, see Douglas, *Standards of Unemployment Insurance*, pp. 219–225.

to study the question. This commission, with Miss Elizabeth Magee as secretary, held hearings throughout the state, and finally at the end of the year produced an extraordinarily able two-volume report, which was by all odds the best American study of the question which had been made.[1] With a wealth of detailed analysis, this committee reaffirmed the proposal for a single pooled fund under public control and with joint contributions. The contributions for workers were fixed at 1 per cent of their wages, while those for employers were to average 2 per cent; but after an initial period the latter might be varied according to merit rating between a minimum of 1 and a maximum of 3½ per cent. This bill was vigorously pushed in the legislature by Senator Harrison and by the labor and reform groups behind it. While it did not pass both houses of the legislature it did arouse public sentiment.[2]

At about the same time that the Ohio report appeared, the American Federation of Labor at its Cincinnati meeting reversed the unfavorable stand which it had previously taken in its two preceding conventions regarding compulsory unemployment insurance and came out with a direct and powerful endorsement of it. This reversal of position was largely caused by the vigorous action at the con-

---

[1] *Report of the Ohio Commission on Unemployment Insurance* (1932, 1933), 2 vol.

[2] For a valuable analysis of the whole situation in Ohio by a skilled participant, see I. M. Rubinow, "The Movement Towards Unemployment Insurance in Ohio," *Social Service Review*, Vol. VII (1933), pp. 186–224.

vention of President John L. Lewis of the United Mine Workers. It is probable also that the opposition of many of the leaders of the A. F. of L. had been weakened both by the severity of the depression and by a growing movement within their own rank and file which was demanding action.[1]

Within the growing movement for insurance, the Ohio plan made increasing headway. Despite the fact that the various state legislatures convened very shortly after the Ohio report was issued, there were almost as many bills introduced in 1933 in the legislatures on the Ohio as on the Wisconsin model.[2] The American Association for Old Age Security, which under the leadership of Mr. Epstein had been the leader in the old age pension movement, broadened its name and purpose to cover the whole field of social insurance and threw its influence behind the proposals for pooled funds. Of the three books which appeared on the subject during 1932, one favored plant reserves,[3] one a combination of industrial and plant reserves,[4] while the third advocated among other features the principle of the

---

[1] Thus, a strong movement in this direction grew up in Ohio.

[2] A study by Donald M. Smith of the University of Chicago shows that of a total of fifty-six bills of this year which he was able to trace and examine, eighteen provided separate employers reserves; sixteen followed the Ohio plan of a pooled fund with merit rating; seven had industry reserves; six were radical bills—two of them of the type later to be known as the Lundeen plan; six bills provided for a pooled fund without merit rating. See Smith, *A Comparison of State Unemployment Insurance Measures*, 1930–1935, p. 4 (M.A. thesis, University of Chicago Library).

[3] Ewing, *Job Insurance*.

[4] Hansen and Murray, *A New Plan for Unemployment Reserves*.

pooled statewide fund.[1] The next two books on the
general subject of social insurance, namely, those
by Epstein and Rubinow, strongly supported the
idea of a pooled fund. In addition there was an
increasing volume of books throughout this period
on the problems and accomplishments of unemployment insurance abroad.[2] It is significant that,
during these legislative sessions, unemployment
insurance bills passed one house of seven state
legislatures, namely, those of Ohio, Maryland,
Connecticut, Utah, Minnesota, California and New
York. While these measures were killed in every
instance in the other chamber, the fact of their
progress was indicative of changes which were going
on in the mind of the public. All these factors
played their part in influencing public opinion.

It was the feeling of most advocates of unemployment insurance at this time, however, that the
states would have to be the primary agencies in
the passage of such acts.[3] It was recognized that
this would create enormous difficulties in the way of

---

[1] Douglas, *Standards of Unemployment Insurance* (1933).

[2] See the series published by the Industrial Relations Counsellors: (1)
Gilson, *Unemployment Insurance in Great Britain*; (2) Spates and Rabinovich,
Unemployment Insurance in Switzerland; (3) Kichel, *Unemployment Insur-
ance in Belgium*; and (4) the earlier study of Bryce Stewart and others on
Unemployment Benefits in the United States. See also Mollie Carroll, *Unem-
ployment Insurance in Germany* (1929) and *Unemployment Insurance in
Austria* (1932); Helen Hohman, *British Social Insurance and the Minimum
Wage*; Douglas and Director, *The Problem of Unemployment*. Among other
books contributing to the movement should be mentioned Calkins, *Some
Folks Won't Work*.

[3] The People's Lobby from the first, however, urged national action; as
did later the advocates of the Lundeen bill.

action because each state would fear that, in assessing its industries to support such a system, it would place them at a great competitive disadvantage with employers in those states which did not take such action. But in view of newness of the subject and the fact that the federal constitution gave no explicit power to the national government to legislate on such matters, the reluctant judgment seemed to be that the chief reliance must be placed on state action. This belief was reinforced by the conservative temper of the Supreme Court. Such federal action as was advocated was in the main confined to the following proposals: (1) laws for those directly engaged in interstate commerce; (2) federal grants-in-aid primarily on a "matching" basis to states which passed unemployment insurance acts; and (3) exemption from the federal income tax of payments made by private employers to unemployment insurance funds.

As a result of the depression and the discussion which was being carried on, the public mind was increasingly coming to favor some form of unemployment insurance. The strongest force working in this direction was the growing realization that our relief system was at best inadequate, humiliating and at times uncertain. The average amounts granted per family scarcely averaged over $20 per month. This amounted to about $4.50 a month or 15 cents a day per person. This was the average for the country as a whole, while in many states the amounts were, of course, much less. There were, in fact, some states where the average monthly grants per family were only between $6 and $10. It was becoming realized that the country needed to provide better protection against unemployment, and that self-respecting persons should not be ground into destitution before grudging aid was given. A strong feeling developed, therefore, for some form of insurance which would be granted without a humiliating means test and which would give the unemployed a buffer before they were stripped of all their slender resources.

The Wagner-Lewis Bill of 1934

In February, 1934, Senator Wagner of New York and Representative David J. Lewis of Maryland jointly introduced a bill which had been drafted in the Department of Labor and which was designed to speed up the process of getting the states to enact unemployment insurance laws.[1] This measure drew its inspiration from the Federal Inheritance Tax Act. This act had been passed after the state of Florida had added an amendment to its constitution in the early twenties which prohibited that state from ever taxing inheritances. The Florida amendment had, of course, been passed to induce wealthy and aged residents of other states to spend their declining years amid the sunshine of Florida to the profit of both the merchants and the real estate owners of that state.

[1] Introduced in the House of Representatives as H. R. 7659, 73rd Congress, 2nd Session.

The states with inheritance taxes, however, felt that their sources of revenue were being depleted by the way the wealthy and their heirs were tending to prefer the taxless attractions of Florida. Similar movements to exempt inheritances from taxation were being started in other states which sought rich residents, and as a consequence the inheritance tax structure of the various states threatened to break down. To meet this situation the national government, in the administration of President Coolidge and with Mr. Mellon serving as Secretary of the Treasury, passed a federal inheritance tax law which provided that up to 80 per cent of the sums thus collected would be returned to those states which had state inheritance tax laws. If a state did not have such a law, however, the federal government retained all the amounts paid in from the estates of residents. This put Florida in a very embarrassing position. It had attempted to draw the wealthy to its shores under the promise of immunity but now, despite this pledge by the state, the federal government had stepped in and taxed them. Furthermore, Florida because of its constitutional amendment was estopped from passing a state inheritance tax and hence was compelled to see all such receipts go to Washington without being permitted to share in them. It is small wonder, therefore, that the civil authorities of Florida decided to attack the federal inheritance tax law on the ground that it was both un-American and unconstitutional. It was alleged to coerce the states into passing state inheritance taxes and hence to violate their sovereign right to determine what sort of revenue system they should have. But when this issue came before the United States Supreme Court in the case of *Florida v. Mellon*[1] that body unanimously declared the federal act to be constitutional. Florida then repealed its constitutional amendment prohibiting it from taxing inheritances and proceeded to pass such a tax in order that it might share in the proceeds of the federal measure.

Such was both the constitutional precedent and the germinal idea behind the Wagner-Lewis bill. It levied a pay-roll tax upon employers equal to 5 per cent of the amounts paid out in wages, but provided that where a state had passed a mandatory unemployment insurance law which came up to certain minimum standards then the contributions paid by employers under such an act would be credited as an offset against the federal tax. In this way, any state which would pass an unemployment insurance law would not be adding to the financial costs of its employers but would merely be transferring for the relief of local unemployment, and, therefore, presumably for the reduction of local taxes, sums which otherwise would go to Washington and be spent for undetermined purposes. On the other hand, states which did not pass such laws would not be able to obtain any unfair competitive advantage for the firms within their borders, since

[1] 273 U. S. 12.

[23]

these would still be compelled to make their payments to the federal government.

The states were, however, to be left free to enact the type of unemployment insurance system which they desired, whether this was to be upon a plant or industrial reserve basis or upon that of a pooled state fund. The states could also, if they wished, levy contributions upon the workers as well as the employers and could themselves make contributions. The minimum standards to which the state laws had to conform were of a very moderate nature. The state laws had, of course, to be mandatory in order to be recognized and were to be administered through a system of public employment offices.[1] The unemployed who went out on strike or who were locked out were not to receive benefits, but those who refused to fill such vacancies were not disqualified from benefits. Nor were those who refused to work for "substantially less" than the going rate of wages or who refused to sign a so-called "yellow-dog" contract binding them as a condition of employment not to join a union or talk with union officials.[2]

---

[1] The basis for these had been laid through the Wagner-Peyser Act of 1933, which gave federal grants-in-aid for a federal-state system of public employment offices. For a devastating description of the nationalized system set up in 1931 by the Hoover administration as a substitute for the previous Wagner bill, see Ruth M. Kellogg, *The United States Employment Service* (1933).

[2] This was indeed but the logical implementation of the Norris-LaGuardia Act of 1932 (47 U. S. Stat. L. 70), which declared the "yellow-dog" contract to be contrary to public policy and unenforceable in the federal courts.

The low benefit provisions of the existing Wisconsin act and the desire upon the part of the sponsors to have this law qualify under the federal act kept down the features to which the state acts were to conform to a ten weeks' benefit period with a minimum weekly benefit of $7 per week. The exemption from the federal tax of all employers with fewer than ten workmen was also due to the fact that the Wisconsin law carried a similar exemption. There was evident, therefore, in this bill a pronounced lack of balance between the rather heavy assessments levied upon industry and the very low benefits guaranteed to the unemployed.

Hearings upon this bill were conducted before a sub-committee of the House Ways and Means Committee in March of 1934.[1] Not only did Secretary Perkins testify in favor of the bill, but the President later declared that he favored it. The proposal, however, met with vigorous opposition from the more conservative Democrats as well as the Republicans and was not pushed by the administration with any real vigor.

Many close observers believed that Congress would, however, have passed the bill if the President had taken a decided stand in favor of it. This, however, he did not do and the session was allowed to end without any affirmative action by Congress in the field either of old age pensions

[1] *Hearings before a Sub-committee of the Committee on Ways and Means*, House of Representatives, 73rd Congress, 2nd Session, on H. R. 7659. See also an article by the author, "Towards Unemployment Insurance," *The World Tomorrow*, Vol. XVII (March 29, 1934) pp. 160–162.

or of unemployment insurance. There was an undercurrent of feeling among many of the progressive members of Congress that the President wanted to delay congressional action in order that he might make the program his own and thus obtain popular approval for it. The friends of the President insisted, however, that his only purpose was to have the problems studied more carefully and that he believed public sentiment was not yet sufficiently crystallized in favor of such a program.

The Declaration of Policy by the President

Whatever may have been his motives the President, while refusing to push vigorously the Dill-Connery and Wagner-Lewis bills, addressed Congress on June 8, 1934, on social security and advocated "some safeguards against misfortunes which cannot be wholly eliminated in this man-made world." He then stated that it was his intention to appoint a Committee on Economic Security which would study the whole question during the remainder of the year and report with a definite program to the new Congress in January, 1935. This committee was shortly afterwards set up by an executive order and consisted of the Secretary of the Treasury, the Attorney-General, the Secretary of Agriculture, the Relief Administrator, and the Secretary of Labor, with the last named serving as chairman. This committee selected Dr. Edwin E. Witte of the University of Wisconsin as Executive Director and built up a staff. It then proceeded to organize a rather bewildering cluster of advisory committees. First, there was an interdepartmental technical board headed by the Second Assistant Secretary of Labor, A. J. Altmeyer, who like Dr. Witte was a resident of Wisconsin. This board was midway between the so-called staff experts at the bottom and the cabinet committee at the top. Then a general advisory council of twenty-three citizens was appointed with Dr. Frank P. Graham, the President of the University of North Carolina, as chairman. This council was supposed to advise the cabinet committee on general problems of policy. Further advisory committees were also set up on medicine, public health, hospitals, dental work, public employment and assistance, and child welfare. Actuarial consultants were also appointed. Then the committee called in November a two-day conference in Washington of interested and invited persons, where various points of view were discussed. Something of a flurry was caused by the fact that the President in his statement to the conference, while endorsing unemployment insurance, also declared that he did "not know whether now is the time for legislation concerning old age." Since popular opinion was presumably far more solidified in favor of old age pensions than it was in the case of unemployment insurance, this statement aroused a great deal of surprise and uncertainty. The Secretary of Labor, however, hastened to remove this impression by declaring that old age pension legislation was still very much on the program of the committee and that the administration as a whole was in favor of it.

CHAPTER II

THE PROBLEMS BEFORE THE COMMITTEE ON ECONOMIC SECURITY

ONCE it was decided to favor some form of federal assistance against indigent old age and for the fostering of unemployment insurance, two issues of fundamental policy immediately arose. These were: (1) What should be the relationship of the national government to the plan? Should it work through the states, and if so in what manner? Or should it set up an outright national system? (2) From the financial point of view, how costly a system should be introduced and how should these costs be distributed? One phase of this latter problem was the distribution of the governmental costs as between federal and state governments; but even more important was the relative degree to which employers, employees and the government should contribute toward them.

These two fundamental issues were, of course, necessarily interconnected. Allied with them were still others—such as the degree of coverage which should be provided; the time for initiating the system; the handling of the accumulated funds, etc. In order to clarify the discussion of the act, it is advisable to go into these issues in some detail.

What Type of Federal Action

Broadly speaking, once some form of federal action was decided upon there were approximately four lines which might be taken. (1) An outright national system could be set up which would disregard state lines and which would provide benefits for old age and unemployment. These benefits could be financed either from public funds or from contributions paid by or levied upon industry and employees, or from a combination of these methods. (2) A system could be created in which the federal government would collect certain taxes and then turn over to the states "block" grants of money which did not need to be matched by these states and which would be sufficient to provide the main benefits. This system of 100 per cent grants was in certain respects virtually identical with a tax remission plan, which will be described later. (3) A system of "matched" federal grants could be carried through which would require some state or local appropriations in addition to the federal monies. (4) A tax offset system could be favored along the lines of the Wagner-Lewis bill. Each of the last three methods involved a joint federal-state relationship and hence inevitably raised a series of questions as to the precise zones of power which each should possess.

A proposal for an outright national old age pension system had been advocated during the preceding session by Congressman Keller of Illinois.

[29]

The idea of an outright national set-up for unemployment insurance was also stressed by many individual students who saw numerous economic and administrative advantages in it, such as the following: (1) It would enable uniform rules and uniform amounts of benefit, whether for old age or unemployment, to be established throughout the country instead of allowing these benefits to vary widely as would tend to be the case under separate state plans. These benefits would also tend to be more adequate than where responsibility was diffused. (2) It would in all probability provide a better administrative personnel since it is a generally accepted fact that the level of employment in the federal service is appreciably superior to that of the vast majority of the states. (3) Administrative records could be relatively centralized and a standardization of forms effected. The country could be divided into some eight or ten administrative districts, each of which would have a set of central records. (4) Being a national system, it would care more adequately for workers who moved from one state to another, and many of whom would otherwise tend to lose their eligibility to benefits under the residence requirements of the various state laws. (5) It would permit the national government to assess a large part of the necessary expenses upon individuals in the upper income brackets and upon the excess profits of corporations. This would be largely impossible to the degree to which the states themselves contributed under the device of "matched" grants. For the states in general lack effective income taxes and tend instead to collect their revenues from taxes on general property, retail sales, and gasoline. State and local taxes tend, therefore, to be regressive and also to single out one class of property-owners, namely, those who own real estate, and to let the owners of intangibles largely escape. Since the tax offset method was designed—so far as social insurance was concerned—to fall on payrolls, this meant that it was ultimately a tax on sales or on wages, or upon employers without regard to their earning powers, or upon a combination of the three. In any event, such a tax would certainly not be so much in conformity with the principle of the relative ability to pay as would a national system financed in the way which has been outlined above.

The arguments against a national system and in favor of some federal-state arrangement were in general political (in the better sense of the term) and constitutional. But some administrative considerations operated as well against the centralized form of set-up. Thus, in the case of old age pensions, the natural unit of administration in most localities is the county. This is the convenient administrative area within which applications can be made, investigations carried out and tentative benefits fixed. In all this a great deal of unpaid service from citizens would be required, while in the larger metropolitan centers fairly effi-

[31]

cient departments manned by professional social workers are already available for such work. It is not too hard a task to gear these county groups into some state plan of administration, but it is far more difficult to have them omit the states as such and be lined up under national control. And this would be the case even if the country were to be subdivided into districts. For the federal government to create its own welfare staff which would man the local services would at once duplicate the local units, constitute a top-heavy administrative set-up and arouse local animosity.

The payment and indeed the administration of the entire system of unemployment benefits would, moreover, have to be carried through by the public employment offices. These had been placed on a federal-state basis by the Wagner-Peyser act of 1933, which had replaced the national system of the Hoover administration. It would have been very difficult to have reversed this whole trend and to have returned to the centralized system of offices which would have been required under a national system of unemployment insurance. The Wagner-Peyser act, therefore, helped to fix the mold into which the unemployment insurance system was to be cast. The believers in a federal system of government were also opposed to organizing the social security program upon a national basis. They feared that it would reduce the initiative and interest which state plans would create; that it would bind the country into an undue uniformity of

rules and benefits without making sufficient allowance for geographical differences; and that it would
not ultimately result in as much progress as what
the late Justice Holmes termed the "interstitial
experimentation" of the states.

There were other powerful considerations which
operated against using a national system wherever
it could be avoided. The states rights sentiment is
still strong in the country and a general movement
towards centralized control of these functions
would undoubtedly have aroused powerful local
prides and jealousies which, when combined with
the opposition of local politicians to letting such
powers escape them, would have endangered the
program. Constitutional doubts and fears were
another factor which worked against the national
method. The constitution, having been drafted
long before there was any real wage-working class
as such, no direct authority was given to the
national government to legislate on such matters.
In order to do so justification would have to be
sought under the so-called "implied powers." It
was feared, however, that the Supreme Court
might well look with disfavor upon such attempts
and that the whole structure of social security
would be razed by an unfavorable judgment.

The ardent advocates of the Wisconsin plan were
also anxious to adopt a federal-state rather than a
national system. For if a national plan were
adopted, the complexities of administration would
prevent the plant reserve system from being used

[33]

and would make pooled funds inevitable. Under a federal-state system, however, Wisconsin could demand and probably retain the right to its own method of plant reserves and its advocates could attempt to get other states to adopt similar systems. These considerations were powerful in operation, since while the Wisconsin system was fast losing favor with the informed public, some of its supporters occupied key positions in the Committee on Economic Security, while still others impinged closely upon it and were able to exercise a decided influence.

During the consideration of these issues, the author suggested a possible device for overcoming the obstacle of constitutionality.[1] This was for Congress to pass not one act but two. The first would have raised the necessary revenues whether by payroll, income, or excess profits taxes, or by a combination of the three. This obviously would be perfectly constitutional. The second would have laid down the scale of benefits to be paid out of the treasury for the unemployed and the needy aged. In view of the fact that the Supreme Court, as Professor Corwin has pointed out,[2] has seldom questioned the right of Congress to appropriate money for virtually any object, this second act would also seem to be constitutional in method. What might, therefore, have well been

---

[1] Paul H. Douglas, "A National Program for Unemployment Insurance," *The New Republic*, Vol. LXXX (October 3, 1934), pp. 215–216.
[2] E. S. Corwin, *The Twilight of the Supreme Court.*

unconstitutional if joined together might have been able to run the legal gamut if put asunder.

This suggestion was not, however, acted upon[1] and the Committee on Economic Security sought instead to create wherever possible a federal-state instead of a national system. In one part of its program, however, the sheer logic of events drove them to adopt the national method. This was in the matter of compulsory contributory annuities for old age. It was decided by the committee and the administration that the use of federally subsidized old age pensions as the exclusive source of protection for the needy would ultimately entail too great a financial burden upon the national treasury. The committee and the President, therefore, decided to introduce a mandatory and contributory system of old age annuities for many of those who in the future would reach the age of sixty-five. Not only would this reduce the governmental outlay, but it would also free those who received pensions from being subjected to a means test as would inevitably result if the only protection were a federal-state old age pension system along present lines. It was also urged that it could be used to provide higher benefits for those who had earned more than the minimum sums during their lifetime.

But once such a mandatory system was decided upon, it was seen to be plainly impossible for it to be administered along state lines. For a large pro-

---

[1] Except that it was later adopted by Congress in the two railway retirement acts of 1935. See Chapter VI.

portion of Americans change from state to state during their working lives and indeed often make frequent changes. It would plainly be unjust for the workers to lose eligibility or their claim to the benefits resulting from past contributions merely because they had moved to another state. On the other hand, the problem of transferring from one state to another the precise actuarial credits of workers, of keeping their records up to date and moving them about and of balancing the claims of the various state funds against each other would be hopelessly and needlessly complicated. The only way to administer such a system, covering a man's entire working life in a country with as fluid and as wide a labor market as ours, is upon a national and not upon a state basis. In the face of this plain necessity, political objections and constitutional fears had to be cast aside.

In the case of outright old age pensions and of unemployment insurance, as well as in that of most of the "welfare" features, the committee, however, preferred to foster state action. So far as old age pensions were concerned, the committee followed the lines of the Dill-Connery bill of the previous session and recommended federal grants-in-aid which were to be matched on the part of the states by at least equal sums. This met with the general approval of most students of the question, although it was opposed by the followers of the Townsend plan, who wanted a national system, and by those who, though favoring state-administered systems, wanted the federal government to meet all the costs by providing a 100 per cent "block" or unmatched grant.

Sharp controversy raged, however, over the best method of stimulating the states to enact unemployment insurance laws. The Secretary of Labor and her legal staff were strongly in favor of the tax offset provisions of the Wagner-Lewis bill and felt that very few minimum standards need be required of the states. As the subject of federal action was, however, studied in greater detail an increasing number of the experts attached to the staff of the committee and an even greater number of those not officially connected with the committee came to see very clearly the grave defects in such a plan and favored instead a 100 per cent block grant from the federal government to the states.

The Defects in the Offset System

The major grounds for this dissatisfaction with the offset plan were the following:[1]

1. It laid down very few standards to which the state plans had to conform in order to obtain

[1] I have drawn here upon a memorandum submitted by the author to the House and Senate committees considering the social security legislation and which, I believe, expresses the general judgment of this group. See *Hearings before the Senate Committee on Finance*, 74th Congress, 1st Session, on S. 1130, pp. 892–896; *Hearings before the Committee on Ways and Means*, House of Representatives, 74th Congress, 1st Session, on H. R. 4120, pp. 1086–1091; see also the memorandum of Dr. Eveline M. Burns, *Hearings before the House Committee on Ways and Means*, pp. 1092–1096; and the testimony of Abraham Epstein, *Hearings before the Senate Finance Committee*, pp. 458–478; 491–516; *Hearings before the House Committee on Ways and Means*, pp. 552–577.

offsets against the tax. This failure to prescribe minimum standards was due in part to the constitutional difficulties of the offset method and in part to its clumsiness from an administrative standpoint. There was a fear that if many standards were imposed upon the states the act would be regarded by the courts as being primarily regulatory in its purposes and hence, under the precedent furnished by the second child labor case,[1] would be declared unconstitutional. As a result the states, under the revised offset plan favored by the Department of Labor, were to be left free to enact virtually any kind of unemployment insurance law which they desired subject to a few simple rules concerning eligibility for benefit. More specifically no standards were set on such vital matters as: (*a*) the mimimum or maximum length of the waiting period; (*b*) the mimimum or maximum length of the benefit period; (*c*) the approximate average percentage of weekly wages to be paid in benefits; (*d*) the minimum and maximum weekly benefits; (*e*) provisions for part-time employment; (*f*) whether plant reserves, industry reserves or state-pooled funds were to be used; (*g*) the salary limits for the inclusion of nonmanual workers.

While some variation and experimentation between the states were admitted to be desirable, it was apparent that under the method proposed, a bewildering variety of provisions was likely to result which would give widely varying degrees of

---

[1] *Bailey* v. *Drexel Furniture Company*, 259 U. S. 20.

protection to the workers in different states and there was great danger that excessively low standards would be set up in many states.

2. The "offset" features of the bill would be relatively ineffective in enforcing such few standards as it prescribed for the states. For if a state violated any of these standards, the only way the offset provisions could be used would be to declare that an employer's contribution to a state fund would not be credited against the federal payroll tax. If this were done, the employers would have to pay a double tax, namely to the nation as well as the state. In practice, the federal authorities would be almost completely unwilling to invoke such a severe penalty against private parties who would not have been guilty of any offense. For if the only way to punish A is to penalize B, then A is not likely to be checked. It was urged, therefore, that in practice the offset feature would be almost completely ineffective in maintaining uniform standards on those few points which were covered in the bill, and that it could not be used to lay down further standards in the future.

3. The offset feature carried with it the almost inevitable corollary that each state would tend to make equal percentage levies upon the payrolls of employers. For any additional tax would expose the employers of a state to that competitive disadvantage which it was the purpose of the plan to remove. But since the average volume of unemployment differed widely as between the states,

this would inevitably result, if each state were treated (as was proposed) as a completely autonomous and separate insuring unit, in a gross inequality of benefits as between the various states. These differences between states in the relative volume of unemployment among non-agricultural workers were computed by the committee's own statisticians on the basis of the census of unemployment in 1930[1] and for the four years 1930–1933. These averages were as shown in Table II.[2]

These statistics showed, therefore, that in April, 1930, there was almost four times as much relative unemployment in the state with the highest percentage (Michigan) as in the state with the lowest (South Dakota). If the four years of 1930–1933 inclusive be taken as a whole, the percentage in the highest state (Michigan) was twice that of the lowest state (Georgia).

It was apparent, therefore, that the equal rates of assessment ,upon employers, which would result from the offset law, would provide for widely varying amounts of benefit, unless balanced in the states where unemployment was higher by contributions from the employees or grants by the state governments themselves. States with a very high volume of unemployment would otherwise be able to pay only a few weeks of benefits to their unemployed, while those with a low volume would

[1] Fifteenth Census (1930), *Unemployment*, Vols. I and II.

[2] *Supplement to Report to the President of the Committee on Economic Security* (1935), pp. 5–6.

TABLE II
Average Percentages of Unemployment by States among Nonagricultural Workers

	April, 1930			1930–1933	
State	Percentage of gainful workers unemployed	Ratio to average of all states, per cent	State	Percentage of gainful workers unemployed	Ratio to average of all states, per cent
All states............	8.5	100	All states...........	25.8	100
1 Michigan.........	13.9	164	1 Michigan........	34.3	133
2 Rhode Island.....	11.2	132	2 Rhode Island....	29.6	115
3 Montana.........	10.7	126	3 New Jersey......	28.8	112
4 Illinois...........	10.3	121	4 Montana........	28.4	110
5 Oregon..........	10.1	119	5 Pennsylvania....	28.3	110
6 Nevada..........	9.8	115	6 Illinois.........	28.0	109
7 Ohio............	9.5	112	7 New York.......	27.8	108
8 Massachusetts....	9.4	111	8 Nevada.........	27.8	108
9 Pennsylvania.....	9.0	106	9 Arizona.........	27.7	107
10 Colorado.........	8.9	105	10 Florida.........	27.1	105
11 New Jersey......	8.9	105	11 Massachusetts...	27.0	105
12 California........	8.8	104	12 Ohio...........	26.9	104
13 New York.......	8.7	102	13 Indiana.........	26.6	103
14 Indiana..........	8.6	101	14 Connecticut.....	26.4	102
15 Washington......	8.6	101	15 New Mexico.....	26.2	102
16 Utah............	8.5	100	16 Utah...........	25.7	100
17 Florida..........	8.5	100	17 Arkansas........	25.6	99
18 Oklahoma.......	8.4	99	18 Colorado........	25.1	97
19 Maine...........	8.2	97	19 Washington.....	24.4	95
20 Minnesota.......	8.2	97	20 Wyoming.......	24.2	94
21 Vermont.........	8.0	94	21 Missouri........	24.2	94
22 North Carolina...	7.9	93	22 Oklahoma.......	24.2	94
23 New Hampshire..	7.9	93	23 Louisiana.......	24.1	93
24 Kentucky........	7.8	92	24 Vermont........	24.1	93
25 Connecticut......	7.8	92	25 California.......	24.0	93
26 Wisconsin........	7.8	92	26 Texas..........	23.9	93
27 Missouri.........	7.7	91	27 Wisconsin.......	23.8	92
28 Louisiana........	7.7	91	28 Minnesota.......	23.4	91
29 Idaho...........	7.6	89	29 Maryland.......	23.4	91
30 West Virginia....	7.4	87	30 West Virginia....	23.2	90
31 New Mexico.....	7.4	87	31 Alabama........	23.2	90
32 Arizona..........	7.4	87	32 Maine..........	21.8	85
33 Wyoming........	7.1	84	33 Iowa...........	21.8	85
34 Texas...........	6.7	79	34 Idaho..........	21.8	85
35 Arkansas.........	6.5	77	35 New Hampshire.	21.8	85
36 Kansas..........	6.2	73	36 Oregon.........	21.7	84
37 North Dakota....	6.1	72	37 Nebraska.......	21.5	83
38 Virginia..........	5.9	69	38 North Carolina..	21.3	83
39 Nebraska........	5.9	69	39 Virginia.........	21.1	82
40 Georgia.........	5.9	69	40 Kansas..........	21.0	81
41 Maryland........	5.8	68	41 Kentucky.......	20.8	81
42 Alabama.........	5.6	66	42 Tennessee.......	20.4	79
43 Iowa............	5.4	64	43 Mississippi......	19.4	75
44 Tennessee.......	5.3	62	44 North Dakota...	18.9	73
45 South Carolina...	5.2	61	45 Dist. of Columbia	18.3	71
46 Delaware........	5.2	61	46 Delaware.......	18.3	71
47 Dist. of Columbia	4.9	58	47 South Dakota...	17.5	68
48 Mississippi......	4.6	54	48 South Carolina..	17.2	67
49 South Dakota....	3.9	46	49 Georgia.........	17.0	66

be able to provide many more. There would be no justification for such unequal treatment, since the unemployed in the states where the benefit period was short would be just as innocent as those where the benefit period was much longer. There would be in fact no justifiable reason for penalizing them because of the accident of their residence. Since unemployment is primarily a national problem proceeding not only from causes outside the individual workshop but also outside individual states, there would seem instead to be a national responsibility for guaranteeing at least a substantial uniformity of benefits as between the unemployed of the various states.

Those who believed in the inadequacy of the offset plan as advocated by the personnel of the Department of Labor urged very strongly that either (a) a sufficient amount of the tax be retained by the federal government and then distributed to the states to ensure this substantial uniformity, or (b) that a different system of cooperation between the federal and state government should be devised. From computations made by the present author it appeared, on the basis of the April, 1930, figures, that an adequate reinsurance fund for the equalization of benefits could have been created by earmarking for this purpose 50 per cent of the sums going to the states.[1] If the total levy were equal to

[1] For the methods used in making this estimate, see Paul H. Douglas, "Two Problems of Unemployment Insurance," *Supplement to Journal of American Statistical Association*, Vol. XXX (March, 1935), pp. 215–220.

3 per cent of the wages paid out this would mean retaining for this purpose a sum equal to 1 per cent and letting the states have an amount equal to 2 per cent. Because of the smaller differences involved in the 1930–1933 figures, the reserve for this purpose could have been somewhat less or approximately one-fourth of the total.

4. The proposed offset plan made no provision for those workers who acquired eligibility in one state and who on moving to another state became unemployed before acquiring eligibility there. It left migratory workers completely out of its protection and did not sufficiently protect those who moved from state to state at less frequent intervals. The numbers in these classes were, however, in absolute terms fairly large, and many of them needed protection more acutely than almost any other group. Yet the proposed plan, by making eligibility occur within a specific state and not within the country as a whole, debarred this class from aid except through voluntary reciprocity provisions agreed to by the separate states.

5. The proposed plan would set up forty-nine different sets of central records and would result in a bewildering variety of forms and administrative records. Those who knew the administrative handling of the unemployment records of the British system at Kew realized the necessity of a relative concentration of these records in at least large districts. Most of the states, it was believed, were too small to handle this work effectively.

6. Perhaps most important of all was the fact that the offset method would confine the financing of unemployment insurance to a levy upon payrolls. For that was the nature of the federal tax. A state could not obtain offsets for its citizens if it wished to finance a portion of the costs from income or excess profits taxes. These could not be offset against a federal tax on payrolls since they would not fall on identical persons or to the same degree upon those who would pay both. Those who wanted to have at least a portion of the cost of unemployment insurance met from the so-called social surplus were opposed to the offset feature on this ground and preferred a substitute proposal which would at least permit those other sources of support to be tapped.

The Advantages of the 100 Per Cent Block Grant

The group which objected to the "offset" method proposed as a preferable substitute a "block" or unmatched grant to the states equal to approximately the full cost of paying standard unemployment insurance benefits. This was also sometimes called "the federal subsidy plan" and "the tax remission system." Under it, the federal government would independently collect the necessary funds whether by taxing payrolls or by using other methods, and would then redistribute these sums to those states which passed satisfactory unemployment insurance laws. Such a system, it was urged, would have distinct advantages over the tax offset method.

1. It would have a better chance of being declared constitutional. While the tax offset system had not previously been used in the field of labor legislation or social reform, the system of federal grants was long established in our constitutional history. Federal land grants to the states to promote higher education and the later appropriations of cash to further research are well known and their constitutionality has never been seriously questioned. These were unmatched or block grants. Federal grants to the states upon a matching basis had been made for numerous purposes, such as forest fire protection, agricultural extension, vocational education, highway construction, the prevention of venereal disease, and the health care of mothers and infants.[1] This method, moreover, had been declared to be constitutional by the Supreme Court in the case of *Massachusetts* v. *Mellon*.[2]

2. The tax remission plan would permit more thoroughgoing and adequate standards to be laid down as a basis for state action. The clearer constitutional basis of the tax remission system would permit them to go further in this direction than under the offset plan. In addition, the fact that the monies would originally be collected by the federal

[1] See A. F. McDonald, *Federal Aid;* Paul H. Douglas, "The Development of a Federal System of Grants-in-aid," *Political Science Quarterly*, Vol. XXXV (June and December, 1920) and Dorothy Kirchwey Brown, *Federal Aid to the States* (1926).

[2] 262 U. S. 447.

government and then remitted to the states would permit the former to require certain minimum provisions in the various state laws.

3. Similarly, it would be much more possible for the federal government to keep the states up to continuing satisfactory standards of administration and of legislation. For the federal government could simply refuse to remit the necessary sums if a state failed to carry out the proper administration of the plans. Uniformity of records and procedures could also be obtained and greater cooperation between the states effected.

4. By withholding a portion of the funds collected and by setting up a national reinsurance fund, aid could be given, under proper controls, to those states with relatively high unemployment, so that a substantial uniformity of benefits could be virtually assured to the unemployed of all states. As we have seen from the discussion of differences of unemployment, it would seem fairly safe if only one-third or one-fourth of the total receipts were retained for this purpose and this would probably also be enough to provide the type of interstate protection described in the next point.

5. With such a central fund it would be possible to take care of those workers who transferred from state to state, and thus make eligibility a matter of working within the country as a whole rather than confining it to employment within a specific state.

6. The way would be left open for other sources of revenue than the payroll tax to be used if and

when, in the judgment of Congress, this became desirable. A small portion of the total taxes could be remitted between the states in the precise proportion in which they were collected, while the major portion could be distributed according to the relative ratio of unemployment.

It will be noted that the tax remission plan, or that for block grants, was midway between the decentralization proposed by the Wagner-Lewis method and the centralization of an outright national system. The collection of the finances would be centralized but the local administration would be decentralized, subject to the requirement that the states should meet certain minimum federal standards. States could also provide benefits in excess of the minimum laid down for the country as a whole by tapping additional sources of funds.

The Final Decision

The system of block grants, or the tax remission plan, was not only advocated by experts within and outside the staff of the committee, but was also favored by a 9 to 7 vote by the Advisory Council.[1] The leading officials of the Department of Labor,

[1] See statement by Dr. Frank P. Graham, the chairman of the Advisory Council in *Hearings before Committee on Finance*, U. S. Senate, 74th Congress, 1st Session, on S. 1130, p. 315. Also Paul U. Kellogg, "Unemployment Compensation," *Survey Graphic*, Vol. XXIV (March, 1935); and Mr. Kellogg's testimony before the Senate Finance Committee, *Senate Hearings on S. 1130*, pp. 900–907. See also the testimony of Helen Hall, *Senate Hearings*, pp. 767–771. The report of the Advisory Council is given in the *Hearings before the Committee on Ways and Means*, House of Representatives, 74th Congress, 1st Session, on H. R. 4120, pp. 882–896.

however, insisted on supporting the tax offset, or
Wagner-Lewis, plan and succeeded in getting the
cabinet committee to agree with them, so that the
bill as presented to Congress embodied this as
the method of stimulating the states to take action
in the matter of unemployment insurance. Little
publicity was given to the recommendation of the
Advisory Council by the officials in power and
it was not until a well-informed article appeared
in the *New York Times* that there was any public
awareness of the situation. After a time, the report
of the Advisory Council was finally made available
when President Graham testified before the House
and Senate committees.

The one major argument that came to be urged
for the offset plan as opposed to the tax remission
system was that, if the latter were later declared
to be unconstitutional, the whole system of unemployment insurance would necessarily collapse,
whereas, even if the tax offset method were finally
rejected by the Supreme Court, the states would
in the meantime have passed acts that would
continue. The federal offset plan might therefore
ultimately disappear with comparatively little loss,
having fulfilled its purpose in getting the states to
take action.

The advocates of the tax remission system, or
the method of block grants, made two replies to
this line of reasoning. First, they pointed out again
that the tax remission system had a far better
chance of being declared constitutional than had

the offset plan. Secondly, they warned that the more conservative state legislators and the outright opponents of unemployment insurance would be sufficiently wary to make any state law that was passed conditional upon the constitutionality of the federal act being sustained. Therefore, if the offset plan were declared unconstitutional, this would be likely not only to tear down the federal scaffolding, but to demolish the structure of the state laws themselves. As we shall see, several state legislatures have already acted as these friends of social insurance feared they would.

The final draft of the bill as prepared by the committee differed in one vital respect from the original Wagner-Lewis plan. The 1934 bill had provided that if a state levied an assessment upon its employers for unemployment insurance which was equal to the full amount of the federal tax, the entire amount of the federal tax would be offset and no monies would be received by the federal government. In the revised form the state levies were to be credited as an offset only up to a total of 90 per cent of the federal tax. The remaining 10 per cent was to go into the federal treasury. The federal government was then to distribute to the states the amounts needed to provide for the administration of the system. Although these latter grants were not formally earmarked as being identical with the sums which the national government received from its one-tenth, it was well understood that this was in fact the source from which the administrative grants were derived. The main reason for this action was undoubtedly the realization that closer federal control over the minimum standards of administration could be obtained through the tax remission, or block grant, plan than by the offset system. To this extent, therefore, those in charge of the legislation tacitly admitted some at least of the criticisms which had been advanced against the Wagner-Lewis plan. It was pointed out that this left the employers making contributions both to the state governments on the one hand and to the federal government upon the other, and that for the sake of administrative convenience it would be preferable that they should make their contributions to one agency, namely, the federal government, which could then assume the task of redistributing the funds among the states.

The committee's bill, therefore, in its entirety finally used virtually every form of national and federal-state action which could be conceived. Thus, a national system was used for contributory old age insurance. The method of federal aid upon a matching basis by the states was employed, as we shall see, in the case of outright old age pensions, the care of dependent children, maternity and child health, etc. The Wagner-Lewis or tax offset plan was used to stimulate the states to take action in the matter of unemployment insurance, while the tax remission plan or outright block grant was used to meet the costs of administering the state plans of unemployment insurance, for county health units and for child welfare.

Financial Problems

Let us now turn to some of the financial problems which were necessarily involved and consider first the financial aspects of unemployment insurance. The statisticians and actuaries attached to the cabinet committee made the following estimates as to the *average* amounts of protection which could be provided for the country as a whole for sums equal to 3, 4, and 5 per cent of the payroll respectively. These are given in Table III.[1]

It is apparent from the above estimates that only relatively limited protection could normally be provided from sums equal to a 3 per cent payroll tax. If accompanied by a three weeks' waiting period, then, on the basis of the 1922–1933 experience, only about thirteen weeks of benefit could be given without allowance for any of the actuarial adjustments. When these allowances were made, the probable weeks of benefit were reduced to only nine. The estimates on the basis of the 1922–1930 experience rates were, of course, appreciably higher and amounted to eighteen and fourteen weeks respectively, if the contribution rate were 3 per cent and the waiting period three weeks. If a four weeks' waiting period were required, then a 3 per cent

[1] See *Report to the President of the Committee on Economic Security,* p. 13; also *Hearings before the Committee on Ways and Means,* House of Representatives, 74th Congress, 1st Session, on H. R. 4120, p. 29.

assessment would, on the basis of the 1922–1930 experience, provide fifteen weeks of benefit. These

TABLE III

ACTUARIAL ESTIMATE OF AVERAGE WEEKS OF BENEFITS WHICH COULD BE PAID (BENEFITS EQUAL TO 50 PER CENT OF AVERAGE WAGE) UNDER A NATION-WIDE SYSTEM OF UNEMPLOYMENT INSURANCE ON BASIS OF VOLUME OF UNEMPLOYMENT FROM 1922 TO 1930 AND 1922 TO 1933

Contri-bution rate, per cent	Waiting period	Standard maximum weeks of benefit			
		1922 to 1933 experience		1922 to 1930 experience	
		Unadjusted	With actua-rial adjust-ments[1]	Unadjusted	With actua-rial adjust-ments[1]
3	4	14	10	20	15
3	3	13	9	18	14
3	2	12	8	17	12
4	4	21	15	36	24
4	3	20	14	32	21
4	2	18	12	28	18
5	4	35	21	48	38
5	3	31	19	48	35
5	2	27	17	46	30

[1] Actuarial adjustments took account of the following: (1) the rule that no employee may draw benefits unless employed forty weeks in the two preceding years; (2) savings from employees voluntarily quitting work or being discharged for proven misconduct; (3) allowance of an additional week of benefits for each six months of contributions without drawing benefit up to a maximum of ten additional weeks; (4) limitation of benefits in the ratio of one week of benefits to four weeks of contributions; (5) compensation for part-time employment; (6) limitation of benefits to unemployment within the normal season; (7) limitation of maximum benefits to $15 per week; (8) estimated increase in costs caused by the fact that benefits will be paid on a full-time wage basis while contributions will be made on the actual payroll, including some part-time; (9) an allowance for the inadequacy of the data; (10) allowances for various contingencies, including an upward drift of costs.

Items 1, 2, 4, 6 and 7 operated to decrease costs; while items 3, 5, 8 and 10 tended to increase them. Balancing these together, the actuaries arrived at a loading of 28 per cent above the unadjusted cost figures.

estimates, it should be remembered, were for the country as a whole. In states with a relatively high ratio of unemployment, they would of course be appreciably lower. The actuaries estimated on the basis of the 1922–1930 experience that even if the volume of unemployment only amounted to between 7 and 11 per cent, 26 per cent of the unemployed would be eliminated by the requirement of a four weeks' waiting period, and 28 per cent more would be on the average unemployed for more than nineteen weeks, and hence would exhaust their claim to benefits. If unemployment ranged between 20 and 30 per cent then it was estimated that 21 per cent of the unemployed would be eliminated by a four weeks' waiting period, while no less than 45 per cent would be unemployed for more than nineteen weeks.[1]

Because of this, various members of the Advisory Council led by Paul U. Kellogg, President William Green of the American Federation of Labor and Helen Hall tried to raise the total funds provided to an equivalent of 5 per cent of the payroll. This, on the basis of the record from 1922 to 1930, would have provided at least thirty weeks of benefits, subject to a waiting period of two weeks. This group wanted the extra 2 per cent to be raised from a tax on incomes[2] if possible. This proposal was defeated in the Advisory Council, as was also a proposal to make the total levy equal to 4 per cent.[3] The final

[1] See *Hearings before Senate Committee on Finance*, 74th Congress, 1st Session, or S. 1130, p. 333.

[2] See the testimony of Miss Hall and Mr. Kellogg before the Senate Committee of Finance, *op. cit.*, pp. 767–770; 900–907.

[3] The margin of votes against the 4 per cent proposal was very slight.

recommendation was to finance unemployment insurance by a 3 per cent levy upon payrolls and this was embodied in the bill presented to Congress. A minority of the Advisory Council, including a number of the employers together with Professor Raymond Moley, advocated requiring the workers to pay a tax to the national government to help finance the system, but this proposal was defeated in the Advisory Council and did not find favor with the officials of the Department of Labor.

So far as the federal grants-in-aid for old age pensions, for dependent children, and for the various health services were concerned, they were to be derived from the general revenues of the government. Their ultimate incidence would therefore be determined in proportion to the amounts which the various economic classes contributed to the support of the national government itself.

Old Age Insurance As a Partial Ultimate Substitute for Pensions

The Committee on Economic Security concluded, as we have stated, that the costs to the federal government would be too great if outright noncontributory pensions were used as the only form of protection for old age. The actuaries of the committee computed that, if no other method were devised to supplement the pensions,

---

At least seven of the members were in favor of the higher tax, namely, Kellogg, Graham, Hall, Ohl, Harrison, Schoenberg and Green. See testimony of William Green, *Hearings before Senate Committee on Finance*, p. 171.

by 1950 the federal grants for this purpose would amount to between 397 and 712 millions of dollars, by 1965 to between 723 and 1,091 millions, and by 1980 to between 857 and 1,294 millions.[1]

This was judged to lay too heavy a financial burden upon the government and to reduce this, as well as for the other reasons which have been stated, there was fairly general agreement that an auxiliary plan for a compulsory and contributory system of old age insurance should be prepared. This would not involve the use of a means test and would graduate benefits to past earnings. But even though it was agreed that this plan should ultimately be self-supporting so that in its maturity each age group would either contribute itself or have contributed for it sums which would be sufficient to provide the annuities granted, there were at least two very important transitional problems, namely, (1) what should be done for those in the upper age groups who were nearing the pensionable age and who because of the relatively few years left in which they could make contributions would necessarily receive only very small earned annuities; (2) whether the full rate of assessment which would be ultimately needed to

---

[1] The higher estimates were based upon the assumption that the dependency ratio of those over sixty-five would rise from 15 per cent in 1936 to a maximum of 50 per cent in 1957, and that the average pension would amount to $25 a month, of which the federal government would pay half. The lower estimate was based on the assumption that the maximum dependency ratio which would be reached in 1961 would be 40 per cent, and that the average pension would be $20 a month. See *Hearings before Senate Committee on Finance*, 74th Congress, 1st Session, on S. 1130, p. 250.

provide the annuities should be immediately imposed or whether in view of the depression and the difficulties involved in building up a huge reserve it might not be better to start at a much lower rate of assessment and only gradually reach the maximum. These issues were naturally inter-related since the lower the initial contributions were, the more inadequate the earned annuities would be. We shall, therefore, consider the latter question first.

The Financial Features of Old Age Pensions

The maximum contributions needed over the course of a working lifetime in order to provide moderate annuities at the age of sixty-five, and certain death benefits, were computed as being approximately 5 per cent of the payroll. It was felt that this would be too heavy an initial burden upon both employers and workers. An immediate addition of one-half of these amounts would send up the production costs of the employers, who would also be bearing the burden of the contributions for unemployment insurance. In view of the great difficulties under which business was laboring during the depression, it was feared that this might cause some businesses to close down and compel others to reduce their scale of operations and to lay off men. It was also felt that such contributions by the workers would be excessive since even those who had jobs, because of short time and wage cuts, would be receiving relatively low weekly earnings and commonly would have heavy further burdens resulting from the unemployment of members of their families. The payment of such sums by those in the lower age groups would also lead to the accumulation of a huge reserve, which by 1980 would probably have amounted to enormous sums.

Not only would the investment of so enormous a sum create grave problems but at least half of it, and indeed as we shall see very much more, would come from the pockets of the wage earners. They would then have to decrease their current consumption and there would be an immediate withdrawal of a large quantity of purchasing power from the field of consumers goods. Unemployment would, therefore, tend to be created in these lines. If the sums thus withdrawn from consumers goods served either directly or indirectly to go into the field of capital goods, they would thus largely counterbalance this tendency. In view of the existing state of the investment market, however, and the reluctance of business to build new factories and install new machinery, etc., there was no surety that these sums would be immediately reinvested. The result might, therefore, be an initial impounding and sterilization of large sums of monetary purchasing power, with a consequent intensification of the depression. Furthermore, even if the sums were later reinvested it might lead to a further lack of balance between the proportion of the national income devoted to the increase of capital goods and the proportion spent upon consumers goods.

For all these reasons, therefore, it was thought unwise to put the ultimate rates of assessment immediately into effect. It was instead decided to start at a low rate and to reach the maximum gradually. The committee recommended that the following scale of contributions should be followed.

TABLE IV

Years	Percentage rate of assessment for compulsory old age insurance	
	Employer	Employee
1937–1941	0.5	0.5
1942–1946	1.0	1.0
1947–1951	1.5	1.5
1952–1956	2.0	2.0
1957 and later	2.5	2.5

The committee therefore favored starting at the low rate of one-half of 1 per cent from each party and not reaching the maximum of 2½ per cent for twenty years, or not until 1957.

This made the difficulty of taking care of those in the upper age groups under the compulsory insurance system even greater. Since the average expectancy of life for males who reach the age of sixty-five is now approximately twelve years, and for females fifteen years, contributions equal to 25 per cent of the wages would be needed for those who were over sixty in order to give them five years later annuities as low as 15 per cent of their earnings. In fact, under the rates fixed by the committee the amount of "earned" annuities would have been very small, as is shown by the following table.[1]

TABLE V

MONTHLY "EARNED" ANNUITIES ACCORDING TO CONTRIBUTION RATES PROPOSED BY THE COMMITTEE ON ECONOMIC SECURITY AND BASED ON VARIOUS LEVELS OF MONTHLY EARNINGS

Age	Years of contributions	$50	$100	$150
60	5	$ 0.24	$ 0.48	$ 0.72
55	10	0.78	1.55	2.33
50	15	1.68	3.35	5.03
45	20	3.02	6.03	9.05
40	25	4.88	9.75	14.63
35	30	7.12	14.23	21.35
30	35	9.79	19.57	29.36
25	40	12.95	25.90	38.85
20	45	16.69	33.37	50.06

Such sums would not furnish any adequate protection for those in the upper age groups. If persons of sixty were later to receive only that which had been directly paid for them, the monthly annuities for the $100 a month man would amount to only $.48, while those of fifty-five and fifty years would receive only $1.55 and $3.35 respectively. The committee, therefore, decided to recommend initial annuities to those who had paid contributions for five years (two hundred weeks) equal to

[1] See *Hearings before Senate Committee, op. cit.*, p. 252.

15 per cent of their average wage, and to increase this by 1 per cent for approximately each of the following five years.[1] A person for whom contributions had been paid for approximately ten years was, therefore, to receive an annuity equal to 20 per cent of his wage. Thereafter the annuity increased at the rate of 2 per cent of the average wage for each year or each block of forty weeks worked. The maximum annuity was to be 40 per cent of average wages. Those who entered the system after 1942 were to receive somewhat smaller annuities.

It will thus be seen that very appreciable sums were to be paid to those in the upper age groups in excess of the amounts contributed by and for them. How then were these added sums to be financed? The committee's plan was in effect for them to be ultimately, though not immediately, borne by the national government. For approximately the first twenty-five or thirty years they were to be advanced from the contributions which were being made by and for the younger workers. Then as these erstwhile younger workers reached the annuity age, the government would make contributions towards their annuities which would repay the advances which these groups had made plus interest at 3 per cent. The financial set-up of the plan by years was estimated by the actuaries to be as follows.[2]

---

[1] Strictly speaking, these rates were for each forty weeks of work. I have treated forty weeks as being approximately equal to a year.

[2] See *Hearings before Senate Committee on Finance, op. cit.*, p. 251.

TABLE VI

ESTIMATED FINANCIAL STATUS OF OLD AGE INSURANCE PLAN AS APPROVED
BY THE COMMITTEE ON ECONOMIC SECURITY
(In millions of dollars)

Year	Net contributions[1]	Interest on reserve[2]	Federal subsidy	Benefit payments	Reserve at end of year
1937	306.0	.....	....	0.7	305.3
1938	308.9	9.2	....	2.0	621.5
1939	312.0	18.7	......	3.3	948.8
1940	314.9	28.4	....	4.8	1,287.3
1945	672.3	106.0	....	190.1	4,123.5
1950	1,073.3	211.9	....	577.1	7,770.7
1955	1,520.0	329.6	....	1,149.6	11,687.2
1960	1,979.2	431.9	....	1,924.8	14,880.1
1965	2,058.3	470.0	....	2,532.8	15,660.4
1970	2,137.5	468.0	507.3	3,112.8	15,600.0
1975	2,216.7	468.0	926.5	3,611.2	15,600.0
1980	2,216.7	468.0	1,387.9	4,072.5	15,600.0

[1] Net contributions equal joint contributions less administrative expenses.
[2] Interest was computed at 3 per cent of the average reserve for the year.

It will thus be seen that the recommended plan contemplated: (1) A maximum reserve of from fifteen to sixteen billions of dollars which would be reached by 1965 and be maintained at an approximately stabilized level thereafter;[1] (2) Government contributions which would begin somewhere between 1965 and 1970,[2] and which would rise to about 1.4 billions of dollars by 1980. After about the year 2000 the federal grants were to be approximately equal to the annual amounts of interest which the system would lose from not having initially built up its reserve from the full contribu-

[1] Stabilized at least in relation to population and earnings.
[2] According to other computations of the actuaries the federal government would have contributed about 166 millions in 1965. See *Senate Hearings*, *op. cit.*, p. 251.

tions required from the older workers to eliminate
any "unearned" annuities.

By such a financial arrangement, the committee
planned to accomplish the following purposes: (1)
The total size of the reserve would be kept down
to minimum limits, thus lessening the problem of
reinvestment and minimizing the withdrawal of
active purchasing power from the field of consumers goods. (2) To pay fairly adequate sums
under the insurance plan to those in the upper age
groups and thus lessen the costs to the federal and
state governments of outright old age pensions
during these years. (3) To free the government
from the cost of subsidizing during the transitional
period these actuarially "unearned" annuities and
thus smooth the financial problem of the national
government. (4) For the government, however, to
ultimately bear the cost of these subsidies but to do
it at a time when presumably the financial skies were
cleared. There were, however, not wanting political
cynics who implied that the postponement of the
governmental subsidies to 1965 or later was due to
the natural desire of almost any administration to
postpone the day of ultimate outlay to a time when
it would have been long out of office. Whether or
not this suspicion had any basis, the fact remains
that the policy was amply justified on other grounds.

Payroll Tax or Income Tax?

Underlying many of the financial issues involved
in old age insurance and unemployment insurance

was the question whether these measures should be exclusively financed by a levy upon payrolls or whether an added tax upon the upper income brackets should not be used to provide at least a portion of the necessary funds.

There were many attacks upon the payroll tax as such. To the degree that the workers made direct contributions under old age insurance, it was pointed out that this decreased the already inadequate incomes of the workers. To the degree that the employers contributed, as they did jointly in the case of old age insurance and exclusively in the case of the federal levies for extending unemployment insurance, it was argued that these amounts would be shifted ultimately to the workers and would make excessively severe inroads upon their incomes. This shifting might take one or both of two forms. In the first place, it might move backward and result in a decrease of wages. In the second place, it might move forward and result in an increase of prices.

It was argued that if the imposition of the taxes were not accompanied by an expansion of bank credit and if consequently no general rise in prices occurred, then wages must ultimately be reduced by the amount of the tax. The reasoning behind this contention was approximately as follows.[1] Under conditions of pure competition, each of the workers,

[1] For the fullest statement of this theory, see Harry G. Brown, *The Economics of Taxation*; and also Dale Yoder, "The Economic Implications of Unemployment Insurance," *Quarterly Journal of Economics*, Vol. XLV (1931), pp. 622-639.

according to the marginal productivity theory, receives the amount added to the social product by the last workman of their group who possesses equal ability. If the employer is compelled to pay for each worker a given percentage for social insurance in addition to his wage, then his outlay for the last worker (or workers) is greater than the value of the social product added by this or any other worker. He will, therefore, tend to dismiss a sufficient number of workers in order to bring the added productivity of what is now the last worker to a higher point, where it would at least equal the wage plus the insurance cos ts.[1] But the dismissal of these workers will create a considerable group of unemployed. These, in order to obtain employment, will offer to work for less than the prevailing wage rather than get nothing. This process would lower the general scale of wages and the movement would be continued until, in order to absorb all of the unemployed, the new wage plus the insurance costs would just equal the old wage without the insurance costs. For this, it will be remembered, was the point where the expenditure upon each of the workers was equal to the amount added to the

[1] From my studies of the probable slope of the marginal productivity curve in my book *The Theory of Wages*, it appears that the elasticity of this curve is not far from −3.0. A 5 per cent increase in wages would, therefore, cause under "pure" competition a decrease of approximately 15 per cent in the numbers employed. This tendency would be slightly mitigated by the fact that the increase in real income to the workers would lead to a voluntary retirement of a certain number from the labor market; and hence would give a higher marginal productivity to those who remained than would otherwise be the case.

social product by the last employee. In this way the entire cost of the employers' contributions would be transferred to the shoulders of the workers.

It may be granted that under conditions of pure competition such would tend to be the results. But in practice the actual working out of these results would not only be impeded by the "frictions" of real life but would also be altered by the fact that pure competition is far more the exception rather than the rule. Pure monopoly exists in some industries and imperfect competition in others. In these cases the workers will originally receive less than the productivity of the last employee.[1] An increase in the outlay for labor will not necessarily cause as much unemployment under these conditions as it would under pure competition and the ultimate result might well be some impairment of monopoly profits. It is probable, however, that in most cases a payroll tax upon employers would even under these conditions be at least partially shifted to the workers.

The argument that the employers' tax would be shifted to the consumers was far less sophisticated. It was tacitly assumed that the increased costs

---

[1] For a fuller development of the theory of imperfect competition, see Joan Robinson, *The Economics of Imperfect Competition;* and Chamberlin, *The Theory of Monopolistic Competition.* In brief, the workers will receive not the marginal physical productivity multiplied by price but the increment which the marginal worker adds to total gross revenue or marginal revenue. This marginal revenue is always less than price under conditions of imperfect competition. The full working out of the effects of imperfect competition upon the theory of distribution is a task which remains to be done.

would compel the banks to issue more credit and lead to an increase in prices.[1] This increase in prices it was declared would take out of the workers' pockets as consumers what had been added to them in social insurance, and hence make the workers really foot the bill for collectively meeting their needs. Here again there was very real truth, if we assume that bank credit would expand and prices would rise proportionately. Two exceptions would, however, be that in some industries prices need not rise by as much as the cost of the insurance payments[2] and, secondly, that since the workers are by no means the sole consumers a portion of the costs could be unloaded upon the well-to-do, the self-employed, etc.

A payroll tax, moreover, by increasing costs more in industries and plants with a high labor content than in those with a low labor content would lead to some readjustment of industries and firms. Thus, hand bakeries would lose ground as compared with mechanized bakeries, and cotton would lose in comparison with rayon. This would at least cause temporary unemployment. There might also be some shifts between industries.

---

[1] Whether this increase in unit prices would under pure competition be equal to, less than or more than the unit increase in labor costs would be the question. Under constant costs it would be the first; under increasing costs the second; and under decreasing costs the third. Modern analysis is, however, more and more pointing to constant costs as the general condition for moderately long-run equilibrium under pure competition. But here again the theory of imperfect competition will cause a substantial modification of the above conclusions.

[2] This point is referred to in the preceding footnote.

On the other hand it was pointed out that a tax upon the upper income brackets would not be shifted, would cause less industrial disturbance and unemployment, since it would fall on economic surpluses rather than on industrial margins, and would be borne by those best able to carry the load. In support of this point of view, the income statistics, computed for 1929 by the Brookings Institution, were frequently cited. These showed that in 1929 the 24,000 families who received more than $100,000 apiece enjoyed a total income which was three times as great as that obtained by the six million families at the bottom who received less than $1,000 a year.[1] This meant that the average income in this upper group was approximately 630 times as much as the average for those at the bottom. Even more striking was perhaps the fact that the total income of the 4,000 families who received over half a million dollars apiece in that year was one and three-quarters times as much as that of the submerged six million families, or on the average about 2,600 times more. The amount of total surplus income available in 1935 was of course much less.

But despite the merits of financing at least a portion of the costs of the social security program in this fashion, the administration chose to reject it and to use instead the levy upon payrolls. Those who favored a 100 per cent subsidy system com-

[1] Leven, Moulton, and Warburton, *America's Capacity to Consume*, pp. 54–55.

[67]

bined with income taxation were overruled on the latter point as well as upon the former.

This attitude of the administration, when combined with Secretary Morgenthau's later appearance before the House Committee when he asked for the removal of all future government grants to old age insurance, made the informed progressives in Congress and the country conclude that the administration had turned to the "right." It seemed opposed to any added levies upon wealth and large incomes in order to carry a portion of the cost of guarding against social insecurities. Progressive sentiment, therefore, rose against the administration on this point during March and April of 1935 but the control over Congress by the President gave them small prospects of any immediate success.

The Omission of Health Insurance

No proposal was advanced by the committee for health insurance. This was the result of four sets of factors. In the first place it was thought this would overload the program. Secondly the full details of a proper plan had not been generally worked out.[1] Public sentiment moreover had not yet been deeply aroused in favor of it. Finally the opposition of the leaders of the American Medical Association and of most state associations was intense, bitter and persistent. Grants for public health work were proposed, however, as a forward step.

[1] Yet see the excellent "model" bill which was drafted by the American Association for Social Security and for which Professor Herman A. Gray and Abraham Epstein were largely responsible.

CHAPTER III

THUNDER ON THE LEFT

THE administration's program was sharply challenged both in Congress and before the public by two plans of a much more radical nature. These were the Townsend Old Age Pension Plan and the Lundeen Bill for Unemployment Insurance.

The Townsend Plan

The Townsend plan burst into nation-wide prominence during the latter part of 1934 and the first part of 1935.[1] It proposed that all persons over the age of sixty irrespective of their personal means were to receive $200 a month from the national government on condition that they fulfill two conditions. These were, first, that they would retire from regular employment; and second, that they would agree to spend the money received within the month. The expenses were to be financed by a national tax on all "transactions." Its sponsor, Dr. Townsend of Long Beach, California, claimed for his method not only that it would (1) care properly for the aged, but also (2) remove unemployment by withdrawing the older workers from

[1] See F. G. Townsend, *Old Age Plan for Revolving Pensions.*

the labor market, (3) increase in some fashion the total quantity of purchasing power and hence build up production and employment and finally (4) speed up the circulation of money and hence help to revive business.

The arithmetic of the Townsend plan was somewhat startling. There were 10.4 million people in 1930 who were sixty years of age and over and by 1935 this number had probably increased to about eleven million. It is probable that at least ten of these eleven millions would have claimed the Townsend pension since the conditions attached to it, namely, that one should retire from industry and spend the money, could scarcely be regarded as onerous. This number of persons each receiving a pension of $200 a month or $2,400 a year would have required a total annual outlay of 24 billions of dollars. Since the national income of 1934 was probably not much, if any, in excess of 48 billions, this would have meant turning over one-half of the national income (on the assumption that prices would not increase and that the real national income would remain constant) to about 8 per cent of the population.

Dr. Townsend declared that his plan could be financed by a 2 per cent tax on transactions. Such a tax would of course pyramid as commodities were moved on through the various processes of fabrication and of marketing. Robert R. Doane, Dr. Townsend's economist, estimated that such a tax on physical goods would yield in 1935 four billions of dollars; if levied on all producer and consumer expenditures, the yield was estimated at six billions, and on all gross transactions and transfers at between nine and ten billions of dollars.[1] The yield, according to Mr. Doane, would have been double these amounts on the 1929 basis of activity. It was clear, therefore, that Dr. Townsend's proposed scale of financing would not have sufficed to pay the full benefits which he promised. Since the total volume of retail sales in 1934 probably did not exceed thirty-two billions of dollars, the tax if levied on material goods alone, and by an amount necessary to raise the needed twenty-four billions, would have necessitated an increase in the final retail prices of about 75 per cent.[2] If levied on services as well as goods it would have increased prices by about 50 per cent. The unskilled laborer receiving $16 a week would, therefore, have had his real income reduced by from one-third to three-sevenths in order that those over sixty years of age might receive $50 a week. These sums, moreover, were to be paid to the aged irrespective of their need and might indeed be claimed by such persons as Ford, Rockefeller, Mellon and Morgan if they were to satisfy the two simple conditions which were required.

What then shall be said about the claim that the Townsend plan would build up purchasing power

---

[1] See *Senate Hearings, op. cit.,* p. 1244.

[2] This is of course on the assumption that the amount of bank credit would expand correspondingly.

and increase production? The initial advance of money to finance the plan would temporarily have increased the total quantity of monetary purchasing power and hence have expanded consumption. It would consequently have probably restored some of the unemployed to work and have raised production.[1] But, thereafter, since the plan was to be financed by a sales tax the result would really not have been a net increase but rather merely a transfer of purchasing power. The purchasing power of those who paid the tax would have been decreased by the same amount as that by which those who received the pensions was increased. After the first stimulus, no additional net increase in purchasing power would, therefore, have been forthcoming. It should also be noticed that the administrative difficulties of collecting the transfer tax from so many different persons would be enormous, while perhaps even more trouble would have been caused by the task of preventing the pensioners from retaining paid employment and of requiring them to spend every month their full pension of $200.

Despite its economic weakness, however, the Townsend plan attracted an extraordinary amount of public support. Many millions of signatures were obtained to petitions asking Congress to adopt the plan, while the letters advocating it which were received by Congressmen probably themselves ran up into the millions. By the middle of February,

[1] Part of this increase in monetary purchasing power would have been counterbalanced by an increase in prices.

1935, Dr. Townsend testified that there were no less than 3,000 Townsend clubs in existence with an average membership of 150 persons in each. Within less than a year the various branches of the Townsend movement took in no less than $85,000 in contributions to further their work of propaganda.

While, therefore, it was impossible to enact the Townsend plan, the widespread popular support which it had obtained probably did weaken the die-hard opposition to the security bill. While the major portion of the sentiment in favor of the bill had been created both by the drift of conditions and by the work of such pioneers as Rubinow, Commons and Epstein, the agitation in behalf of the Townsend plan did help to break down opposition to the idea of greater social security and to obtain support for the idea in quarters which would have been unaffected by more soberly drafted proposals. At the same time, however, it pitched the hopes and claims of its supporters on far too high a level and without educating them in the realities of the problem served to make them dissatisfied with any practical step taken. In short, the way in which the Townsend plan was suddenly taken up by millions well illustrates an all too general tendency of the American mind. That tendency is to ignore almost completely, during periods of relative prosperity, any defects in the social order and any well thought-out program for their improvement but to embrace enthusiastically during periods of depression hasty and ill-considered schemes which are impossible of fruition.

The Lundeen Bill

The other plan which was advanced from the left was the Lundeen bill for unemployment insurance. This proposal had been previously advocated by various left-wing groups and it was introduced into Congress in 1934 by Representative Lundeen (Farmer-Labor) of Minnesota[1] and again introduced by him in 1935.[2] This bill provided for the payment of unemployment compensation out of the funds of the national government to all unemployed persons over the age of eighteen years for as long as they were out of work through no fault of their own. It thus included those who were then out of work as well as those who would lose their jobs in the future and it covered self-employed persons such as farmers, merchants, professional workers, etc., as well as those who worked for wages. It furthermore made no exemptions among the workers themselves as the administration's bill later did for farm laborers and domestic workers, but was instead all-inclusive. The amount of the

[1] H. R. 7598, 73rd Congress, 2nd Session, 1934. See also the *Hearings* on this bill; D. W. Douglas, "What Kind of Unemployment Insurance," *Social Work Today*, Vol. I (May, June, 1934) pp. 3–6; Mary Van Kleeck, "The Workers Bill for Unemployment and Social Insurance," *New Republic*, Vol. LXXXI (December 12, 1934), pp. 121–124.

[2] H. R. 2827, 74th Congress, 1st Session, 1935. See also *Hearings* on this bill.

benefits was to be at least equal to the full prevailing local rate of wages but in no case was to be less than $10 per week, plus $3 for each dependent. Those who were given only part-time employment were to receive the difference between their earnings and the local wages for full-time. The cost of these benefits was to be paid for by the government out of taxes on inheritances, gifts, and incomes of over $5,000 a year, and no payroll levy was to be made upon either the employers or the employees. It was not however to be administered by the government but by bodies elected by "workers' and farmers' organizations," under rules approved by such groups. In the last draft of the bill the same provisions were also to be carried out for all workers and farmers who were unable to work for any reason, whether this inability was caused by sickness, old age, maternity, industrial injury, etc. The original proposal was thus widened to include social protection against all forms of involuntary lost time and not merely against unemployment alone.

The foregoing description of the Lundeen bill will have indicated why many came to support it. It promised self-respecting aid to those who were then unemployed and did not merely confine itself to those who in the distant future might lose their jobs. Its appeal was, therefore, immediate. Furthermore, it was inclusive. It barred no one and reached out to include the farmers, the professional workers and the self-employed as well as the wage-

earners. Its scale of benefits was far more ample
than that provided either by relief or by any insurance system which was likely to be set up. It demanded that the unemployed should be guaranteed
enough to give them at least a minimum of physical
subsistence and should not be provided with less
than this either by relief or by insurance. This of
course made a strong appeal to the unemployed
and those on relief and this appeal was increased
by the provision that the administration of the
system was to be in the hands of the workers and
farmers and not to be conducted by the government. To men and women who were smarting under
the rules laid down by relief officials where almost
complete destitution was required before aid would
be given, this provision, as well as the more ample
scale of benefits, seemed fundamental. Finally the
plan proposed to care for the unemployed on this
scale and in this manner for as long as they were
unable to find suitable employment instead of
dropping them at the end of a given period as would
inevitably be the case under the projected unemployment insurance laws which were to be passed
by the states.

The main driving force behind the Lundeen bill
was originally furnished by the communists. But
many noncommunists came to support it because
they believed it to be the most thoroughgoing and
adequate proposal which had been put forward for
taking care of the unemployed. To many it seemed
to be merely the American replica of the demand of

the British Labour Party that the unemployed should be given "work or maintenance." While officially opposed by the American Federation of Labor, it was endorsed by a number of city federations and by a very much larger number of local unions. It was also supported by a surprisingly large number of social workers led by Miss Mary Van Kleeck of the Russell Sage Foundation.

Many old-time advocates of unemployment insurance, however, pointed out several crucial defects in the bill which to them made the proposal highly impracticable.

1. The bill proposed to compensate for the unemployment of self-employed persons. But how, it was asked, could it be determined whether in fact such a person was unemployed; when for example was a doctor, a lawyer or a farmer unemployed? The test as to whether a wage or salaried worker was unemployed could be made fairly definite. Was his name on the payroll of industry? If not, he could properly be regarded as out of work. But no such test could be imposed upon the self-employed. How few patients, for example, did a doctor have to have before he could be so classified, or how few clients a lawyer? How low must a merchant's sales have to fall before he could obtain aid, and would a farmer be compensated during the winter months? When it is remembered that the bill also provided that part-time workers were to have their incomes brought up to the prevailing local wages, it will be seen that still further complications would

[77]

be created in the case of these self-employed workers.

The advocates of the Lundeen bill replied that these criticisms were after all but minor in nature and that all these problems could be easily ironed out by the administrative commissions which would be elected by the workers and farmers themselves. The opponents of the plan rejoined that this merely begged the issue and that these commissions would still have these problems to settle.

2. It was furthermore alleged that the proposed administrative set-up was thoroughly illogical. The government supplied all the funds for the payments but had virtually no control over them. The commissions chosen by the farmers and workers would naturally wish to protect the interests of those who elected them and to whom they would be responsible. In consequence, it was feared that the decisions of such bodies would be overwhelmingly in favor of the applicants, and the result would be a wholesale raiding of the public treasury.

3. This would be increased, it was charged, by the fact that the compensation granted would at the least be equal to what the applicant could earn if employed, while in a large proportion of the cases it would be more. It will be remembered that the bill did call for benefits at least equal to going wages but not less than $10 a week for each worker, plus $3 for each dependent. If workers were paid as much when they were unemployed as when they had a job, what incentive, it was asked, would there

be for them to seek employment? Furthermore in the case of many workers who had dependents, they would actually receive very much more if unemployed than if they had a job. Thus, an unskilled laborer with a wife and four dependent children would receive $25 a week if he were unemployed, whereas he might be fortunate to receive $16 a week if employed (i.e., 40 hours of work at 40 cents an hour). Under such conditions, it was alleged, malingering would flourish; men would not try to obtain work; and the administrative boards controlled by those who were drawing the benefits would not put sufficient pressure upon them to make them do so.

Finally, it was pointed out that when Soviet Russia had a system of unemployment insurance, it did not pay benefits equal to 100 per cent of wages, but instead only about 35 per cent of the customary wage and that for a limited period of time.[1] It was, therefore, asked whether it was not inconsistent of the admirers of Soviet Russia to ask a capitalistic nation to provide a far more liberal scale of benefits relative to its wage structure than Russia itself had granted.

Proponents of the Lundeen bill replied to all this by saying, first, that if men had the chance to work

---

[1] See the chapter by the author on social insurance in the volume *Soviet Russia in the Second Decade*, edited by Chase, Dunn and Tugwell; also *Russia after Ten Years* (International Publishers), pp. 44–49. Benefits equal to 100 per cent of wages were, however, granted in the case of sickness and accidents without any appreciable stimulus to malingering at least up until 1928.

they would do so and they would not lie idle merely because they could get as much money. Secondly, that where the benefits exceeded the prevailing wage, this differential would withdraw workers from the labor market and by making labor more scarce would raise the wage rate until it at least equaled the unemployment benefits. The benefits to the unemployed could thus be used as a lever to compel industry to pay a living wage to those who were employed. In a sense, therefore, this proposal meant that the benefits could be used to finance a tacit strike to make the scale of benefits the scale of wages.[1] Finally, the Lundeenites declared that it was quite proper for a wealthy and prosperous country such as the United States to pay a scale of benefits which a poor country like Russia, which had always been industrially backward, could not afford.

4. The final fundamental objection to the Lundeen bill was that it would involve a financial burden which would be too heavy for the country to bear. Since there were at least ten million unemployed who would have to be paid either the going rate for their labor or more, this would have meant at the very least an annual average of $1,000 and a minimum yearly total outlay for unemployment of ten billions of dollars. The addition of similar

---

[1] The bill explicitly provided that the benefits were to be paid to those who refused to work for "less than average local or trade-union wages." It would not have been difficult to have formed unions which would have demanded that the relief scale should furnish at least the minimum rate for unskilled labor.

provisions for those unable to work because of old age and illness would have required at the very least close to another ten billions. The Lundeen bill, therefore, in its mature form called for almost as large an outlay as the Townsend plan, although it aimed to benefit a wider group who were in greater need and to finance the expenses in a more democratic way.

It was apparent, therefore, that, even if the public agreed to pay such relief benefits, they could scarcely be financed out of the existing national income. Some of the supporters of the bill tried sincerely to prove that this could be done, but it is probable that there were others who realized that this was impossible and who indeed partly advocated the plan because they knew it could not be fulfilled under the existing set-up. Many of the advocates believed that if these benefits were once established and if it developed that they could not be paid out of the existing national income, the people of the country would then demand a reorganization of industry and would insist that men be put to work producing for each other under a program of production for use rather than profit. In the minds of some there was, therefore, an unquestionable desire to use the Lundeen plan as an initial wedge to obtain the socialization of industry. There were many advocates of the plan who did not go so far as this. The hearings on the bill before the House Committee on Labor disclosed such support for the measure that this committee by a close vote

[81]

recommended its passage.[1] The administration forces, as we shall see, prevented the bill as such from coming to a vote but when it was offered in the House as an amendment to the administration's bill it obtained approximately fifty votes.

The Lundeen bill, however, like the Townsend plan, had an effect upon the course of legislation and we may expect it to exercise a continuing influence upon the future trend of unemployment insurance. The radical and sweeping nature of its proposals enabled the administration forces to say to the indifferent and to the conservative that unless the latter accepted the moderate program put forward by the administration they might later be forced to accept the radical and far-reaching provisions of the Lundeen bill. As is generally true in political strategy, the center was thus able to use the left as a club against the right.

But perhaps even more important may be the effect which the Lundeen bill will have in the future. The state systems of unemployment insurance which will be set up will necessarily furnish the workers with only a partial and incomplete protection against unemployment. Unless all signs fail, a large section of the working class will continue to advocate the basic principle of the bill, namely, that those unemployed through no fault of their own are entitled to maintenance on the basis of at least a minimum of physical subsistence. This has already become the fundamental issue which is

[1] See *Report No.* 418, 74th Congress, 1st Session, March 15, 1935.

being pushed by the more militant members of the British Labour Party.[1] Fundamentally the issue which was joined between the administration's bill and the Lundeen plan was the question whether "social-reform" capitalism can provide adequate security against the great social risks of industry. If such a program of social reform provides only partial protection for limited periods of time to restricted groups in the population, while the great social risks still continue in a widespread and severe form, we may expect the agitation for the principles of the Lundeen bill to continue and to increase. A demand for a new organization of industry and politics may well accompany it. This will make it possible to provide the more adequate protection which will be claimed. Social-reform capitalism will then undergo a most severe test.

[1] See the able discussion of this point by Mrs. Helen F. Hohman in her *British Social Insurance and the Minimum Wage.*

CHAPTER IV

THE LEGISLATIVE HISTORY OF
THE SECURITY ACT

THE friends of the social security movement urged the necessity of speed upon the administration if it were to obtain cooperative action from the states in the near future. For virtually all the state legislatures were meeting during the early months of 1935. Most of them would, however, adjourn their regular sessions by the middle of the spring and would not normally reconvene for nearly two years or until the beginning of 1937. It was, therefore, pointed out that quick action in drafting the bill and in its consideration by Congress were essential if the program were to be accepted by any considerable number of states in 1935 or indeed even before 1937.

The Bill As Introduced

It was not, however, until the fifteenth of January that the Committee on Economic Security made its report[1] and on the seventeenth that the bill was introduced into Congress by Senator Wagner in the upper branch and by both David

[1] *Report to the President of the Committee on Economic Security.* See also *Supplement to Report to the President of the Committee on Economic Security.*

[84]

J. Lewis of Maryland and R. L. Doughton of North
Carolina in the House. Representative Lewis, it
will be remembered, had, during the preceding
Congress, jointly sponsored with Senator Wagner the unemployment insurance bill, while Mr.
Doughton had then been either indifferent or opposed to it. The latter now, however, also attached
his name to the draft,[1] and under administration
guidance it was referred to the Ways and Means
Committee, of which he was chairman. This reference to the Ways and Means Committee instead of
to the House Committee on Labor seemed somewhat illogical to some and was explained by certain
cynical students of the political scene on the
ground that the administration feared that the
relatively progressive or radical Committee on
Labor would so liberalize the provisions of the
measure that the administration would be forced
into a more radical position than it wished to
assume. With the far more conservative Committee
on Ways and Means no such fears need arise. Justification for this action was, however, found in the
fact that the measure involved public appropriations together with further contributions by or
taxes upon employers and employees. It might,
therefore, be said with some propriety to be a matter with which the Ways and Means Committee
should deal. Similarly, in the Senate the bill was

---

[1] It was intimated by several newspaper correspondents that this was done
in order to obtain credit in the public eye for an act which was about to
pass.

[85]

referred to the Committee on Finance rather than to that on Labor.

Hearings started in the House on January 21 and in the Senate on January 22. As the bill began to be studied, however, it was soon discovered that the technical job of drafting which had been confided to the legal staff of the Department of Labor had been poorly done. There was little or no logic in the sequence of topics covered and some of the language was ambiguous and, indeed, in places unintelligible.[1]

In the bill, as it was introduced, there were a number of salient features which need to be noticed. Under the old age pension section, fifty million dollars was appropriated for the year ending June 30, 1936, and one hundred twenty-five millions of dollars for each of the subsequent years. It was

---

[1] Thus, the outline of the bill (H. R. 4142 and 7260; S. 1130) was as follows:

Title   I Appropriations for old age assistance.

       II Appropriations for aid to dependent children.

     III Earnings tax (for old age insurance).

    IV Social Insurance Board. Under this were included: (*a*) The provisions governing the payment of monthly annuities under mandatory old age insurance; (*b*) Allotments to states for the administration of unemployment insurance.

      V Annuity certificates.

    VI Imposition of Tax (offset method for unemployment insurance). This title contained in fact a jumble of material. The definitions under this title were given towards the end, being preceded by the levying of the further tax and provisions for allowable credit. The sections of the bill which granted additional credit where the contributions of individual employers were reduced because of progress in stabilization were almost totally incomprehensible.

   VII Maternal and child health and child welfare.

 VIII Appropriations for public health.

provided that in order for any state to receive the
federal aid for this purpose it was necessary that:
(*a*) The plan should be state-wide and if administered by counties or localities should be mandatory
upon them. The state should itself participate in a
substantial financial manner. (*b*) There should be
one central state authority which would be in general charge of the administration of the pension-
system. To this body individual claimants might
appeal if they were denied by the local authorities,
and it was also charged with the duty of making
the necessary reports to the federal administration. (*c*) The pensions granted must, when added
to the private incomes of the aged person, furnish
"a reasonable subsistence compatible with health
and decency." The decision as to what this "reasonable subsistence" would be was to be in the hands
of the federal authority administering this section
of the act. (*d*) The pensions could not, at the least,
be denied to citizens of the United States who in
other respects were eligible. This clause aimed to
do two things. It made it optional for the states to
grant pensions to aged aliens and it sought to place
some protection, if they were citizens, around
Negroes and other racial minorities and groups
which might locally be oppressed; so that if they
were otherwise eligible they could not be denied
pensions. (*e*) The pensions were ultimately to be
granted to all those of sixty-five years and over
whose incomes and that of their families were insufficient to provide the "reasonable subsistence"

mentioned on page 87. Following a suggestion which had originally been made by. Mr. Epstein in 1934 the states were now given a period of grace until 1940 during which they could confine the benefits to those of seventy years and over. This was done because so many of the existing state laws had fixed seventy years as the age of eligibility. (*f*) The state laws must not deny benefits to those who had resided in the state for five of the ten years preceding the date of application. This was a much lower residence requirement than that which had been imposed by the majority of the existing state laws, for these had naturally been framed with a view to preventing an influx of aged persons into the pioneering states.

The amount of the federal aid was to be one-half of the pension paid by the state subject to a monthly maximum grant by the federal government of $15. The general administration of the grants for old age assistance was to be given to the Federal Emergency Relief Administrator,[1] who had the power to compel the respective state authorities to establish such "methods of administration" as were approved by the administrator. If a state failed to come up to the legislative and administrative standards laid down, the federal administrator then had the right to withhold from that state the federal grants.

---

[1] The Federal Emergency Relief Administrator was also given charge in the original draft of the allotments for aid to dependent children or what are popularly known as mother's pensions.

So far as the mandatory taxes for the purpose of providing old age insurance were concerned, the scale of payments prescribed was that which has already been outlined in Chapter II. These taxes were to be collected by the Bureau of Internal Revenue under the direction of the Secretary of the Treasury and were to be effected through the purchase of special stamps, etc. The bill, as introduced, provided for an extraordinarily wide degree of coverage by specifying that the contributions were to be made by and on behalf of all manual wage-workers and all salaried employees under sixty years of age. It was not, however, to be levied on that portion of a worker's salary which exceeded $250 a month. No occupations or industries were to be excluded except public employment and the railways.[1] Farm laborers, domestic servants and employees of non-profit seeking organizations were definitely included. Similarly, no firms were excluded because of smallness of size, and the firms with one employee were included along with the giant corporations.

The monthly annuities which were to be paid to these insured persons who reached the age of sixty-five and for whom contributions had been paid for at least two hundred weeks were to be those previously outlined in the second chapter. Those for whom taxes were paid only after 1941 were to receive in annuities a basic 10 per cent of their aver-

---

[1] At that time it was thought that the railway workers were provided for under the Railway Retirement Act.

age wage plus 1 per cent for each year over five (i.e., for each forty weeks beyond the first two hundred weeks) for which such contributions had been made.

Let us now turn to the unemployment insurance provisions of the original bill. It provided during the first two years of 1936 and 1937 for a sliding scale of payroll taxes upon industry based upon business conditions. The normal tax was supposed to be 3 per cent of the payroll, which was of course to be solely paid by the employers. But it was provided that if the index of production of the Federal Reserve Board during the year ending September 30, 1935, was less than 84 per cent of its 1923–1925 average the payroll assessment was then to be only 1 per cent. If the index was between 84 and 95 per cent the assessment was, however, to be 2 per cent.[1] In order that an employer might obtain a credit up to 90 per cent of the federal tax, it was necessary that payments to the unemployed should not begin until two years after the contributions first began to be made under the separate state laws. The payments of the state benefits were to be made through the public employment offices of the states and the sums collected by the states were to be deposited in a federal unemployment trust fund under the direction of the Secretary of the Treasury. These monies might be invested in government bonds or any obligations which were

[1] It was provided, however, that the assessment for 1937 could not be less than that for 1936 even though the index of production were lower.

guaranteed both as to principal and interest by the federal government.

It will be remembered that the funds for the administration of the unemployment laws of the various states were to be supplied from 100 per cent grants by the federal government. Although it was not explicitly stated, it was understood that these sums were in turn derived from the one-tenth of the federal payroll tax against which offsets could not be credited. An initial appropriation of 4 million dollars was made for the fiscal year ending June 30, 1936, but the total amounts which could be distributed for this purpose were to be 49 millions a year in subsequent years. In return for these grants, the Social Insurance Board, which was to administer this and certain other sections of the act, was to require that all positions under the state unemployment insurance acts were to be "filled by persons appointed on a nonpartisan basis and selected on the basis of merit under rules and regulations prescribed and approved by the Board." The board was also to see that the administrative rules and practices of the states were calculated to insure full payment of the benefits.

The scope of the payroll tax for the purpose of stimulating the states to take action in the field of unemployment insurance was indeed broad. It included employers with four or more employees, except government and public agencies. The employers were taxed on their entire payroll and not merely on those of manual workers and salaried workers under a specified amount. This meant that the taxes would be collected on the salaries of executives, etc., who might not come under the protection of the various state funds, or who if they did would be given only comparatively small benefits in relation to their salaries.

The states were left largely free to adopt almost any type of insurance system which they wished. They could put into effect state-wide pooled funds, plant reserves, or industry funds composed of subgroups of employers. Provision was also made to recognize plans for guaranteed employment. It was provided, however, that those who contributed to plant and industry funds could obtain an offset against the federal tax only if they also contributed 1 per cent of their payrolls to a pooled state fund in order to help provide a reserve for other industries. The offset provisions for the plant reserve plans were unfortunately almost completely unintelligible to the average reader. Their intention was, however, to enable these employers to credit against the federal tax not only the amounts which they actually contributed but also the amounts which they were freed from contributing because of the relative stabilization of labor within their establishment or industry, which they had either effected or which had just "happened."

In addition there were, as I have indicated, appropriations for general welfare and health purposes. The sum of 25 million dollars was to be appropriated to provide federal aid to the states for the care in their homes of dependent children under the age of sixteen on condition that the states would furnish twice as much money as the federal grants. This was to be handled by the Federal Relief Administration and was intended to supplement and to extend aid already given by most states under the so-called "mother's pension" laws. A further annual appropriation of 4 million dollars was also provided to aid maternal and infant care. This was designed to continue the work which had been started after the war under the Sheppard-Towner act, but the federal appropriations for which were later discontinued. Unless prevented by "exceptional circumstances" the states were expected to match these latter federal grants by an equal appropriation, although some federal funds were to be made available to the poorer states without this requirement of matching. The administration of these funds was given to the Children's Bureau, which had been the agency to administer the rather short-lived Sheppard-Towner act. An annual sum of 3 million dollars was provided in the form of federal aid for the care of crippled children, and these sums "except in the case of severe economic distress" were to be matched by equal amounts from the states. Another one and a half million dollars was to be granted for various child welfare purposes. The major portion of this, as in the other welfare grants, had to be matched by corresponding state appropriations, but some was left free to be allotted outright to the most hard-pressed states. Finally there was an appropriation of 10 million dollars yearly for public health. Eight-tenths of this was to be turned over by the U. S. Public Health Service to the states for the purpose of developing public health work. These were outright grants which did not require matching. The remainder, or 2 million dollars, was to be retained by the Public Health Service for research into the problems of disease and sanitation.

The general administration of the unemployment features of the act as well as those dealing with old age insurance was confided to the Social Insurance Board of three members, who were to hold office for six years and receive a salary of $10,000 a year. The bill called for the placing of the board inside the Department of Labor and the approval of the Secretary was required for the appointment of officers, attorneys and experts. This would of course have made the Secretary of Labor the dominant force in the administration of the system. Much the same issue was coming up simultaneously in connection with the National Labor Relations Board, which was being proposed in connection with the Wagner Industrial Disputes bill, and where the Secretary of Labor was urging that a similar arrangement be made. Finally, the "officers, attorneys, and experts," of the board could be appointed without regard to civil service provisions, but other employees could not.

The Hearings on the Bill

Hearings on the bill were started on January 21 before the House Committee and on the following day before the corresponding committee of the Senate. They were continued until February 12 before the former body and until the twentieth of that month before the latter. The witnesses before these committees may be divided into four groups: (1) Those who explained the bill and argued in favor of it. This group included such persons as the Secretary of Labor, Senator Wagner, and Director Witte. (2) Constructive critics of the plan, who although approving of many features in the bill, believed it could be improved in other respects. Representatives of this point of view were Messrs. Paul Kellogg, Abraham Epstein, William Green, President of the A. F. of L., Dr. Frank P. Graham and Miss Helen Hall. (3) Advocates of widely differing plans, such as those of Dr. Townsend and Congressman Lundeen. (4) Opponents of social insurance. Among this group should be listed James A. Emery, representing the National Association of Manufacturers, and James L. Donnelly of the Illinois Manufacturers Association. It was noticeable, however, that Henry I. Harriman, the President of the United States Chamber of Commerce, did not attack the main features of the bill and that some of the opposition was not directed against the ultimate merits of the proposal as such, but rather took the ground that the time was not

[95]

then ripe for action and that Congress should postpone approval until business conditions were better. The reply which was made to this contention by the advocates of social insurance was that if the nation were to wait for prosperity before it instituted the plan, it would never start at all because by then the driving force of public sentiment would be removed. We would then blunder into the next depression without any reserves being accumulated to protect the unemployed just as we had blundered into the present depression. It should be noted that one business group, namely, the National Retail Dry Goods Association, was ardently in favor of the program and produced an extremely intelligent and public-spirited report on the subject.[7]

The most important change of policy which was made by the government during the hearings was in the field of contributory old age insurance. As has been pointed out, the original plan proposed by the Committee on Economic Security called for low initial rates of contributions and for a slow raising of these rates so that the maximum contribution rate of 5 per cent would not be reached for twenty years. It also carried with it annuities for those in the upper age groups which would be in excess of the sums provided by the contributions by and for these older workers. These "unearned" annuities, as will be remembered, were to be initially advanced from the contributions made by the younger workers who would not for many years be eligible for their annuities, but these advances were to be repaid with interest by government contributions which would begin between 1965 and 1970. Secretary Morgenthau, however, appeared before the House Committee on February 5 after the hearings had been under way for two weeks with the proposal that all future government contributions were to be eliminated from the contributory old age insurance portion of the bill and that this plan was to be put on a strictly "self-supporting" basis.[1] This change of policy was popularly supposed to be favored by the President. In order to eliminate the future government grants, two sets of changes were proposed. In the first place, those who retired during the next thirty years were to receive smaller annuities than had been originally proposed. Secondly, the rates of contribution were started at a higher level, namely, at 1 per cent each from the employers and workers, instead of half that amount as the bill had provided. The rates rose more rapidly thereafter to a maximum of 6 per cent instead of to the previous maximum of 5 per cent. Thus, the rates paid by each party were to increase by one-half of 1 per cent every three years in place of every five years. At the end of twelve years, or by 1949, the new plan provided that each party would contribute 3 per cent, whereas the former plan had provided

[1] *Hearings before Committee on Ways and Means*, House of Representatives, 74th Congress, 1st Session, on H. R. 4120, pp. 897–911.

that the maximum of 2½ per cent apiece would not be reached until 1957.

In effect, therefore, this new plan called: (1) For cutting down the annuities paid to those who would retire within the next thirty years; and, if they were still in need after these annuities were paid, for meeting the difference out of the noncontributory old age pension systems. (2) For having the workers of the younger generation finance out of their payments not only the protection for their own old age but also the excess of payments being made to those in the upper groups over the contributions made by and for them. The younger workers were, therefore, asked to provide not only for their own future but in part also for the future of those who were more advanced in years. (3) For the permanent payment by future generations of 1 per cent more than under the original plan.

A necessary consequence of this was, of course, the accumulation of much larger reserves for contributory old age annuities. These were naturally built up more rapidly out of the larger contributions and were not drawn down as much as before by the advances to those in the upper age groups. Thus, by 1950 the original bill envisioned a total reserve of approximately 7.7 billions of dollars; while the Morgenthau plan looked forward to a reserve in that year of approximately 18.7 billions of dollars, or nearly two and a half times as much. The original plan had also provided for an estimated reserve of about 15.3 billions in 1965; while under the schedules proposed by Secretary Morgenthau this would probably amount to no less than 42.1 billions. Under the first plan the reserve was never supposed to raise above the maximum of 15.3 billions, but Secretary Morgenthau's proposal called for the building up by 1980 of a total reserve of no less than 50 billions of dollars.[1]

Despite the fact that the House hearings closed by February 12, it was not until nearly two months later, or April 5, that the Ways and Means Committee reported out a revised bill. Part of this delay was caused by the necessity of improving the technical drafting of the bill, which emerged in a much clearer and more logical fashion after having been revised by the committee. A part of the delay was, however, due to the slowness with which Congress faced the work during the first three months of the session. The failure of the administration to assume active leadership at this time and some resentment in the House against the administration accounted also for the lost time. Many Congressmen were opposed to the omnibus character of the measure and resented the administration's attitude that it must be "all or none." There were many who did not like to be forced to adopt a vast series of untried measures in the original drafting of which they had had no part.

[1] The estimates of these reserves as finally prepared by the Senate Committee on Finance and the House Ways and Means Committee were however somewhat less.

The Bill As Reported by the Ways and Means Committee

The bill as reported[1] to the House made numerous changes in the original draft, which may be listed as follows.

1. The requirement that the amount of the state pensions to aged persons must as a minimum assure "a reasonable subsistence compatible with decency and health" was sharply qualified so that this was to be done only so far as was practicable under the conditions in each state. One reason for this change was the fear on the part of many southern Senators and Representatives that the earlier provision might be used by authorities in Washington to compel the southern states to pay higher pensions to aged Negroes than the dominant white groups believed to be desirable. Conversely, this very fact made the articulate and informed Negroes prefer either a national system of old age pensions or one under which the national government could control the minimum payments made by the state and could prevent discrimination against the Negroes as such. With a considerable amount of political strength in the north the Negroes believed they could better protect their race in the south under national rather than under state control. In fairness to the south, it should be

---

[1] See *Report of Committee on Ways and Means on the Social Security Bill*, House of Representatives, 74th Congress, 1st Session, Report No. 615; H. R. 7260; 74th Congress, 1st Session, Union Calendar No. 186 as reported on April 5, 1935.

added that there were Congressmen from other sections of the country where there were unpopular racial or cultural minorities who wanted to have their states left more or less free to treat them as they wished. The desire of some states not to expend much money for this purpose was also a strong factor.

Another change may also have been connected with this issue. The earlier draft had provided that if a number of other qualifications such as age, need, etc., were met, assistance could not be denied to anyone who was a citizen of the United States. This was altered slightly so as to read that no "citizenship requirement' could exclude any such citizen. This might pave the way for legitimatizing the exclusion of aged Negroes, Indians and other racial groups from pensions on other grounds than citizenship.

2. The following groups of workers were excluded from paying contributions to the compulsory old age insurance fund, namely, agricultural laborers, domestic servants in private homes, casual labor, those over the age of sixty-five, seamen, those in public employment and finally those employed by non-profit seeking organizations. The argument for the exclusion of this last group was led by representatives of the pension funds of the various denominations who claimed they were already providing for the old age of ministers, etc., and that the churches should not, therefore, be compelled to pay twice. What was sometimes omit-

ted in such statements was the fact that there were, however, other employees of religious, educational and charitable organizations who were not hired on an annual basis and who consequently were not protected by these private funds. The exclusion of this group from the federal provisions left them, therefore, without any protection. It was estimated that the number of persons covered by these provisions would be, according to the 1930 figures, about 25.8 millions. This was a little over one-half of all those gainfully employed in 1930 and about two-thirds of all those who worked for wages or salary.[1]

3. The higher scale of contributions advocated by the Secretary of the Treasury was adopted.

4. The monthly annuities which were to be paid to the insured workers who reached the age of sixty-five were to be computed on a somewhat different method, namely, on the total income received by the workers during their insured lifetimes. This was graduated on the following basis: (*a*) On the first $3,000 of total wages, the monthly annuities were to be at the rate of one-half of 1 per cent of the total. This would mean an annuity of $15 a month if the person had earned a total of $3,000 while insured. (*b*) On the amounts earned between $3,000 and $45,000, or on the next $42,000, the monthly annuity was at the rate of one-twelfth of 1 per cent of this amount. Thus, if a man had earned a total of $15,000 the added

---

[1] House of Representatives, 74th Congress, 1st Session, Report No. 615, p. 14.

annuity on the last $12,000 of this would be $10 a month, making a total annuity of $25 a month. A person earning a total of $45,000 would receive a total monthly annuity of $50. (c) On all sums earned over $45,000 the monthly annuity was to be at the rate of one-twenty-fourth of 1 per cent.

The minimum monthly benefit was to be $10 and the maximum $85. This plan, therefore, provided for a somewhat larger proportionate scale of benefits to the lower paid workers and to those employed in insured occupations for comparatively short periods of time. The committee also estimated that the reserves would ultimately be somewhat less than the amounts which the Treasury had believed. It estimated this reserve at 32.8 billions of dollars by 1970, whereas the Treasury's estimates had been for 46.4 billions. The new figure was, however, over double that involved in the original proposal.

5. The provision of voluntary annuities for self-employed workers and for those excluded from mandatory old age insurance was eliminated. This was done on the ground that such voluntary insurance would put the government into competition with potential private business. While in the past the private insurance companies had not sold many annuities to members of these groups, they hoped to have more success in the future and the committee did not wish to disturb their development of this field.

6. So far as the payroll tax to stimulate the states into taking action on unemployment insur-

ance was concerned, the same industries were excluded as in the case of mandatory old age insurance. In addition, however, all firms employing fewer than ten employees were exempted. It was estimated that this last exemption reduced the coverage by approximately 5.4 million workers,[1] or to a total on the basis of the figures for 1930 of 22.0 millions; and allowing 4 per cent for growth the estimated coverage came to nearly 22.9 millions for 1936.

7. The states were no longer permitted to set up plant reserves or industry reserves as alternative types of unemployment insurance, but instead were required to set up only those funds "all the assets of which are mingled and undivided, and in which no separate account is maintained with respect to any person." This was a severe blow to the advocates of the Wisconsin plan who, as has been hinted, occupied some powerful positions of vantage in the Washington scene. The committee, however, had been led to its conclusion by at least three powerful sets of considerations. In the first place, they had come to see the great inadequacy of the plant reserve system in periods of depression and the pronounced inequalities of benefits which would result under it. Secondly, the complicated problems of drafting the offset provisions so as to give credit to employers, under the Wisconsin plan, for contributions which they did not make as well

[1] House of Representatives, 74th Congress, 1st Session, Report No. 615, p. 15.

as for those which they did, naturally made them feel inclined to avoid these difficulties by removing the possibility of the plant reserve system. Finally, added doubts about the constitutionality of the measure would have been created, according to their belief, if the plant reserve system were to be recognized. For such a system would be accompanied by unequal rates of contributions by the various establishments. Some firms which would pay nothing for unemployment insurance would then be given the full 2.7 per cent credit against the federal payroll tax, while other establishments would have to pay state contributions of 2.7 per cent in order to obtain such an offset. Since there is a constitutional provision that all federal taxes must be uniform, such sharp differences would, it was believed, strengthen the case of those who would attack the law on constitutional grounds.

8. The payroll taxes designed to stimulate the states were made less complicated than in the earlier draft. It was now provided that the payroll tax for 1936 should be 1 per cent, and that it should rise to 2 per cent for 1937 and to its maximum of 3 per cent by 1938. The earlier provisions which graduated this tax according to the degree of recovery were, therefore, eliminated.

9. The administrative responsibilities were, in certain vital respects, altered. The Social Security Board was removed from the Department of Labor and was given independent powers of appointing and fixing the compensation of members of its staff.

This was, of course, a defeat for the Secretary of Labor. The administration of the grants for old age pensions, or old age assistance, was taken from the Federal Relief Administration, as was originally proposed, and was given instead to the Social Security Board. This board was also entrusted with the work of supervising and directing the systems of old age insurance and unemployment insurance. A relative unification of the social insurance functions in an independent body was, therefore, proposed. The board's powers were also increased by giving to it, rather than to the Relief Administration, the administration of the allowances for dependent children, or the so-called mother's pensions. The Children's Bureau of the Department of Labor, however, was still kept in charge of grants for the health care of mothers and infants and of those for crippled children.

10. The powers given to federal authorities for setting minimum standards for the personnel of the state bodies administering the various provisions were drastically curtailed and in fact virtually abolished. Thus, under the sections providing for the state administration of unemployment compensation and of old age pensions the board was specifically deprived of any power to lay down provisions for the states to follow in the "selection, tenure of office and compensation of personnel." A similar denial of powers was written into the sections dealing with the grants for aid to dependent children. The reason assigned for this

refusal was the familiar one of states rights. It was argued that the states should be free to administer these laws in virtually any way they wished and should not be compelled to follow standards laid down by a central government, which could not know the local situation as they did. One reason was, undoubtedly, the fact that the standards of personnel which would be set by the federal government would be far higher than those to which the vast majority of states, with the honorable exception of states like New York, Massachusetts and Wisconsin, would conform. In other words, there was every probability that the local political machines would not be allowed to dominate these state services if the federal administrative bodies were given control over the standards to be followed locally in selecting the personnel. But added to this consideration was a real fear on the part of many of a centralized bureaucracy and a zeal for local autonomy. Unfavorable reactions to the whip of administrative patronage as practiced by the chairman of the Democratic party, Mr. Farley, also contributed to this desire to remove federal control over state personnel standards.

The Republican minority of the Ways and Means Committee in general declared that they favored more liberal federal aid for old age pensions than was provided, and endorsed in a lukewarm fashion the unemployment insurance sections. They declared themselves opposed, however, to the compulsory old age insurance sections.

About a week's discussion was given to the bill upon the floor of the House, but this debate was unfortunately not on a very high level.[1] Fears were expressed by several Representatives that the government grants to the states for old age pensions would merely permit those states which already had such pensions to decrease their own appropriations for this purpose by the amount of the federal grants. It was thus suggested that the federal aid would in a large proportion of cases be given to the states rather than to the old people.

A revised Townsend plan was presented by Representative Monaghan of Montana as a substitute for the old age features of the bill. This called for a special 2 per cent tax upon all transactions and bequests. Only the amounts thus raised were to be distributed in pensions to those over the age of sixty. In this way, it was hoped to meet one of the previous objections to the Townsend plan by confining the outlay to the amounts thus collected. In order to avoid a further criticism, the pensions were not to be paid to those whose incomes were more than $2,400 a year.[2] Precisely how large a pension would have been provided by this plan was somewhat uncertain. The best estimates seemed to indicate somewhere about $50 a

[1] See *The Congressional Record*, 74th Congress, 1st Session: pp. 5650–5659, 5708–5743; 5801–5825; 5830–5836; 5900–5930; 5987–6023; 6044–6048; 6066–6107; 6112–6120; 6162–6196; 6202–6214; 6258–6289.

[2] See *Congressional Record*, 74th Congress, 1st Session, pp. 6163–6165, for the text of this revised measure.

month or $600 a year. This, however, was voted down 206 to 56.[1]

Similarly, the Lundeen bill, which was backed by the Farmer-Labor and Progressive congressmen, including those attached to the two old parties who were members of the so-called "Mavericks," was put forward only to be defeated 204 to 52.[2]

Other amendments which were designed to liberalize the old age pension features of the bill were uniformly defeated. Thus, a proposal to raise the maximum federal grant to $20 a month so that with a corresponding pension from the state the total pension might be $40 a month was voted down 121 to 85.[3] Another amendment to lower the age of eligibility from sixty-five to sixty years was also rejected, by a vote of 115 to 13.[4] Similarly, proposals to raise the amounts initially appropriated by the federal government for old age pension grants to 500 millions and to 150 millions failed. Another amendment which proposed to give the states these grants even if they did not match them with equal sums failed of passage. An attempt to reject the old age insurance features of the act was then defeated by a vote of 128 to 65.[5] One amendment to include an appropriation for aid to the blind was lost by a vote of 100 to 54,[6] but created

[1] *Ibid.*, p. 6169.
[2] *Ibid.*, p. 6175.
[3] *Ibid.*, p 6177.
[4] *Ibid.*, p. 6189.
[5] *Ibid.*, p. 6278.
[6] *Ibid.*, p. 6265.

favorable sentiment which later led to its inclusion in a modified form by the Senate.

The opposition to the bill as a whole finally more or less collapsed and it was passed by the House on April 19 by a vote of 371 to 33,[1] in substantially the form in which it had been reported by the Ways and Means Committee. The minority was composed of slightly more than a score of conservative Republicans together with a handful of the most ardent advocates of the Townsend and Lundeen bills, who regarded the administration bill as being so incomplete as to be worse than nothing.

The Draft of the Senate Finance Committee

The Senate Finance Committee went over the House bill and on May 13 reported the measure out favorably, but with a certain number of further amendments.[2] These changes, some of which were extremely important, were embodied in the new draft.

1. All references to the necessity for the state old age pensions to provide "a reasonable subsistence compatible with decency and health" were eliminated. Here again the desire on the part of many senators from the south and other portions of the country to prevent authorities in Washington from telling their states what they should pay to members of racial minorities helped powerfully to discard

[1] *Ibid.*, p. 6290.
[2] See 74th Congress, 1st Session, Senate Calendar, No. 661. Report No. 628; H. R. 7260, Calendar No. 661.

this clause, while a desire to economize on state expenditures was another factor.

2. Persons of sixty-five years and over who were in receipt of annuities under the compulsory age insurance features were required to give up their jobs if employed, on penalty of forfeiting these monthly benefits. This was done for a dual reason, namely, (*a*) to remove the older workers from the labor market so that any unemployed younger workers might have a better chance of gaining employment; (*b*) to eliminate what the committee termed "the anomaly that employees over sixty-five may draw old age benefits while earning adequate wages in full-time employment."[1]

This statement reveals in a convincing fashion that the committee regarded the compulsory old age insurance as partaking far more of the nature of relief than of insurance. They ignored the fact that the contributions of the workers gave them a strong right to keep on working if they so desired and they failed to take into account the cases where an aged person might well need both his earnings and his annuity to protect him or those dependent upon him in any adequate fashion. They also paid little attention to the administrative problems of enforcing any such rule.

3. The sale of voluntary annuities to those not covered by the compulsory old age insurance provisions, which had been eliminated by the House, was again authorized. This time, however, the

[1] Senate Report No. 623, *op. cit.*, p. 3.

administration of this feature was given, as Secretary Morgenthau had requested, to the Treasury Department, instead of as originally provided to the Social Security Board.

4. The requirement that all unemployment insurance benefits must be paid through the public employment offices of that state was modified so that this would apply only to the extent that such offices existed and were so designated by the states. This was in line with the general tendency of the committee to weaken virtually every clause which looked in the direction of central control and to leave the states as free as possible to act as they wished.

5. The coverage of the tax for unemployment insurance was broadened so that instead of excluding firms which employed fewer than ten employees, it was now only to exclude those who employed less than four.

6. The states were again given the opportunity of establishing systems of plant or industry reserves if they wished and a provision was further added that firms were permitted to offset against the federal tax credits thus granted them for so-called "stabilization."

The forces behind this return to the original draft were many. They included of course the proponents of the Wisconsin system of plant reserves, who though now fewer in number than they had been some months earlier were still highly placed and influential.

In the various state funds it was also urged that the previous requirement providing that the contributions of all the employers must be mixed without segregation would not only invalidate the Wisconsin and Utah[1] laws, which provided for plant reserves, but also the New Hampshire act, which though it set up a pooled fund provided for the segregation of the separate accounts for each employer as a bookkeeping aid preparatory to the introduction of a system of merit rating.[2] Senator LaFollette of Wisconsin was particularly active in seeking to give the states the option to introduce plant reserves, since it would otherwise be necessary to transform the Wisconsin law, to which there was naturally attached in that state a great deal of pioneering local pride.

Finally, the decision on May 6 of the United States Supreme Court in holding the Railway Pension Act to be unconstitutional[3] furnished a further impetus to restore the option of choice to the states. This act had set up one combined pension fund for all the railroads in order that the insolvency of any railroad would not deprive its aged employees of uniform benefits. The majority opinion of the court held that this was unjustifiable among other reasons on two grounds: (*a*) The age of entrance into the railroad service differed

---

[1] The Utah law had only recently been passed.

[2] For a description of the principles behind the New Hampshire act, see Herman Feldman, "Application of Merit Rating to Unemployment Insurance," *Social Security* (1935), pp. 164–178.

[3] *Railroad Retirement Board* v. *Alton Railroad Company*, 55 Supreme Court, 758.

from carrier to carrier and consequently the costs of providing uniform benefits for old age would vary as between roads. (*b*) The requirement by the act that the roads were nevertheless to pay uniform contributions into the fund amounted to taking property from some "without due process of law." It was argued, therefore, with some cogency, that if the federal act restricted the states to such pooled funds this decision might furnish a precedent upon which the Supreme Court might well declare the act to be unconstitutional. This argument, therefore, served at least to neutralize the contention that the adoption of the plant reserve system would violate the requirement that federal taxes must be uniform. This decision represented a new element introduced into the situation subsequent to the passage of the bill by the House.

7. The Social Security Board was again placed under the Department of Labor instead of being an entirely independent department. In support of this restoration the committee declared that "this type of legislation the world over is almost invariably under the direction or supervision of the labor department or its equivalent. By placing the Social Security Board under the Labor Department, considerable saving in administrative costs may be anticipated. The committee regards it as inadvisable to create new independent agencies, particularly where their functions are closely related to the major functions of an existing department."[1]

[1] 74th Congress, 1st Session, Senate Report No. 628, p. 3.

It should be noted, however, that no explicit power was given to the Secretary of Labor to pass on appointments, salaries, etc., as was originally provided. Instead the board was authorized to appoint and fix the compensation of its employees. It is possible, however, that the Secretary of Labor could still have claimed the implicit power to control these matters of personnel on the ground that the board was within the department and therefore subject to the secretary.

8. The administration of the grants-in-aid to the states for dependents' allowances or mother's pensions was placed under the Children's Bureau rather than under the Social Security Board. This bureau had been entrusted with the administration of the grants for the health care of mothers and infants and for the other child-health measures. It was, therefore, thought proper to give it this further field, for which its previous studies had also prepared it, in order to integrate the administration of the various forms of aid to children.

9. A new title was added appropriating $3,000,-000 annually to be allotted to the states for the payment of pensions by the states to the permanently blind. As in the case of old age pensions, the federal government was to meet half of the cost of these pensions but was not to pay more than $15 a month for any one person. The Social Security Board was put in charge of this work.

The Bill on the Floor of the Senate

When the bill came up before the Senate for action on June 18 and 19, three important changes were made in the measure as reported out from committee. In the first place, the power of the Social Security Board to sell voluntary old age annuities to the some twenty-two million gainfully employed persons not covered by the compulsory old age insurance was again eliminated. The movement to strike out this feature was led by Senator Lonergan of Connecticut, a state which is the home of many private insurance companies. Senator Lonergan's main argument was that the private insurance companies were beginning to develop the business of selling old age annuities and that the government should not enter into competition with them. This argument prevailed despite the reading into the record of a letter from President Parkinson of the Equitable Life Assurance Company that he welcomed the plan because he believed it would popularize the idea of insurance just as the War Risk Insurance Act had done. Nor was the fact that the government sale of annuities would eliminate most of the selling expense attached to the private policies and hence enable a larger amount of protection to be bought with a given amount of contributions any more persuasive.[1]

[1] For the discussion of Senator Lonergan's amendment, see *The Congressional Record*, 74th Congress, 1st Session, pp. 10018–10023.

Another movement which developed considerable strength upon the floor of the Senate was to
reduce the financial burden to be borne by the
poorer states in meeting their portion of the costs
of old age pensions. It was pointed out that not
only were many of the states poor in comparison
with the general average for the country as a whole,
but that in many cases their financial resources
were so crippled that it was extremely doubtful
whether they could provide their half of a monthly
pension of $30. It was feared that the aged in those
states would, therefore, suffer greatly because of the
relative poverty of the people and the governments. To meet these needs, which were chiefly
advanced on behalf of the southern and mountain
states, Senator Borah of Idaho introduced an
amendment which provided that the federal grant
need not be limited to $15 a month and need not be
matched equally by the states. It was instead
provided that the minimum pension should be $30
a month and that the government contribution
should be added to grants by the states until the
total reached this amount. Under this amendment
it would have been possible for the states and
localities to have appropriated $1 a month per
person and the federal government would then
have been compelled to give the remaining $29.
This amendment would, of course, have tended very
distinctly to shift the financing of the system towards a national basis and had this been done the
administration of the system in all probability

would sooner or later have followed the same course. It was defeated, however, by a vote of 60 to 18.[1]

Somewhat allied to this issue was an amendment which was successfully sponsored by Senator Russell of Georgia and which was designed to enable federal aid to be paid for old age pensions for the first two years to those states which did not themselves make grants. At the time this amendment came up, there were thirty-three states with such laws (shortly afterwards two more, Illinois and Florida, were added) and therefore fifteen (later thirteen) without them. Of the states with these measures, only Arkansas and Kentucky, with its completely inoperative law, were southern states. Twelve of the fifteen states which did not have such laws were, on the other hand, south of the Mason and Dixon line, and it was, therefore, these who would profit most from such an amendment. The reason assigned by Senator Russell for his amendment was that some of these states were prevented by lack of constitutional authorization, as in Georgia, from appropriating money for old age pensions, and that he did not believe that the aged poor in these states should be penalized because of this fact. The amendment provided that the amount of the federal grant for the aged in these states was not to exceed $15 a month. These sums were to be paid to those persons sixty-

[1] For the debate and vote on Senator Borah's amendment see *The Congressional Record, op. cit.,* pp. 10014–10017.

five years or older who were designated by the authorized state public welfare body as being entitled to receive them.[1] The Social Security Board was apparently empowered to set up or designate the agency to make and administer these payments during the transitional period.[2] By July 1, 1937, however, the states were expected to have old age pension laws on their books and to be making contributions themselves to match the federal grants.[3]

This amendment went through without apparent opposition, although it was feared by many students of the question that it would constitute a dangerous precedent which might continue after 1937. Thus, the states without laws might continue not to pass them and the federal government in 1937 might again be asked not to abandon the needy aged in these states. It was feared that it might also deter some states with laws from revising them to conform with the standards laid down in the bill. There was, in short, the possibility that the amendment would open the way for many of their states to dump their responsibilities upon the federal government instead of cooperating with it to fulfill them. It might thus pave the way for a dual system of pensions, namely, one which in some states would be upon a federal-state basis and in

[1] This state body was to be designated by the governor but was to operate under rules laid down by the Social Security Board.

[2] See *The Congressional Record, op. cit.*, p. 10023.

[3] For the discussion on this amendment see *The Congressional Record, op. cit.*, pp. 10023–10024.

others be nationally financed with inadequate grants to the aged.

The most important change made was, however, the authorization that private pension plans could, with certain safeguards, be substituted for the all-inclusive old age insurance system and the legalization of this "contracting out." Such a proposal had been made by Senator Clark of Missouri in the executive sessions of the Senate Finance Committee but had been voted down by it. He brought the issue before the floor of the Senate in an amendment which aroused the most vigorous debate which had occurred in connection with the entire bill. In bringing the amendment before the Senate as a whole, Senator Clark attempted to safeguard his proposal for exemption by attaching the following conditions which a private plan must meet in order to be approved by the Social Security Board.

(1) The plan was to be available without limitation as to age, to any employee who elected to come under it. (2) The benefits payable at retirement and the condition as to retirement were not to be less favorable than those provided in the act. (3) The contributions of the employer and employee were not to be kept with the company's ordinary funds but were to be deposited with a life insurance company, an annuity organization or a trustee approved by the Social Security Board. (4) Termination of employment was to constitute withdrawal from the plan, while the worker could

himself withdraw later voluntarily even though he continued to be employed by the company. (5) When the employee thus withdrew before the age of sixty-five, the company system was to pay into the treasury of the United States an amount which would be equal to the taxes which otherwise would have been payable by both employer and employee on the past service of the worker together with interest at 3 per cent compounded yearly. (6) If an employee died, his estate was to receive at least as much as it would have obtained under the act. (7) The employer and employee were to pay into the private funds at least as much as they would have paid into the general old age insurance fund. (8) The Social Security Board was to have the full right to call for reports and to audit and inspect the books of the separate company plans. (9) Finally, according to an amendment of Senator Schwellenbach's, it was provided that no employer was to require the workers, as a condition for obtaining or retaining employment, to come or remain under such a private plan.

These qualifications seemed on the surface to safeguard the proposal against the various dangers which were customarily involved in private pension plans and Senator Clark made a very able case for his proposal. He stressed the need for flexibility and argued against having all cases of old age insurance administered by one central organization. He declared that there were numerous private plans which already gave greater benefits than those provided by the act itself, and argued that these were likely to be discontinued if no such exemption were granted. For few employers, he argued, would be able to pay not only the required amounts into the general old age insurance but also the amounts needed to maintain their private plans.

Senators Wagner, LaFollette and Harrison led the fight against the exemption of the private pension plans and stressed the fact that it would result in an adverse selection of risks in which the private plans would get the younger and the government system the older workers. Constitutional objections were also raised against the Clark amendment which will be described later.[1]

The forces in favor of the exemption were too strong and the Clark amendment was adopted by a vote of 51 to 35.

After the amendments which have been described were passed, the bill as a whole was approved by the overwhelming vote of 76 to 6.[2] The

[1] See *The Congressional Record, op. cit.,* p. 10014. For the debate on the amendment see pp. 9912-9936; 10008-10014. The sources of strength for the bill were of an interesting nature: A firm of insurance brokers furnished a great deal of the driving strength, and some companies with private plans bestirred themselves. With one exception, however, the insurance companies themselves seemed to have kept hands off.

[2] *The Congressional Record,* pp. 10010-10013. The six senators who voted "no" were Austin, Hale, Hastings, Metcalf, Moore and Townsend. All except Senator Moore are Republicans, and all are from the North Atlantic states. The following conservative Democratic senators did not vote: Byrd, Glass, Gore, Tydings and Smith. The first two, it was announced, would have voted "no." Senators Gore and Tydings merely answered "present" when their names were called.

bill was then sent to conference to reconcile the difference between the form in which the measure passed the Senate and that in which it passed the House.

The Bill in Conference

A joint conference committee of the two houses went to work and succeeded by the middle of July in reaching an agreement on most of the points of difference with the exception of the Clark amendment and some minor points.[1]

The Russell amendment was compromised in conference to provide that where a state was prevented by its constitution from paying out money for old age pensions, the federal grants could be paid up until July 1, 1937, provided that the political subdivisions of the state participated financially to the degree to which the state would otherwise have been asked to do. This in effect gave the states with such constitutional inhibitions approximately two years in which to remove them and provided that in the meantime their aged could receive federal grants if the local and county governments would make the required appropriations. After July 1, 1937, in order to receive the federal grants the states themselves would, however, be expected to participate in the financial support of the pensions. This on the whole seems a fairly satisfactory solution of the difficulty although

[1] See 74th Congress, 1st session, House of Representatives, Report No. 1540 (July 16, 1935).

[123]

there is, of course, always the danger that the so-called " period of grace" may be extended beyond the time set and that it may harden into a permanent practice. Were this to occur it would be unfortunate and it might lead to an extension of the discredited county option method into states which now have mandatory state-wide laws.

So far as unemployment insurance was concerned, the House conferees receded and permitted the LaFollette amendment to be retained. This permitted states which so desired to adopt the Wisconsin system of plant reserves. The scope of the payroll tax to induce the states to pass unemployment insurance laws was also compromised by providing that it was to fall on employers of eight or more workers instead of the House requirement of ten or the Senate provision which reduced this number to four.

The House, however, had its way so far as the independence of the Social Security Board was concerned. It was made completely independent instead of being placed in the Department of Labor under the general direction of the Secretary. Moreover, the administration of the grants-in-aid to the states for the care of dependent children was taken out of the hands of the Children's Bureau of the Department of Labor and given to the board. A number of other agreements were reached which were too detailed to analyze here.

No agreement could, however, be reached on the Clark amendment and it was decided to refer this question back to each house for a further statement of its opinion. The House voted overwhelmingly against the amendment on the ground that it would ruin the entire system of old age insurance, but the Senate on its side equally refused to give ground. A further deadlock ensued which was finally broken by an agreement that the act would be passed without the Clark amendment but that a joint legislative committee should be set up to study the matter during the interim between the sessions and to report to Congress when it reconvened in January, 1936. Since the old age insurance provisions were not to take effect until 1937, Senator Clark was willing to agree to this compromise since it still gave Congress sufficient time to amend the old age insurance features in this manner should it be deemed desirable.

The Act, with these alterations, was then quickly passed by both Houses of Congress during the week of August 5 and was signed by the President on August 18.

Part Two

THE FEDERAL SECURITY ACT

CHAPTER V

UNEMPLOYMENT INSURANCE

AS has been pointed out, the Social Security Act does not itself set up a system of unemployment insurance but instead aims to make it easier for the states to set up such systems for themselves. The act does this by crediting contributions by employers to mandatory state systems of unemployment insurance as offsets against a special federal tax on payrolls. This federal tax is levied exclusively upon employers and not upon the employees. It amounts for 1936[1] to 1 per cent of all wages and salaries, to 2 per cent for 1937 and to 3 per cent for all subsequent years. These taxes are to be collected by the Bureau of Internal Revenue and are to be levied upon the wages and salaries paid out during the preceding year. They are to be levied upon all salaries irrespective of the amount received. This was done in part because it was felt that the constitutionality of this provision would be endangered if certain incomes were completely exempted from the federal tax. The tax in support of old age insurance meets this situation by exempting that portion of personal salaries which were over $3,000 a

---

[1] Included in this are the cash values of all payments in kind.

year. But no such exemption is provided in the case of unemployment insurance, and the tax is levied upon the salaries of the heads of corporations as well as upon the low stipends of clerks and craftsmen. These taxes like those on incomes may be paid in a lump sum or in four quarterly installments.[1] Employers who are not in the exempted industries and who have employed eight or more individuals during twenty weeks of a given year must pay this tax but those who have employed fewer than this number are exempted. Seven sets of industries and types of labor are, moreover, completely exempt irrespective of the number of workers employed in specific establishments. These exemptions are: (1) Agriculture. (2) Domestic service in a private home. Hotels, laundries, restaurants, etc., however, which employ eight or more workers are included. (3) Shipping within the navigable waters of the United States. This exemption applies to officers and members of the crew but apparently does not apply to longshoremen or other workers around wharves, etc. (4) Services of members of the immediate family, except that where children of over twenty-one years are employed by their parents they are to be counted as individuals and taxes are levied on the amounts paid to them if the establishment is of sufficient size. (5) The service of the federal government or one of its instrumentalities. This would apparently also exempt government corporations and authorities such as

[1] See Section 905 of the act as given in the Appendix.

the Alaska railroad, the Tennessee Valley Authority, etc. (6) The service of a state government or its subdivisions and authorities. This not only will exempt the employees of state governments but those of local governments as well. The local and state authorities will, therefore, not have to make any payments at all under this clause. This will also be the case for interstate authorities such as that of the Port of New York, etc. (7) Agencies not operating for profit and carried on for religious, charitable, scientific, literary, and educational purposes.

It will be realized in all this that, of course, all self-employed persons are exempted but that all employed individuals whether paid on the basis of wages or salaries are included and will count as integral parts of the required number of workers. This inclusion of the higher salaried workers under the taxing provisions will tend either to raise the salary limits included in the state acts or to abolish them entirely and cause everyone to be taken in. In any event, the provision of maximum weekly benefits will reduce the proportionate protection which those in the upper salary groups will receive.

It should be noted that these taxes are to be levied upon those employed in interstate commerce and the states are explicitly empowered to tax incomes received in these occupations.[1] The

---

[1] Section 906. "No person required under a state law to make payments to an unemployment fund shall be relieved of compliance therewith on the ground that he is engaged in interstate commerce or that the state law does

federal government in short at least temporarily waives its right to include these workers in a separate national system and permits them instead to be assimilated into the various state systems. Some administrative problems will undoubtedly arise in this connection, but in the case of the railroads the shop workers, clerks, section hands, etc., will undoubtedly be handled rather readily by being included in the systems of the states where they work. Train crews whose regular run extends across state lines will present a more difficult problem but their earnings can be taxed and they can be paid benefits in the state in which they live and are paid. The chief difficulty will however arise with those workers who are paid in one state and who live in another.

Against these federal taxes, the employers may credit as an offset the amounts which they contribute under an approved state unemployment insurance fund with the added qualification that the total amount of such credits shall not exceed nine-tenths of the federal tax for that year. This means that the maximum offsets given to employers under the present terms of the bill are 0.9 per cent for 1936; 1.8 per cent for 1937, and 2.7 per cent for 1938. If a state, therefore, levies assessments against its employers amounting to 1.0 per cent for 1936 and then mounting to 2.0 and 3.0 per cent for 1937 and 1938 respectively, these employers

not distinguish between employees engaged in interstate commerce and those engaged in intrastate commerce."

will still have to pay 0.1 per cent to the federal government for 1936 and then 0.2 per cent and 0.3 per cent in the two subsequent years.

In those states which do not have unemployment insurance laws, the employers covered by the federal tax will pay the full amounts directly into the federal treasury. In the states which do pass unemployment insurance acts, the employers will make two sets of contributions. The first will be under their state system and will presumably be made currently. The second will be made to the federal government for the one-tenth of the federal tax which the government will retain. As long as a state does not assess its employers more than nine-tenths of the federal tax, the enactment of a state system will not increase the expenditures of employers, but will merely transfer sums which would otherwise have gone to the federal government into funds or reserves destined for the relief of unemployment within their state. To the degree to which the state assessments upon employers are, however, in excess of 0.9 per cent for 1936, 1.8 per cent for 1937 and 2.7 per cent for 1938 and subsequent years, the required contributions from the employers will constitute an addition to, instead of a reapportionment of, the federal taxes.

As has been stated, these offsets will be granted only if the state laws under which the contributions are made come up to certain minimum standards. These minimum standards are very few in number and are specified in the act. They deal with the handling of the funds and the circumstances and rules attending the payment of benefits rather than with the amount or duration of the benefits to be paid. The states are left free to adopt any scale of benefits they wish and to fix at their pleasure the waiting period and the maximum period of benefit. The specific standards to which the state laws must conform are as follows.

1. The benefits to the eligible unemployed must "be paid through public employment offices in the state or such other agencies as the Board may approve." It is fortunate that the previous freedom given the states to designate as disbursing agencies other institutions than the employment offices was removed in conference and that the approval of the board for such action was required instead. This should result in the whole system's being soundly based on a comprehensive network of public employment offices. This prerequisite for sound administration is, in consequence, virtually ensured.

2. The states are not to pay out any benefits until two years after the date on which the assessment of contributions is made under the state law. Since eight of the present nine state laws on this subject do not go into effect until January 1, 1936, this will mean that no benefits can be paid by them before 1938. It will be virtually impossible for any other states which pass similar acts this year to put their laws into effect at any earlier date and, therefore, their benefits also cannot begin before

1938. In many cases the actual starting point will be at an appreciably later time.

3. All monies received by the states in their unemployment funds shall immediately be paid over to the Secretary of the Treasury to the credit of the Unemployment Trust Fund, which will later be described.

4. All money withdrawn by the states from this Unemployment Trust Fund shall be used solely for the payment of unemployment benefits. No administrative expenses are to be paid from it, since these are to be provided from a separate source.

5. All state systems must pay unemployment benefits to persons who would otherwise be eligible if these unemployed workers refuse to accept new work under any of the following conditions:

a. "If the position offered is vacant due directly to a strike, lockout, or other labor dispute." In other words, no state system can use unemployment insurance as a means of exerting pressure upon an applicant to take a job which has been vacated because of a labor dispute.

b. "If the wages, hours, or other conditions of the work offered are substantially less favorable to the individual than those prevailing for similar work in the locality." This means that applicants may refuse work which pays "substantially less" than the going rate, or which has substantially poorer working conditions attached to it, and may still be eligible for benefit. The States

[135]

are not, however, required to pay benefits to workers who refuse work which is only slightly less favorable than the prevailing conditions. In other words, it is possible for the states to set up a "zone of tolerance" below the prevailing rate. Within this zone, a worker may be asked to take employment, and if he refuses he may be denied benefits. This makes it possible for wage levels to be made more flexible than the opponents of unemployment insurance have charged would be the inevitable consequence of such an act. For in periods of depression unemployment insurance need not be used to maintain workers who rigidly insist that they must have the precise going rate and no other. Within this "zone of tolerance," whose width will depend upon the definition which is given to the term "substantial," there may, therefore, be adjustments of wages (if the states permit it), which in periods of stress may serve to lower costs and permit plants which otherwise might reduce operations to go on. But the workers are, however, protected from any severe exploitation by the requirement that if the unfavorable difference between the proffered job and those similar to it in the locality is "substantial," the states must permit the unemployed person to refuse it and still draw benefit.

The states are apparently to be given the initial determination of what are "substantially less favorable" terms of employment. This power is, however, subject to control by the Social Security Board if they try to stretch the terms too far.

Thus, their laws must originally not define the term more broadly than the federal act. On the other hand, it is possible for the state laws to set a more narrow "zone of tolerance" or to abolish it entirely by paying benefits to those who refuse to work for any amount which is under the prevailing scale, however slight the difference may be. Similarly, if in the administration of the act, the states deny benefits to persons who refuse to work for wages which in fact are "substantially" below the prevailing scale, then the Social Security Board would apparently have the power to step in on the ground that the administration of the state law was defeating its purpose. The board could then shut off the funds which the state would otherwise receive for administrative costs and it could also invoke the very clumsy weapon of denying the offset privilege to the employers of that state.

This somewhat lengthy discussion can perhaps best be summarized by saying that the Social Security Board will have the general power of fixing the outside limit of the lower wage which workers must accept on penalty of losing benefits, but within that limit the states may fix it as they will. They may greatly narrow or completely abolish the so-called "zone of tolerance."

c. The third type of job which an unemployed person can refuse and still be eligible for benefits is where as a condition of employment a worker is "required to join a company union or to resign from or refrain from joining any bona fide labor organization." This means that the protection of unemployment insurance is not to be taken away from any one who refuses to sign or agree to a "yellow-dog" contract. This type of contract, already denied legal protection in the federal courts by the Norris-LaGuardia act, and declared to be illegal by the Wagner Industrial Disputes Act for industries "affecting inter-state commerce," is, therefore, still further weakened by the Social Security Act. For this act will insure maintenance for a limited period to those who refuse to work under such terms.

6. The sixth and final standard to which the state laws must conform is that the benefits promised to the unemployed shall not be vested rights but may be altered at will by the respective state legislatures.

Plant Reserves, Guaranteed Employment and the Offset Provisions

The LaFollette amendment recognizes two other types of insuring units besides the state-wide pooled funds. These are: (1) Employer reserves, which may be those of a single employer or those of a group and which pay benefits only to those employed by the employer or employers who make up the insuring unit. (2) "Guaranteed employment accounts," where the employer or group of employers instead of providing payment at past wages for periods of unemployment guarantee their workers a given minimum amount of employment within a given year. This minimum amount is thirty hours of wages for each of forty weeks during the year or a total of 1,200 working hours. For each week of work guaranteed above forty, the guaranteed hours per week may be reduced by one. Thus, a firm which guarantees fifty weeks of employment will only have to guarantee twenty hours per week or a total of 1,000 hours. A probationary period of employment within the enterprise of not to exceed twelve weeks may also be required before the worker can become eligible for the guarantee.

This amendment, therefore, not only permits the weaknesses of the plant reserve system with its inequality of benefits but also makes possible further inadequacies by permitting the guaranteed employment plans to operate on a rather low level of employment. Thus, a firm which in good times was accustomed to work fifty-one weeks of forty hours each and hence to afford a full-time worker 2,040 hours of employment need offer only 1,200 hours of employment and indeed possibly only 1,000 hours in order to escape paying benefits. If a firm, therefore, employed these men for forty weeks at only thirty hours a week, it need not pay benefits either for (*a*) the ten hours of lost time in each of the forty weeks, or (*b*) the eleven weeks in which no work at all was offered. Under an ordinary unemployment insurance system a worker would at least receive benefits for the eleven weeks of lost employment subject to the deduction of a given waiting period.

[139]

The act attempts to throw some safeguards around the employer reserve system and the guaranteed employment accounts. This is done through the regulation of the conditions under which extra credit for offsets may be granted. It is appropriate, therefore, to discuss at this point the nature of these extra credits.

Since the argument in favor of employers reserves and guaranteed employment is that they will stimulate the employers to stabilize employment it becomes necessary for the tax offset to credit employers not only with the amount of the contributions which the employers actually make under the state laws, but also with the contributions which they would otherwise have made but from which they are freed because of their supposed success[1] in stabilizing employment. For if a firm which otherwise would have had to pay 2.7 per cent as a reserve against unemployment is able by these means to reduce its payments to 1.0 per cent, the hoped-for incentive would be entirely removed if this merely meant that it would have to pay the difference of 1.7 per cent into the treasury of the federal government. In order to meet this situation and to permit the employers to retain as much of these economies as possible, they are permitted to credit as offsets not only the amounts which they actually pay in contributions under the state laws

---

[1] I use the term "supposed" in no derogatory sense but merely to imply that in reality the favorable employment record of a firm may not have been caused primarily by the efforts of that firm but rather by business conditions as a whole.

but also the amounts less than the highest contributions of any employer in their state which they do not pay. In no case, however, can the total credit exceed nine-tenths of the federal tax or reduce the one-tenth which the federal government must receive.

In order at least partially to safeguard the abuses which might develop from granting these added credits the following provisions are laid down concerning the conditions under which they may be given:

1. Where a state-wide pooled fund lowers the contributions of individual employers or groups of employers under a merit rating plan, this system of merit rating must be based upon at least three years of insurance experience. This is done to prevent firms which have a favorable employment experience for only a year or two from being given reductions which their later experience might belie. This will not remove the danger, however, that a plant or industry may have low unemployment for three years but may experience high unemployment later because of technological conditions, a shifting of demand or a prolonged business depression.

2. Where employer reserves are either required or permitted, the extra credit will be given only: (*a*) where the reserve has been able to pay benefits throughout the preceding year; (*b*) where the reserve amounts to at least five times as much as the largest annual sum paid out in benefits during

any one of the preceding three years; and (*c*) where the reserve equals at least 7.5 per cent of the wages paid out during the last year.

In the case of the "guaranteed employment accounts" the lower rate is permitted only where the guarantee was fulfilled in the preceding year and where the account amounts to not less than 7.5 per cent of the total wages bill of the firm in the preceding year.

These provisions, since they will undoubtedly reduce some of the potential abuses of plant or employer reserves, prevent the payments of the employers from being lessened before their individual or industry reserves are built up to certain minimum amounts. They make these methods less attractive to the employers than the Wisconsin plan and therefore will lessen the pressure of the owners of industry to have the states adopt that system. But they do not remove the following great defects of that type of reserves: (*a*) The total reserve of an individual plant or industry may, because of a sharp decline in business, be insufficient to provide normal benefits to their unemployed, whereas a broader distribution of risk would furnish the financial basis for more adequate benefits. (*b*) The extra payments which will have to be made by the employers if their reserves do not come up to these standards will go into the federal treasury rather than into their own reserves and consequently will not be available to pay benefits to their unemployed. About the most that can be said for this provision is that it will offer some inducement for a state, if it is resolved to pass a law of the employer reserve type, to enact a somewhat better law than might otherwise be the case. In so doing, it decreases the financial gain which certain employers would derive from a reserve system, but it does not guarantee an equality of benefits to the unemployed within any given state.

The Investment of the Funds

The monies collected by the state unemployment funds are to be deposited immediately with the federal treasury in an "Unemployment Trust Fund." While this will be invested as a single fund, separate accounts will of course be set up for each state and the appropriate state agencies can requisition sums from these accounts with which to pay current benefits.

The Secretary of the Treasury is authorized to invest such a portion of the fund as is not required to meet current withdrawals. These investments may be made only in the United States securities or obligations which are guaranteed as to both principal and interest by the federal government. The federal government may itself issue special obligations which will be sold solely to the fund.

One purpose behind these provisions is to give added powers to the treasury to reduce business depressions. Thus, if the treasury feels that it is desirable to check an undue expansion of credit, the federal government can sell to the Unemployment Trust Fund special bonds or short-time notes and will receive in return the credits of that account. These credits can then either be kept idle by the treasury or be deposited with the Federal Reserve Banks. In either event the employers will indirectly turn over to the government checks which are drawn upon the banking system of the country. It will be the banking system which will owe the government this money, and to meet these obligations the banks will be compelled either: (*a*) to withdraw funds which they have deposited with the Federal Reserve System and hence curtail their power of multiplying credit upon the basis of their deposits with the Federal Reserve System, or (*b*) to try to build up their deposits with the Federal Reserve by presenting more commercial paper, etc., for rediscount. In either event, it is hoped that this will somewhat curtail the amount of bank credit which can be lent industry, and hence dampen down speculation, the rise of prices and the use of short-time credit to finance long-time investments.

On the other hand, if it is felt that credit should be made easier and loans expanded, the treasury may use the funds originally derived from the insurance system to buy bonds in the open market. This will give to the banks more credits which they can deposit with the Federal Reserve System and these increased reserves will permit them to make more loans. But as we have seen during this depression, while the increase in the liquid resources of banks may make possible an increase in loans, it by no means ensures it. To make such a potential increase actual, business must want to borrow more and the banks must desire to lend more. On a pronounced down swing of business neither of these conditions is likely to be the case. Open-market purchases are, therefore, likely to be ineffective at such times.

The unemployment insurance fund will, in short, give the treasury more funds which it may use in cooperation with the Federal Reserve Board in an effort to contract and to expand credit at the appropriate times, and hence more fully to stabilize business. The added powers may help the government, if it has the necessary courage, to check in some degree too great an expansion of credit. But its success in expanding credit is likely to be somewhat less.

Interest equal to the average on all government obligations will be paid on the government securities in which the fund is invested, so that the treasury and not the unemployed will pay for any loss of interest occasioned by using the funds for stabilization purposes.[1]

---

[1] For an early program for using the insurance funds for the purposes of stabilization, see Douglas and Director, *The Problem of Unemployment* (1931), pp. 486–489. For a fuller discussion, see also my *Standards of Unemployment Insurance*, pp. 180–182, and *Controlling Depressions*, Chaps. V and XIII. For testimony before the House Committee on this point, see Alvin H. Hansen, *House Hearings on H. R.* 4120, pp. 372–376.

Federal Grants to the States for the Administration
Of Unemployment Insurance

Title III of the act provides outright grants from the federal government to the states for the administration of unemployment insurance. These funds are in reality derived from the one-tenth of the payroll tax authorized under Title IX, which will be retained by the federal government even though every state were to pass an unemployment insurance law. But no such organic connection between Title III and Title IX is admitted in the act itself. Instead, the grants authorized under Title III are made without any explicit reference to the source from which they are really derived and are treated as though they came solely from the general fund. This was done because of the belief that had the 10 per cent of the payroll tax which the government retained been earmarked specifically for the payment of the administrative costs to the states of unemployment insurance, the case for the constitutionality of the system would have been appreciably weakened. In order to strengthen the constitutionality of the act, the two titles were, therefore, widely separated from each other and a legal fiction is maintained that they have no connection with each other. The legal theory which is built up is that the added revenue which will flow into the possession of the federal government will then merge with the general funds of the government and hence will not be the separate source from which the expenditures authorized in Title III are derived. It can then be argued that these revenues are derived from the general resources of the government into which the various sources of revenue have been inextricably mixed and which by this process will have lost their separate identities.

All this may be sound from a legal standpoint but in terms of reality it must frankly be recognized that the act as a whole commits the government to certain expenditures in Title III and then in Title IX gives to the government sufficient added revenue from which these expenses can be met. While it is true that the receipts which will be derived from Title IX exceed those specifically authorized under Title III,[1] it is clear from a logical point of view that the outlay under the earlier title was in fact intended to be met from the revenues provided by the latter. This is a somewhat sad commentary upon the political contrivances and legal fictions which an inflexible and written constitution forces upon those who are seeking to adapt

---

[1] The appropriations under Title III are 4 million dollars for the year ending June 30, 1936, and 49 millions for the succeeding years. The revenue derived from Title IX will exceed this by the time the 3 per cent maximum is reached, and possibly even by the time the payroll levy is 2 per cent. But administrative costs, if we judge from German and English experience, are likely to equal one-ninth of the benefits or one-tenth of the total costs. See my *Standards of Unemployment Insurance*, pp. 122–123. It was not by accident, therefore, but rather from the very structure of unemployment insurance itself that the federal government was authorized in Title IX to retain one-tenth of the tax on payrolls instead of for example one-twentieth or, as in the federal inheritance tax, two-tenths.

the activities of the government to the needs of the times.

The appropriations are made under Title III and are solely designed to meet the administrative costs to the states of their systems of unemployment insurance. They cannot, in fact, be used for any other purpose. These appropriations for the fiscal year ending June 30, 1936, amount to 4 million dollars and to 49 millions for all subsequent years. If these sums are not enough more can of course be appropriated later. Nor can the states in turn meet part of the administrative costs from the contributions which they may ask from their employers since these amounts must be paid into the Unemployment Trust Fund and must be used exclusively for the payment of benefits. It will be very difficult indeed for the states to disentangle any amounts which they may collect from the workers and use them for administrative purposes rather than for benefits. In practice, therefore, the exclusive source of funds for the administration of the state systems of unemployment insurance will be derived from the federal government. This in turn will throw a moral obligation upon the national government to increase these grants if and when the present appropriations prove insufficient to meet the actual needs,

The relative amounts to be granted to the various states for administrative purposes are not fixed definitely by the act, but the Social Security Board is instead given large discretionary powers. It is provided, however, that the board shall take into consideration the relative population of the states, the numbers covered by the respective state acts and the cost of proper administration. No specific weights are, however, assigned to these factors and the board is specifically authorized to take such others into consideration as it "finds relevant." The board, however, shall refuse to authorize payments to a state if the state law does not: (1) Provide "such methods of administration (other than those relating to selection, tenure of office, and compensation of personnel) as are found by the Board to be reasonably calculated to insure full payment of unemployment compensation when due." Here, however, the specific removal of all matters relating to the choice, tenure and payment of the administrative personnel from the control of the Social Security Board makes the powers of the board under this clause very weak and shadowy indeed. (2) Grant an "opportunity for a fair hearing before an impartial tribunal for all individuals whose claims for benefit are denied." (3) Provide for periodic reports to the board along such lines as the latter may direct. (4) Make available to the federal authorities in charge of public employment or public works the names, occupations, etc., of those receiving unemployment benefits and their rights to further benefit. This last requirement is designed to lay the statistical basis for a possible future program of work relief for those who will exhaust their claims to standard benefit.

In addition, the payment of the grants for administrative expenses is also made contingent upon three conditions which, as we have seen, are also required in order that offsets against the federal tax may be credited. These are: (1) That the benefits must be paid through the public employment offices which are set up in the states, or through "such other agencies as the Board may approve." (2) That the state shall immediately pay over all sums received by its unemployment fund to the Secretary of the Treasury, who will then credit it within the Unemployment Trust Fund to the state in question. (3) That it must use all money which it requisitions from the federal Unemployment Trust Fund exclusively for the payment of benefits and that it cannot use any of it for administrative purposes.

Finally, the board is given limited power to shut off the grants to a state if it develops that in the actual processes of administration a substantial number of persons are denied compensation to which they are entitled or if some of the basic requirements of the state laws which have just been enumerated are in practice denied. Reasonable notice of any such intention on the part of the board must be given the state agency and the agency has the right to be heard.

CHAPTER VI

PROTECTION AGAINST INDIGENT OLD AGE

AS has been emphasized, the act provides two types of protection for the aged, namely, federal aid to the states for old age pensions or old age assistance and compulsory old age insurance to the wage-earners and salaried employees in all but the excluded industries and occupations.

Federal Aid to the States for Old Age Pensions

The federal government will grant sums to aid the states in providing assistance or pensions to aged persons provided the laws of these states measure up to certain minimum standards. The federal government will pay half of such pensions up to a total of $30 a month. This means that the maximum monthly amount which the federal government will contribute for any one person will be $15. The states can, of course, pay larger or smaller monthly pensions than $30. If they pay more, they will have to bear the full burden of all payments over $30. Thus, with a monthly pension or grant of $40, they and their political subdivisions will have to provide $25. If they provide pensions which are less than $30, then the federal grant is reduced equally with their own. If $20 is for example paid as a pension, $10 of this will come as a grant from the federal government while the remainder will have to be met by the state and the localities. In addition, the federal government will provide a further amount equal to 5 per cent of its total grants to a state which can be used for administrative purposes or for pensions but for no other purpose.

In order that a state plan of old age assistance may be approved, it must conform to the following standards:

1. By 1940, the age of eligibility for pensions must not be above sixty-five years, although up to that time the age requirement may be as high as seventy years. The states may, however, fix earlier age requirements than sixty-five years if they deem it wise. If they do, the federal government will not make any contributions.[1] This will probably prevent virtually all the states from lowering the age of eligibility below this point.

2. The plan must normally be in effect in all political subdivisions of the state and must be mandatory upon them. In other words, only state-wide acts will normally be recognized and it is planned to eliminate the optional plans as rapidly as possible. In states, however, which have constitutional provisions preventing them from establishing such a system or making a financial contribution to it, the localities are permitted, up to

[1] That is, it will not contribute to the pensions for those under 65. It will still continue to pay its share for those above this age.

[152]

June 30, 1937, to accept such a system and to match the federal grants with equal appropriations of their own.

3. Subject to the qualification which has just been noted, the states must themselves furnish some of the funds needed to match the federal grants. They do not necessarily have to provide all the needed money but they must provide some. They cannot transfer the entire financial responsibility to the localities and counties. There is no minimum amount that a state is required to provide and it could discharge its legal obligation with a nominal grant.

4. Federal aid will not be applied toward any pensions paid to aged persons who are in public institutions. One of the purposes of old age pensions thus far has been to provide a substitute for public institutional care and to enable the aged to be provided for either in their own or in other private homes. There is nothing in the act which restrains the states from paying pensions to aged persons who are in private institutions, and if they do so the federal government will match their grants up to the legal maximum.

5. Either the state plan must provide for the outright administration of the pension system by a single state agency, or if this is not done, there must be a single agency which will supervise the administration of the plan by local or county authorities.

6. Persons whose claims for old age assistance are denied must be guaranteed the right of appeal to

and a hearing by this administrative or supervisory state agency.

7. The plan must "provide such methods of administration, other than those relating to selection, tenure of office, and compensation of personnel, as are found by the Board to be necessary" for efficient operation. Here, however, the specific exclusion of all federal control over personnel almost emasculates this section. The result may well be in many states that political spoilsmen will be placed in charge of the administration of the old age pensions.

8. The state agency which administers or supervises the plan must make all necessary reports to the Social Security Board.

9. The state system shall not impose any residence requirement which excludes persons who have resided in the state five years out of the nine preceding the date of his application for a pension provided that he has had a continuous residence during the year preceding his application. Since most of the states with old age pensions now require ten years or more of such prior residence this will necessarily compel a revision of their existing laws if they are to qualify for the federal grants.

10. No citizenship requirement can be imposed which excludes any citizen of the United States. This provision is doubtless included to protect Negroes or members of other minority racial groups from discrimination at the hands of local or state officials. The door against such discrimination

may, however, not be closed completely, for such citizens may still be denied pensions on other grounds than an additional requirement relating to citizenship.

11. Finally, if a state later recovers from the estate of a person who received old age pensions any amount in respect to such a pension previously paid him, then this sum is to be shared equally with the federal government.

Federal Appropriations

For the first year, which is to end June 30, 1936, the act pledged that the federal government would appropriate the sum of $49,750,000. It was believed that this was sufficient since the total cost of the state old age pensions in 1934 was approximately 32.2 millions of dollars. For succeeding years there are to be appropriated the full amounts which will be needed to provide the federal grants for pensions plus an added allowance of 5 per cent for administrative purposes. No maximum total is fixed. Dr. Witte in his testimony before the House Committee estimated that by the second year as the system became relatively universalized the total cost to the federal government for this purpose would be 125 millions of dollars.[1] This would involve total expenditures by all governments of at least 250 millions of dollars. This sum will probably increase in future years for at least two and probably three reasons. In the first place, there will be a

[1] *House Hearings, op. cit.*, p. 87.

larger number of old people. Secondly, there is a general tendency for the proportion of the old people who apply for and receive a pension to increase. Moreover, in those countries which have adopted old age pensions, there is a pronounced tendency for the size of the pensions to increase and for the age of eligibility to be lowered. Just how much of an increase in the total outlay for pensions will be caused by these forces is, at best, conjectural. The establishment of mandatory old age insurance for all wage-earners and the lower salaried workers will, of course, after a time reduce the future outlay on outright pensions from what it would otherwise have been. The actuaries attached to the President's Committee on Economic Security estimated that this reduction by 1980 would be as much as 60 per cent.[1]

The grants to the states are to be made quarterly by the Social Security Board and are to be paid in advance upon the basis of estimates which are to be made by the state authorities and checked over by the board itself. If the board overestimates or underestimates the amount of the federal obligations for a given quarter, it is to deduct these differences from or add them to the allowances for the next quarter. By this method the states are relieved of the burden of the current financing which would be theirs if they had to pay all the current expenditures and be reimbursed for the share of the federal government only at the end of a

---

[1] *Report of the Committee on Economic Security*, p. 28.

fiscal quarter or year. The Social Security Board is also given the power to follow up the operation of the state old age pension plans. If it develops that, in practice, age, residence or citizenship requirements are imposed which are not permitted in the laws themselves, then after due notice and a fair warning the board may suspend the payment of subventions to the state in question and continue to do so until the situation is rectified. It may use the same penalty if other required conditions are not fulfilled. The state authority must, however, be given sufficient notice of these charges and be afforded the opportunity for a fair hearing.

Compulsory Old Age Insurance

Compulsory old age insurance is designed to supplement and to reduce the need for state old age pensions. The taxes or contributions required to provide the necessary funds are levied under Title VIII of the bill, while the scale of monthly annuities and benefits is specified under Title II. Here, as in the unemployment insurance features of the bill, the revenue portions are separated from the sections which appropriate money because of the belief that this will enable the act better to run the constitutional gamut.

The taxes specified under Title VIII are levied upon both employers and employees. This is in contradistinction to the taxes imposed in order to stimulate state action in the field of unemployment insurance, which are only imposed upon the employers. These taxes also apply to all businesses, except those which are specifically excluded, whereas the other tax is levied only upon those which employ eight or more workers. On the other hand, the taxes for the provision of old age annuities are not assessed upon that portion of a worker's remuneration which exceeds $3,000 a year, whereas the other tax, as we have pointed out, is levied upon the total sums paid out in wages and salaries without regard to the amounts paid to any specific individual. The list of occupations excluded is substantially the same, save for slight differences, as in the case of the tax for unemployment insurance. It includes agricultural labor, domestic service in a private home, casual labor not in the course of an employer's trade or business, maritime service within the navigable waters of the United States, federal employment, employment by state or local governments, and also employment by a non-profit-seeking organization in the fields of religion, charities, science, literature, and education. The differences are as follows: (1) All workers over the age of sixty-five are excluded from this tax while this group is included in the tax offset plan. (2) The tax levied for old age insurance does not apply to casual laborers who are employed in other services than those connected with their employers' trade or business. There is no such explicit exemption in the case of the tax offset system except as these workers might fall under the exclusion of domestics. (3) The tax offset plan however excludes children under the age of twenty-one who are employed by their parents, while that for old age insurance does not. One further difference between the two taxes should be noted. That for unemployment insurance starts in 1936 while the levy for old age insurance does not begin until the following year, or 1937. The taxes for old age insurance are levied equally upon employers and workers—beginning, as has been stated, with 1 per cent from each and rising to 3 per cent by 1949, according to the following scale.[1]

TABLE VII

Period	Percentage payments on wages and salaries under $3,000 a year	
	Employer	Employee
1937–1939	1.0	1.0
1940–1942	1.5	1.5
1943–1945	2.0	2.0
1946–1948	2.5	2.5
1949 and subsequent years	3.0	3.0

The employers are, of course, to pay their own tax and also to advance the taxes levied upon their own employees, recouping themselves for this

[1] The term "wages" is defined to include not only outright money payments but also "the cash value of all remuneration paid in any medium other than cash."

[159]

latter amount by deducting the sums in question from their wages. The taxes are to be collected by the Bureau of Internal Revenue under the direction of the Secretary of the Treasury and this bureau is to furnish to the Post Office Department the necessary stamps, coupons, etc., needed. The post offices throughout the country are to sell these stamps, etc., to the employers and the Post Office Department will then turn over to the treasury the monthly receipts from this source. The post office in turn is to be reimbursed for its expenses in connection with the sale of these stamps.

In return for all this, when persons in the insured occupations[1] reach the age of sixty-five, they are to receive according to Title II, monthly annuities for as long as they live, subject to two qualifications which will be mentioned now and one which will be discussed later. The first two qualifications are that a claimant must have been employed during each of at least five years and must have received in all at least $2,000 in wages or salary. This will debar those who are over sixty years of age on January 1, 1937, from receiving benefits under this section. The scale of monthly annuities is to be computed on the earnings received from the included occupations according to the following scale:

1. On the first $3,000 so received at a monthly rate of one-half of 1 per cent of this total.

---

[1] The scope of employment in which benefits will be paid under Title II is identical with that used for the levy of taxes in Title VIII. This indicates the actual interconnection between the two titles.

2. On the total sums between $3,000 and $45,000 at a monthly rate of one-twelfth of 1 per cent.

3. On all sums received over $45,000 at a monthly rate of one-twenty-fourth of 1 per cent.

The way in which this formula will work out can quickly be seen if we analyze a few illustrative cases.

Let us first take a man who has been employed for five years in the included occupations but whose total wages for the entire period have been only $2,000. This man would receive a monthly annuity throughout the remainder of his life which would be equal to one-half of 1 per cent of this amount, or $10. Since no one whose total earnings were less than $2,000 will receive an annuity, it follows that $10 a month will be the minimum paid.

Let us now take a man who has been employed in included occupations for thirty years and has received on the average $1,500 a year, or total earnings of $45,000. His monthly annuity would be computed as follows:

The first $3,000 at ½ of 1 per cent = $15.00
The next $42,000 (i.e., $45,000 − $3,000)
    at $\frac{1}{12}$ of 1 per cent   = $35.00
    Total   = $50.00

Let us now compute the monthly annuity for a man who has been employed for forty-five years at an average of $2,000 a year or who has received total earnings of $90,000. His monthly annuity will be figured in the following manner:

[161]

The first $3,000 at ½ of 1 per cent   = $15.00
The next $42,000 at 1/12 of 1 per cent = $35.00
The next $45,000 at 1/24 of 1 per cent = $18.75
       Total   = $68.75

No one can receive an annuity of more than $85 a month or $1,020 a year. This, in effect, means that no annuities will be paid on that portion of people's incomes which over the course of a lifetime have exceeded $129,000[1] in the included occupations.

The act also provides that a worker's account is not to be credited with any earnings which in a given year exceed $3,000. Such amounts therefore will not raise the annuities that he is to receive. Since it is also the case that neither the worker nor his employer will pay taxes on any sums in excess of $3,000, we have here in this parallel treatment a clear indication of the actual interconnection of Title II with Title VIII.

Moreover, since it will require forty-three years for a worker to be credited with $129,000 of earnings, even if he received each year the allowed maximum of $3,000, it follows that the upper limit of the monthly annuities is based approximately on the maximum income with which an employee can be credited over the course of his working lifetime.

The sums thus paid in annuities are exempt from attachment or from the operation of bankruptcy.

[1] Such earnings would yield a monthly annuity of $85 since the $84,000 in excess of $45,000 would give an annuity of $35 to add to the $50 annuity to which the first $45,000 of earnings would entitle one.

They cannot be assigned and are in fact strictly nontransferable. They are to go to the aged persons who qualify and to no one else.

Because of the fact that the rate of annuities is appreciably lower on the higher increments of income than on the lower, it will be seen that the system is designed to favor those with smaller total earnings. This, in turn, will benefit not only those who throughout their life have low earnings in the included occupations, but also those who are now relatively old and have only a few years remaining in which to receive wages and salaries and also those who in the future may enter the included occupations at an advanced age or leave them after a short period of employment.

The table on page 164 shows the monthly annuities which will be paid to persons with total accredited earnings of varying amounts.

The scale of annuities may perhaps be explained more simply by saying that the monthly benefit will be $5 on each $1,000 of the first $3,000 of insured earnings; $5 for each $6,000 of the next $42,000, and $5 for each $12,000 of insured earnings thereafter.

Those who will be over sixty years when the act goes into effect and who hence will not be eligible to receive annuities when they are sixty-five will, however, when they reach that age, be paid a lump sum of 3½ per cent of the total earnings they have received in the insured occupations. The same arrangement will prevail in the future for those who cannot qualify for annuities because they have not

TABLE VIII
Monthly Annuities Payable at Sixty-five Years under Old Age Insurance Plan Based upon Total Earnings in Insured Occupations

Total accredited lifetime earnings under insurance	Monthly annuity	Total accredited lifetime earnings under insurance	Monthly annuity
$ 2,000	$10.00	$39,000	$45.00
3,000	15.00	40,000	45.83
4,000	15.83	41,000	46.66
5,000	16.66	42,000	47.50
6,000	17.50	43,000	48.33
7,000	18.33	44,000	49.16
8,000	19.16	45,000	50.00
9,000	20.00	46,000	50.42
10,000	20.83	47,000	50.83
11,000	21.66	48,000	51.25
12,000	22.50	49,000	51.67
13,000	23.33	50,000	52.08
14,000	24.16	51,000	52.50
15,000	25.00	52,000	52.92
16,000	25.83	53,000	53.33
17,000	26.66	54,000	53.75
18,000	27.50	55,000	54.16
19,000	28.33	56,000	54.58
20,000	29.16	57,000	55.00
21,000	30.00	58,000	55.42
22,000	30.83	59,000	55.83
23,000	31.66	60,000	56.25
24,000	32.50	65,000	58.33
25,000	33.33	70,000	60.42
26,000	34.16	75,000	62.50
27,000	35.00	80,000	64.58
28,000	35.83	85,000	66.67
29,000	36.66	90,000	68.75
30,000	37.50	95,000	70.83
31,000	38.33	100,000	72.92
32,000	39.16	105,000	75.00
33,000	40.00	110,000	77.08
34,000	40.83	115,000	79.17
35,000	41.66	120,000	81.25
36,000	42.50	125,000	83.33
37,000	43.33	129,000	85.00
38,000	44.16	All over 129,000	85.00

been employed in insured occupations for five years or because they have not received $2,000 in wages or salaries from such occupations. Once the full rate of contributions is established by 1949, this will mean that these persons will have returned to them approximately the amounts which they have contributed after this date plus interest. The payments on earnings prior to 1949 will be somewhat heavier because the workers will not have made the full contributions of 3 per cent during this period.

If a person dies before reaching the age of sixty-five, his estate will also be paid 3½ per cent of his total insured earnings, or a rough approximation to what he will have contributed during the course of his lifetime. This payment of a death benefit is virtually necessary under a contributory insurance system in order to provide some protection for the dependents of those who die before they reach the pensionable age. For otherwise the type of insurance given would be something of the nature of the old tontine system, which primarily rewarded survivors rather than compensated dependents for the loss of the deceased.

If an insured person, moreover, dies after he has reached the age of sixty-five but before the total of the benefits received by him have equaled 3½ per cent of his insured earnings his estate is entitled to the difference between his two sums.[1]

These last two provisions, therefore, make the plan in part one of compulsory savings in which the

[1] If these lump-sum payments upon death do not amount to more than

[165]

insured will at a minimum have returned to them or to their estates the amounts they have themselves contributed. The contributions of the employers are then used to provide annuities in excess of these amounts for those who survive for some time after the sixty-fifth year.

No annuities will be paid out during the first five years, or from 1937 to 1941 inclusive. During this period the workers who reach sixty-five will be paid the lump sums which have been mentioned, amounting to 3½ per cent of their insured earnings. The annuities proper will, however, begin in 1942. There will be built up during the preceding five years a considerable reserve. This will be increased in subsequent years as the younger workers make their payments to provide for their own future. The "unearned annuities" which will be paid to the older workers who reach sixty-five will be met out of the higher contributions of the employers and the younger workers. As a result, the size of the reserve will grow rapidly. According to the estimates prepared by the Senate Committee on Finance,[1] the reserve will grow at the following rate and from the following sources.

$500, they are to be paid directly to those heirs who are legally entitled to them without the delay and expense of their being subjected to the laws governing the administration of estates (see Section 205 of Title II).

There is also a provision (Section 206 of Title II) for recapture by the government from the estate of deceased persons who received greater benefits than those to which they were entitled and also more than 3½ per cent of total earned income.

[1] 74th Congress, 1st Session, Senate Calendar No. 661, Report No. 628, p. 9.

TABLE IX

ESTIMATED STATUS OF RESERVE UNDER NATIONAL OLD AGE INSURANCE
SYSTEM
(In millions of dollars)

Fiscal year ending June 30	Appropriation for reserve (derived from taxes)	Interest on reserve	Benefit payments	Balance in reserve
1937	255.5	0	1.9	253.7
1938	513.5	7.6	7.2	767.5
1939	518.5	23.0	14.5	1,299.5
1940	662.2	38.8	22.0	1,973.6
1945	1,137.0	173.0	191.2	6,883.9
1950	1,783.3	371.5	505.5	14,031.7
1955	1,861.2	615.8	887.8	22,115.7
1960	1,939.1	844.2	1,379.9	29,543.9
1965	2,016.9	1,040.9	1,844.0	35,898.5
1970	2,094.8	1,210.9	2,303.5	41,366.7
1975	2,172.7	1,341.8	2,872.1	45,368.3
1980	2,180.5	1,406.0	3,511.3	46,942.7

According to these estimates the reserves by 1945 will be approximately 6.9 billions of dollars and by 1950 about 14 billions of dollars. By 1960, it is estimated that the reserve will be slightly under 30 billions of dollars, and that it will reach a maximum of about 47 billions by 1980. Thereafter, if population remains constant, payments will just balance total income from contributions and interest,[1] so that the fund will remain at this level. Should the population begin to decrease, the size of the reserve would, of course, shrink. Even if we make allowance for the fact that the increase in payrolls and hence in contributions may

[1] The interest rate is to be 3 per cent compounded annually.

[167]

not show so high a secular rate of growth as the actuaries assume, there can be no doubt that enormous reserves will be built up under the present system.

The accumulation of these reserves will beyond doubt greatly decrease the amount of purchasing power which otherwise would be spent upon consumers goods. This will most certainly be the case for the contributions made by the workers. The contributions by the employers will in turn tend to be shifted either backward to the workers in the form of lower wages or forward to the consumers in the form of higher prices. In either event they also will decrease the real outlay on consumers goods. Since our society seems to have suffered during the twenties from too large a proportion of the national income being reinvested and too small a proportion being used for consumers goods, the withdrawal of such huge amounts from current consumption may well help to create a further state of unbalance in the future.

According to the law, the reserves are to be invested only in government bonds or obligations, upon which the rate of interest is to be not less than 3 per cent. In this way, it is hoped ultimately to buy up virtually the entire national debt and thus deprive private individuals of the opportunity of owning tax-exempt government bonds. The purchase of these bonds by the Secretary of the Treasury for the insurance reserve will, however, release these amounts for the investment market and may well lead to overdevelopment there. In addition, the existence of such a large market for government bonds may unduly stimulate the construction of public works, which may not be of an income-producing kind, and which may necessitate extra taxation to make up for the interest which is thus lost.

Relationship between Old Age Pensions or Assistance and Old Age Annuities and Insurance

The old age pensions are to be given to "aged needy" persons and consequently will necessarily involve some kind of a means test to determine whether or not an applicant is needy. The annuities, on the other hand, are to be paid as a matter of course without regard to the financial resources of the annuitant or his relatives. They are to be based on past earnings rather than present need. The millionaire President of a company will at the age of sixty-five receive an annuity based on the first $129,000 of his accredited salary totals or upon whatever his accredited total may be.

The old age annuities are intended to decrease in the future the number of pensioners from what they would otherwise be. They will, however, by no means eliminate the necessity for pensions as such. For while old age insurance will cover employed workers in such industries as manufacturing, mining, construction, trade, etc., it will not include either self-employed workers such as farmers, merchants, etc., or those employed in the ex-

[169]

cluded occupations. In all about 23 millions or 47 per cent of the 49 million occupied workers in 1930 will not come under the old age insurance features. Those who become old and needy in this excluded group can be protected only by old age pensions or assistance. It should also be remembered that the system of compulsory old age insurance only indirectly protects wives who are not gainfully employed through the protection which is given to their husbands. Should they survive their husbands, the lump-sum payments given to them will fail in a large percentage of cases to care for them properly, and pensions will consequently be needed. Many unemployed and aged spinsters will also need pensions. Similarly, pensions will be needed where it is found that an annuitant does not receive enough to provide for his aged wife, mother, etc. A part of such families would be supported by the annuity system and a part by old age pensions.

The pensions will also be needed to supplement the annuities wherever the latter, plus the private income and resources of the annuitant, are, in the judgment of the state authorities, too low. Thus, if the monthly annuity only amounts to $10, $15 or even $20, and if this is the only source of support which an aged person has, then an old age pension will in general be needed to supplement these amounts. If the aged husband has also a wife of pensionable age the need will be still greater. Furthermore, since no annuities will be paid until 1942, old age pensions must bear the exclusive brunt of the burden until that time. Moreover, for some time thereafter, because of the low average of the insurance annuities which will be paid, they will still have to bear the major share.

One last distinction to be noted between the pensions and the annuities is that the former will be paid and administered by the state and probably in many cases by the local governments, while the annuities will be paid by the federal government.

The Requirement That Annuitants Must Leave Gainful Employment

As a result of action by the Senate, the law requires that persons over the age of sixty-five are not to receive the annuities as long as they are regularly employed. When they cease to be so employed they can begin to receive the annuities but not before.[1]

This requirement that the aged must leave regular jobs in order to obtain their annuities was undoubtedly dictated by two sets of considerations. The first was that those who had regular jobs would not be in need of annuities, while the second was a desire to clear the labor market of the older employees in order to make a place for the unemployed young workers.

---

[1] If a person over sixty-five had previously received the annuity when not entitled to it because he had been regularly employed, eligibility for the annuities would not commence immediately upon the cessation of employment. The annuities would be discontinued for a period equal to that during which the benefits were illegitimately received.

This provision, however, is in part a confusion of the idea of relief with that of insurance. The workers will have made direct contributions for half of their annuities and indirectly they will have paid for most of the employers' contributions as well. When the system is throughly established, they will therefore have earned their annuities. To require them then to give up gainful employment is, in reality, attaching a condition upon insurance which they have themselves bought.

This provision will also be difficult to enforce. For, strictly interpreted, it would prevent an aged person from keeping a small shop or operating a farm. All sorts of difficulties will arise in the attempt to ferret out such facts and to keep those over the age of sixty-five from having some gainful job.

It is, however, true that some justification can be advanced for this requirement during the transitional period. For some time, the older workers will receive unearned annuities at the expense of the younger generation. It may therefore be argued that in return they should be asked to leave industry in order to make more certain that the younger workers will have a job. In any event however this requirement should not continue beyond the transitional period.

Pensions for Railway Workers

In 1934 Congress passed a compulsory pension and retirement system for all railway employees who were sixty-five years of age or who had completed thirty years of service in the industry.[1] This act had a fourfold purpose: (1) It aimed to provide for the old age of superannuated railway employees. (2) By so doing, it aimed to speed up the retirement of these workers and thus open up positions for younger workers who, because of the depression and under the seniority rule, had been forced out of their previous jobs and onto the waiting lists. (3) By eliminating the older workers from employment, the safety and efficiency of transportation and commerce would be furthered. (4) The private pension plans which were in effect on railways employing 82 per cent of the workers were menaced by the depression and many were in danger of being abandoned or abridged. This would have deprived large numbers of men of the protection which had been promised and upon which they were, in whole or in part, dependent. The result, it was feared, would have been widespread labor unrest. In order to prevent this and to protect transportation as well as the workers concerned, a mandatory system was introduced which would ensure annuities to the older workers.

The retirement annuities were to be based upon the length of the period during which a worker had served and upon his average wage. Briefly stated, the annuities were to equal the number of years of service (but not to exceed thirty) multiplied by

[1] Public Document No. 485, 73rd Congress (S. 3231). Employees of express and pullman companies were also included.

2 per cent of the first $50 of the average monthly basic wage, 1½ per cent of the next $100 and 1 per cent of the next $150. No amounts over $300 a month were to be considered in computing the annuities. A person of sixty-five years of age, who had been employed for thirty years and who had averaged a monthly basic wage of $200, would have received the following monthly annuity:

1. $1 (i.e., 2% on first $50) × 30   = $30
2. $1.50 (i.e., 1½% on next $100) × 30 = $45
3. $0.50 (i.e., 1% on next $50) × 30   = $15
                                                                        ———
Total monthly annuity................ $90

The maximum monthly pension which could be received was $120, and this could only happen if the annuitant had averaged $300 a month and had retired after thirty years of service at an age of not less than sixty-five. The act was meant to provide present and not merely future pensions. It therefore was to apply to those then on the rolls of the company and indeed even to those who had been employed within a year prior to the passage of the act. In computing the pensions for this back service, the average earnings of a worker during the period 1924–1931 were to be used, but so far as future service was concerned, the pensions were to be based upon the records of actual earnings.

A worker who had been employed for less than thirty years would receive at the age of sixty-five a proportionately smaller pension, based on the number of years which he had worked on the railways. Thus, if a man had been so employed for only ten years and, as in the illustration cited above, had averaged $200 a month, then he would be paid only $30 a month instead of the $90 which the thirty-year man would receive. If a worker retired before he reached sixty-five, the annuity was to be decreased by one-fifteenth for each year below this point. Thus, in the case which has been used for illustrative purposes, if the worker, after finishing thirty years of employment, retired at the age of sixty, he would have received $60 a month instead of the $90 which would have been his had he stayed until he reached the age of sixty-five years.

In return for these annuities, a recipient was compelled ordinarily to leave railroad work at the age of sixty-five, although he was permitted to stay on for five more years if he and the carriers would annually agree in writing to extend the period for another year. By seventy, however, all workers had to retire.

In order to finance these pensions—the cost of which for the initial year was estimated at $90,000,-000—the act required joint contributions from employer and employee, based upon the wages paid, and specified that the rate for the former was to be twice that for the latter. Initially the rates were set as 2 per cent from the workers and 4 per cent from the carriers, but the Railway Retirement Board was given the power to alter these rates later if changes were needed to keep the fund solvent.

These high rates were necessary in order to provide annuities for the extremely large number of older employees who, largely because of the seniority system, had become a relatively more important part of the working force as the numbers employed had shrunk during the preceding decade.[1]

This pooled pension system was intended to supersede the numerous private plans of the railroads, many of which had been menaced by the depression, except where the private schemes had promised superior advantages. The funds of the system were to be handled by the federal treasury and the plan administered by a Railway Retirement Board of three members.

The act was, however, almost immediately attacked as unconstitutional by the railways and in May of this year (1935) the United States Supreme Court by a 5 to 4 decision upheld this contention.[2] The majority opinion was given by Justice Roberts, who, in this instance, joined the four so-called "conservative" judges, namely, McReynolds, Butler, Sutherland, and Van Devanter. The majority opinion first criticized the constitutionality of the act because it required the payment of pensions: (1) to those who had left during the last year, some of whom had been discharged for cause; (2) to those previously employed and discharged for cause but who had found

[1] The desire of the roads to save themselves from a pension burden was probably another reason why older workers were kept on the active lists.

[2] *Railway Retirement Board* v. *Alton Railroad Company*, 55 Supreme Court, 758.

[176]

employment on another line; (3) to those about to retire who themselves had made no contributions.

Passing then to more fundamental issues, the majority declared the act to be a violation of the "due process" clause because it required the pooling of contributions from the various companies and because it was stated to be outside the powers vested in Congress to regulate interstate commerce. Despite previous decisions of the Supreme Court upholding the pooling of contributions in the case of workmen's compensation[1] and the guarantee of bank deposits[2] the majority in the present case declared "the provisions of the act, which disregard the private and separate ownership of the several respondents, treat them all as a single employer and pool all their assets regardless of their individual obligations and the varying conditions found in their respective enterprises cannot be justified as consistent with due process."

The majority then declared that the "fostering of a contented mind on the part of an employee" could not in any just sense be regarded as "a regulation of inter-state transportation." For, if it were, the court reasoned, "there is no limit to the field of so-called regulation" and equal claims could be made for free medical attention, clothing, food, housing, education, etc. The majority then asked the following rhetorical question, which it proceeded to answer to its own satisfaction: "Is it not

[1] *Mountain Timber Co.* v. *Washington*, 243 U.S. 219.
[2] *Noble State Bank* v. *Haskell*, 219 U.S. 104.

apparent that they [i.e., the purposes cited][1] are really and essentially related solely to the social welfare of the worker and therefore remote from any regulation of commerce as such? We think the answer is plain. These matters lie outside the orbit of Congressional power."

The majority brushed aside decisions upholding safety laws, employers liability acts, the regulation of hours of work, provision for the exchange of facilities by railways, joint rates, etc. as having a "direct and intimate connection with the actual operation of the railroads," which pensions were presumed by them not to possess. In a final paragraph, the court caustically termed the law as "an attempt for social ends to impose by sheer fiat noncontractual incidents upon the relation of employer and employee, not as a rule or regulation of commerce and transportation between the states, but as a means of assuring a particular class of employees against old age dependency."

The dissenting opinion of the minority judges, Hughes, Brandeis, Stone and Cardozo, was sharply phrased and pointed. Delivered by Chief Justice Hughes, it began by admitting that certain incidental features, such as the inclusion of all employees whose service had been terminated during the preceding year, were unconstitutional but it nevertheless stoutly defended the constitutionality of the main features of the act. Justice Hughes pointed out that the continuance of

[1] Author's comment.

many of the voluntary plans was menaced by the depression and that, if these systems were discontinued or curtailed, serious labor troubles of national importance and injurious to transportation might follow. The widespread adoption of such private pension plans by the carriers was declared to be proof that they were "not deemed to be foreign to the proper conduct of their enterprises." To further the transformation of these voluntary plans into a compulsory system was defended on the ground that there was no adequate basis for concluding "that the advantages of a pension plan can be only such as the carriers contemplated or that the benefit which may accrue to the service from a sense of security on the part of employees should be disregarded . . . that benefit would not be lost, because the sense of security was fostered by a pension plan enforced as an act of justice."

The minority also criticized the majority opinion on the ground that while it assumed Congress had the power to compel the elimination of the older employees, it denied that body the right to pass a pension act. "The Government's power is conceived," declared the Chief Justice, in a pointed thrust, "to be limited to a requirement that the railroads dismiss their super-annuated employees, throwing them out helpless without any reasonable provision for their protection." This "argument," observed Justice Hughes, "pays insufficient attention to the responsibilities which inhere in the carriers' enterprise. Those responsibilities, growing out of their relation to their employees, cannot be regarded as confined to the contractual engagement."

Justice Hughes then went on to point out that it was admitted Congress had the power to regulate and to prescribe compensation for accidents to employees of the railways and that this principle had indeed been stoutly affirmed by Justice Sutherland himself, when as a United States Senator he had formerly headed a joint committee to investigate this very subject. Justice Hughes then sharply inquired, "What sound distinction, from a constitutional standpoint, is there between compelling reasonable compensation for those injured without any fault of the employer and requiring a fair allowance for those who practically give their lives to the service and are incapacitated by the wear and tear of time, the attrition of the years?"

"I perceive no constitutional ground," he stated, "upon which the one can be upheld and the other condemned.

"The fundamental consideration which supports this type of legislation is that industry should take care of its human wastage, whether that is due to accident or age. That view cannot be dismissed as arbitrary or capricious.

"It is a reasoned conviction based upon abundant experience. The expression of that conviction in law is regulation. When expressed in the government of inter-state carriers with respect to their employees likewise engaged in inter-state commerce, it is a regulation of that commerce. As such, so far as the subject-matter is concerned, the commerce clause should be held applicable."

The minority opinion then went on to consider the contention that the pooling of contributions was a violation of the "due process" clause of the Fourteenth Amendment, and cited previous decisions of the Supreme Court in the field of workmen's compensation (*Mountain Timber Co. v, Washington*, 243 U.S. 219) and the guarantee of bank deposits (*Noble State Bank v. Haskell*, 219 U.S. 104; *Abie State Bank v. Bryan*, 282 U.S. 765) that it was not. Justice Hughes then pertinently referred to the "recapture" clause of the Transportation Act of 1920, which required carriers to contribute a portion of their earnings in excess of a certain amount, in order to provide a fund which was then to be used in making loans to the weaker carriers. This clause had been upheld by the court as constitutional in two cases (*New England Divisions Case*, 261 U.S. 184; *Dayton-Goose Creek Railway Co. v. United States*, 263 U.S. 456). Justice Hughes then analyzed these cases with what must seem to the average layman to be excellent logic to show that their underlying principle was "that Congress has the power to treat the transportation system of the country as a unit for the purpose of regulation in the public interest, so long as particular railroad properties are not subjected to confiscation," and went on to observe "in the light of that principle

... I am unable to see that the establishment of a unitary system of retirement allowances for employees is beyond constitutional authority. Congress was entitled to weigh the advantages of such a system, as against the inequalities which it would inevitably produce and reach a conclusion as to a policy best suited to the needs of the country."[1]

In the closing days of the last session (1935), Congress attempted to meet the situation which had been created by the decision of the court that it could not under the commerce clause set up a pension system for the railway workers. Instead of legislating under this provision, it chose instead to operate under the spending and the taxing powers of Congress.

Under the first power, it adopted a system of annuities substantially similar to those which had been provided in the former act. There were, however, two modifications. In order to remove the objection which even the minority members of the court had raised against including those who had left the railway service during the preceding year, the annuities were to be confined to those who, after March 1, 1936, were employed by the carriers. It was furthermore provided that if, by the joint agreement of worker and carrier, the former remained in the service after the age of sixty-five, his annuity was to be decreased by one-fifteenth for

[1] Justice Hughes cited the followng decisions as confirming this point of view: *Atlantic Coast Railway Co.,* v. *Riverside Mills,* 219 U.S. 186, 203; *Railroad Commission* v. *Southern Pacific Co.,* 264 U.S. 331, 343, 344.

each such year of continued service. As in the former act, however, he was definitively required to retire by the age of seventy.

The general administration of these annuities was given to a Railway Retirement Board of three members, but the annuities were to be paid from the treasury. A joint committee of three senators, three representatives and three other members, all of whom were to be appointed by the President, was set up to study the whole question of railway retirement and annuities and to report to the President and Congress by January 1, 1936. This was aimed to be in time for further legislation before the act went into effect two months later.

A companion act was then also passed by Congress which levied taxes upon the earnings of railway employees totaling 7 per cent. Half of this amount is to be paid by the workers and half by the carriers. The total assessment is, therefore, 1 per cent greater than that provided by the first act. But, since the burden, following the precedent set in title VIII of the Social Security Act, is to be shared equally by carriers and workers, it follows that instead of the former bearing two-thirds of the total assessment they are now to bear one-half of 1 per cent less than under the act of 1934.

Whether this use of the taxing and spending powers of Congress will be upheld by the courts as constitutional is, of course, still a moot issue. It was admitted during the debates in the Senate, however, by opponents of the measure that this newer method, and in particular the separation into different acts of the revenue-raising features and the expenditures upon annuities, greatly strengthened the constitutional prospects for the system. If these laws are upheld, then the railways and their immediately allied industries will be exempted from the operation of the old age insurance features of the Social Security Act itself.

CHAPTER VII

GRANTS FOR WELFARE PURPOSES

THE Social Security Act covers a broader
scope than unemployment and old age
alone. It also provides for no less than seven
further sets of federal subventions, namely, (1)
assistance to dependent children, or what is more
commonly termed "mother's pensions"; (2) maternal and child health; (3) the care of crippled
children; (4) the care of neglected children in
primarily rural areas; (5) vocational rehabilitation;
(6) pensions for the blind; (7) public health.

Assistance to Dependent Children (Mother's Pensions)

The mother's pension movement started in 1911,
when Illinois and Missouri first passed such a law.
By 1933, however, no less than forty-six states and
the District of Columbia had such legislation and
there were but two states, Georgia and South
Carolina, which did not have such provisions. The
purpose of these acts was to prevent homes from
being broken up by the death, removal or disability
of the chief breadwinner, and to permit the mothers
to bring up their children in their own homes
instead of being compelled to place them in institutions. This principle has been steadily extended

[185]

throughout the last quarter of a century. Not only have more and more state acts been passed and more localities within the areas covered have come actually to give such aid, but the legal grounds for assistance have also been widened. Originally the primary reason recognized for the pension was the death of the husband and father, and the grants were popularly called "widow's pensions." This is still the predominant cause, which accounts for approximately five-sixths of the pensions granted.[1] But aid is also given in many cases where the father has deserted his family or is imprisoned, where he is mentally or physically disabled, and where the parents are divorced. In 1931 there were no less than 93,620 families who were receiving such aid as compared with 45,825 ten years earlier;[2] while the number of children who obtained assistance was approximately 253,000, or over a quarter of a million. By 1934, it was estimated by the Children's Bureau that 109,000 families were receiving aid and that 280,000 children were being assisted in this fashion.[3] It should be noted, however, that the majority of the state laws are only permissive and that even in the twenty states and territories where the system is supposedly mandatory, in practice many of the counties, especially during the depression, have been either unable or unwilling to make any payments whatsoever.

[1] *Mothers Aid*, 1931, U. S. Children's Bureau (1933), p. 25.
[2] *Ibid.*, p. 8.
[3] *Public Welfare News*, American Public Welfare Association, Vol. III (July, 1935), p. 3.

Only seventeen of the states provide for direct financial participation on their part, while the remaining twenty-nine throw the entire burden upon the local governments.[1] Of the states which do contribute towards the cost only two, Arizona and New Hampshire, furnish the entire amount. Eight[2] may provide up to one-half and three[3] up to one-third the grant given. The total amount of such aid given amounted in 1931 to approximately 33.9 millions of dollars.[4] During 1934 the sum devoted to this purpose was approximately 37.5 millions, of which only a little less than 6 millions of dollars came from the states as such.[5] In June, 1931, the average monthly grant per family was approximately $32. This naturally varied according to the size of the locality. In cities of over 100,000 population the monthly average per family was $43.50, while in localities under this size the average was $22.51, or only about half as much. In 1934, however, the average grant per family was approximately $29 a month, or slightly less than it had been three years earlier. The average allowance per child was, however, only a little over $11 a month. The following table shows the absolute and relative

---

[1] See *Tabular Summary of State Laws Relating to Public Aid to Children in Their Own Homes in Effect Jan. 1, 1935,* Children's Bureau, U. S. Department of Labor, Chart No. 3.

[2] I.e., California, Delaware, Illinois, Maine, North Carolina, Pennsylvania, Rhode Island, Vermont.

[3] I.e., Connecticut, Massachusetts and Wisconsin.

[4] *Mothers Aid,* 1931, p. 28.

[5] *Public Welfare News, loc. cit.*

TABLE X

MOTHER'S AID IN 1931

State	Number receiving aid		Number families aided per 10,000 families	Total expenditures for mother's aid, thousands of dollars	Average monthly expenditures per family aided	Average per capita expenditures
	Families	Children				
New England:						
Maine....................	608	1,763	8	220.6	$30.16	$0.28
New Hampshire.........	175	516	4	41.7	19.77	0.09
Vermont................	90	239	3	25.2	21.11	0.07
Massachusetts..........	2,817	7,235	7	2,343.0	69.31	0.55
Rhode Island...........	388	1,253	6	241.7	55.09	0.35
Connecticut............	959	2,679	6	553.7	45.91	0.34
Middle Atlantic:						
New York..............	18,423	48,686	15	10,025.6	52.62	0.82
New Jersey.............	7,000	19,361	13	1,753.7	30.03	0.43
Pennsylvania...........	6,066	18,674	6	2,499.9	37.45	0.26
East North Central:						
Ohio...................	7,708	21,262	12	1,947.5	21.68	0.29
Indiana................	1,083	3,387	4	325.8	26.73	0.12
Illinois................	6,087	17,004	8	1,905.2	26.11	0.26
Michigan...............	6,555	18,030	14	2,837.0	37.04	0.61
Wisconsin..............	7,052	18,188	24	1,833.2	21.66	0.62
West North Central:						
Minnesota..............	3,455	9,990	14	1,208.8	29.35	0.47
Iowa...................	3,242	7,829	13	797.2	20.81	0.32
Missouri...............	307	1,134	2	86.5	26.22	0.06
North Dakota..........	978	2,644	18	270.8	22.93	0.48
South Dakota..........	1,290	3,324	20	325.0	21.78	0.52
Nebraska...............	1,453	4,141	11	309.4	17.81	0.24
Kansas.................	342	954	8	58.7	14.05	0.13
South Atlantic:						
Delaware...............	314	818	13	83.6	23.69	0.35
Maryland...............	121	450	1	45.8	30.52	0.04
Dist. of Columbia......	161	595	3	125.2	65.83	0.26
Virginia................	110	309	4	21.3	16.52	0.08
West Virginia..........	334	876	5	63.8	15.46	0.10

TABLE X. (Continued)

State	Number receiving aid		Number families aided per 10,000 families	Total expenditures for mother's aid, thousands of dollars	Average monthly expenditures per family aided	Average per capita expenditures
	Families	Children				
South Atlantic—Continued:						
North Carolina[1]						
South Carolina[1]						
Georgia[1]						
Florida	433	1,461	2	$82.4	$16.64	$0.03
East South Central:						
Kentucky[2]	2,298	5,241	20	282.2	10.01	0.24
Tennessee[3]	117	405	..	63.0	46.40	0.11
Alabama[1]	190	556	3	60.3	26.78	
Mississippi	45	110	4	5.3	11.11	0.05
West South Central:						
Arkansas	131	355	5	21.4	4.33	0.06
Louisiana	69	206	3	8.2	10.06	0.03
Oklahoma	1,896	5,166	12	140.1	7.29	0.09
Texas	475	1,383	4	64.8	12.07	0.06
Mountain:						
Montana	839	1,969	18	242.8	24.78	0.53
Idaho	230	619	6	36.3	13.16	0.09
Wyoming	95	279	11	25.3	22.55	0.29
Colorado	650	2,166	7	204.9	26.50	0.23
New Mexico[4]						
Arizona	131	414	3	25.3	17.25	0.06
Utah	628	1,906	19	90.5	11.77	0.28
Nevada	167	374	23	47.3	24.76	0.64
Pacific:						
Washington	2,517	5,605	16	558.6	19.66	0.36
Oregon	862	2,127	11	191.8	21.35	0.20
California	4,729	11,615	8	1,785.2	31.40	0.31
Country as a whole	93,620	253,298	10	33,885.5	$31.97	$28

[1] No mother's aid law in 1931.
[2] Only Jefferson County (Louisville) gave mother's aid.
[3] Most of families aided were in cities.
[4] Mother's aid law not in operation in 1931.

numbers receiving aid in 1931 by states, the amounts expended and relative costs.[1]

The most striking fact which emerges from this table is the inadequate way in which the southern states, except Florida, have adopted this system. Indeed, in the fifteen states which may properly be termed southern,[2] there were only approximately 12,500 children who were being aided in this fashion or about 5 per cent of the total number aided in the country as a whole. Of this 12,500, approximately 40 per cent were in Florida, leaving only about 7,200 in the remaining fourteen states. Whereas the average number of families aided in the country as a whole was approximately 10 out of 10,000, the ratios in the south were much lower, amounting to 5 per 10,000 in West Virginia and Arkansas; 4 in Virginia, Mississippi and Texas; 3 in Tennessee and Louisiana; 2 in North Carolina and Missouri; and 1 in Maryland. In addition, the average grants per family tend to be appreciably less in these states than in the country as a whole. Whereas the country-wide average was approximately $32 a month, the average in these states seldom exceeded half of this amount and was commonly below even this. In Texas the average was $12.07; in Mississippi $11.11; in Louisiana $10.06; in Florida $10.01; while in Arkansas it was but $4.33. The

[1] These figures are drawn from the bulletin of the Children's Bureau, *Mothers Aid*, 1931, cited above; see pp. 28-29; 16-19.

[2] That is, Maryland, Virginia, West Virginia, North Carolina, South Carolina, Georgia, Florida, Kentucky, Tennessee, Mississippi, Alabama, Missouri, Arkansas, Louisiana and Texas.

Oklahoma average of $7.29 was also extremely low.

The combined result of relatively low grants to comparatively few children was, of course, low per capita outlays. In contrast with the country-wide average of 28 cents the southern averages were only from one-ninth to three-eighths of this. It should not be thought, however, that the only area of low payments was the south. On the contrary, Vermont, New Hampshire, Indiana, Idaho, and Arizona had also exceedingly low per capita expenditures for this purpose. The low expenditures of these states was in no sense a sign that there was little or no need. To a much greater degree it indicated a lack of action in the face of such need.

Some of the states, on the other hand, made comparatively good records. In New York, for example, aid was given to nearly 49,000 children or to about one-fifth of the total number aided in the country. The average grant per family was also rather liberal in that state, being nearly $53 a month. Other states with relatively liberal programs were Massachusetts, New Jersey, Wisconsin, Michigan, Minnesota, South Dakota, North Dakota, Montana and Nevada.

It should be realized, however, that great inequalities existed within as well as between states. Thus, in Illinois there were some counties in 1934 where the average grant per child was only from $2.00 to $3.00 per month, while there were other counties where the corresponding averages were

[191]

$16, $20 and $22.50.[1] This condition was more or less typical throughout the middle west at least and it indicates that even where the average for a state may seem fairly decent, this frequently conceals grossly inadequate payments in certain localities.

While the record between 1931 and 1934 showed some progress, the need was and is much greater than the accomplishments. Thus, in the early summer of this year (1935) there were about 7,400,-000 children under sixteen years in families receiving relief and it was also estimated that there were 358,000 families where there was no adult male breadwinner and where the mother was either widowed, divorced or separated from her husband.[2] In view of this situation, the 280,000 children and 110,000 families who were being aided under the mother's assistance laws formed but a fraction of those who really needed such aid. No pensions were being given in approximately half of the 3,100 counties of the country; the grants, as we have seen, were frequently shockingly low; eligibility was restricted and waiting lists in many localities were long. All this certainly indicated the need for federal aid.

This need was increased by the announced policy of the government and of the Federal Relief Administration of turning back to the states the support of the so-called "unemployables." This policy, it

[1] Testimony of Miss Grace Abbott, *House Hearings, op. cit.*, p. 495.
[2] *Public Welfare News, loc. cit.*

was estimated, would double the number of families for whom pensions should be provided.[1]

Title IV of the Social Security Act attempts to meet this need by providing federal subventions to the states for such assistance to needy and dependent children. The federal grants are to be equal to one-third of the total amounts expended in a state for this purpose, but are not to exceed $6 a month for the first child in a given home or $4 for each succeeding child. The state and local governments will, therefore, receive aid from the federal government only as long as the total monthly grants do not exceed $18 for the first child in a home and $12 for each of the succeeding children. Above these points the state and local units must bear the cost alone. It would be interesting to determine the reason, if any, why the federal grants for this purpose should amount to only one-third while those for old age pensions amount to one-half.

The act limits the federal subventions to needy dependent children under the age of sixteen who have "been deprived of parental support or care by reason of the death, continued absence from the home or physical or mental incapacity of a parent" but who are living in the homes of comparatively near relatives. This definition at once puts some pressure upon the states to broaden their laws.

The federal grants, however, are only made to a given state on condition that both its law and administration satisfy certain conditions. These

[1] *Ibid.*

are parallel in nature to the conditions required in the case of the federal grants for old age pensions and are as follows: (1) There must be a state plan for aid to dependent children which must "be in effect in all the political subdivisions of the state." Even though the plan is to be administered by the counties and localities it must be mandatory upon them. The practice of the majority of state laws in merely permitting the counties and localities to grant such assistance is, therefore, sharply reversed by this provision. Under the present act aid to needy and dependent children must be put into effect throughout the states which accept federal aid for this purpose. (2) Each state must itself contribute towards the support of the plan. Since nearly two-thirds of the states which now have laws make no financial contribution themselves, this provision will compel them to assume some financial responsibility if they are to get any federal aid. (3) There must be a single state agency which either administers the plan itself or which supervises its administration by the local authorities. (4) Anyone whose claim with respect to aid for a dependent child is denied has the right of appeal to and of a hearing before this state agency. (5) The Social Security Board may provide for such methods of administration as it deems necessary for the efficient operation of the plan and the state agency is to make such reports as the board may require. Just as in the case of unemployment insurance and old age assistance, it is, however, expressly stipulated that the board is to have no powers whatsoever over the "selection, tenure of office and compensation of personnel." (6) No plan must require from a child more than a year's residence in a state as a condition for receiving aid. Where the child is less than a year old, the state can also require that the mother shall have lived in the state for one year immediately prior to the birth. There is no requirement however, as in the House draft, that the grants must provide a reasonable minimum of subsistence. They may instead be as small as the states choose to make them.

If these grants lead to a widespread acceptance of this title, they will require the states to help support and direct the granting of the allowances for the children. This will operate, along with the Federal Emergency Relief Administration and the old age pensions, to lead the states into setting up more or less unified state welfare departments. Along with these other programs it will make the states assume more positive financial responsibility for the relief and welfare of their citizens and it will become more difficult for them to evade their responsibility in such matters by turning back the needy upon the localities and counties. But the states and the localities may pay too low grants because of their reluctance to spend the sums required for adequate amounts.

The act appropriates for this purpose during the first year, ending June 30, 1936, the sum of 25 million dollars. One-quarter of a million dollars ($250,-

ooo) is to be used for administrative expenses incurred by the Social Security Board in the administration of the act. The remainder, or $24,750,000, is to be distributed in the form of subventions to the states. For subsequent years there is to be appropriated a sufficient amount to fulfill the purposes of this title of the act. These sums are not specified in the present act, but are apparently to be included from year to year in the general appropriation act.

The fact that no precise limit is placed upon the total of these federal subventions permits the board, as in the case of old age assistance or pensions, merely to see that after the states once come up to the required conditions, they should meet their share of the total costs. Once this is done and a state and its localities between them provide for two-thirds of the cost, the federal subvention follows. These, like the other grants, are also paid quarterly in advance upon the basis of a prior budgeted estimate of probable costs. There is also the usual provision that any differences of the actual outlays from these sums is to be subtracted from or added to the grants for the succeeding quarter.

Maternal and Child Health

The subventions provided for this purpose in Title V constitute in effect a revival of the Sheppard-Towner act. This law was passed in 1921 and was designed to help reduce the very high rates of maternal and infant mortality which then prevailed in this country.[1] During the seven years it was in effect $1,240,000 was granted annually as a subvention to the states for maternal and infant care. Although the act was bitterly opposed by the conservative business interests of the country, its constitutionality was upheld in the case of *Massachusetts* v. *Mellon* (262 U.S. 447) and under it all but three states joined in cooperating with the federal government. Although it is difficult to determine just how large a part these services played in the reduction of infant mortality, it is nevertheless a fact that the death rate for this group fell appreciably.[2] Maternal mortality, on the other hand, stubbornly remained high.[3] In 1929, the federal grants for this purpose were discontinued. During the depression, the state appro-

[1] In 1920 the maternal mortality per 10,000 live births was 80. This was easily the highest in the western world. It was almost twice that of England and Wales and about three times the rate for Sweden and Norway. See testimony of Miss Katherine Lenroot, Chief of the Children's Bureau, *House Hearings, op. cit.,* p. 292. The infant mortality rates per 1,000 white children under one year in the original registration states were as follows:

Year	Males	Females
1910	123.3	102.3
1920	92.4	73.6

The death rates for Negro and Indian children were of course greater. Testimony of Dr. F. L. Adair, *House Hearings, op. cit.,* p. 513.

[2] Again, if we take the original registration states, the rate for white males fell from 92.4 to 61.8 and for white females from 73.6 to 49.2. See testimony of Dr. Adair, quoted above.

[3] It was 68 in 1921; 70 in 1929; and 67 in 1930.

priations for such work declined from $2,158,000 in 1928 to $1,157,000 in 1934, or a decrease of nearly one-half.[1] Prior to 1929, the infant mortality rate in the cities had been higher than in the country districts. Since that date this has been no longer true, and the rates are instead higher now in the rural sections than in the urban centers.[2]

The Social Security Act appropriates $3,800,000 annually for maternal and child health beginning with the year ending July 30, 1936. These sums are to be made available in allotments to the states according to the following method of apportionment:

1. Each state is to receive $20,000 a year irrespective of its size.

2. The sum of $1,800,000 is to be apportioned annually according to the relative number of live births in that state as compared with that for the country as a whole.

3. A further sum of $980,000 is not to be apportioned according to any mechanical formula but is to be allotted by the Secretary of Labor according to the financial need of a state for carrying out the program. Some consideration is, however, to be given to the relative number of live births.

The state in order to qualify for these federal subventions must have its maternal and child health program approved by the Children's Bureau

---

[1] Senate Report, No. 628, Calendar 661. 74th Congress, 1st Session, p. 20.

[2] This failure of the rural areas to progress may have been due to the lapsing of the Sheppard-Towner act.

of the Department of Labor. Together with its local subdivisions it must at least match the sums allotted under formulas (1) and (2) which have been mentioned above and which total $2,360,000. The states and their localities do not, however, have to match the $980,000 which is to be apportioned according to relative need. If this section of the act is, therefore, accepted by all the states, $5,700,000 will be appropriated at the least for maternity and infancy care. This is about five times as much as the amounts spent by the states alone in 1934.

In order that a program may be accepted it must provide for the following features: (1) Some financial support by the state itself. A state cannot, therefore, unload all its responsibilities upon the localities. (2) Either the plan must be actually administered by the various state health agencies or it must be supervised by these bodies. It is indeed a most significant fact that while the national administration of this grant is confided to the Children's Bureau the administration and supervision in the states are given to the established health agencies. For most students of public affairs will remember the fierce struggle which was waged during the twenties as to whether the Children's Bureau or the United States Public Health Service should administer the Sheppard-Towner act. In that struggle most of the welfare workers and the organizations devoted to the protection of children favored the Children's Bureau, while the portions of the medical profession who approved of such work at all favored the Public Health Service. The present formula is clearly an attempt to harmonize these conflicting claims. While national control is given to the Children's Bureau, it is explicitly stated that state control is to be exercised by the state health services. (3) The plan must provide such methods of administration as will operate the plan with efficiency. In keeping with the general policy there is to be no federal control whatsoever over the appointment, tenure or payment of any of the state or local personnel needed to administer the system. (4) Reports from the state health agency must be made as the Secretary of Labor may require. (5) "The extension and improvement of local maternal and child health units." (6) Cooperation with medical, nursing and welfare groups and organizations. (7) The development of demonstration services in needy areas and among groups in special need.

These plans are to be passed upon by the Chief of the Children's Bureau. If they are approved, the Secretary of Labor will then authorize the Secretary of the Treasury to make the necessary payments to the given states. The Department of Labor, operating presumably through the Children's Bureau, is also given the power to withdraw its approval of a state program, if, after adequate notice to and a proper hearing of the state health agency, it finds that these principles are not in practice being observed. The usual provisions are made for the periodic advance of the allotments.

Services for Crippled Children

While full statistics are lacking, it is estimated that there are from 300,000 to 500,000 crippled children in the country, of whom the largest single group are those who have suffered from infantile paralysis.[1] Much can be done for this latter group if treatment is given in time. The personal interest of the President in this matter through the Warm Springs Foundation and other agencies has helped to arouse support on the part of the general public and undoubtedly helped to include this feature in the Social Security Act.

An annual appropriation of $2,850,000 is provided for this group. Each state is to receive $20,000 a year and the remainder is to be apportioned by the Secretary of Labor according to relative need. In the determination of this comparative need the relative number of crippled children in need of such treatment and the costs of such treatment are to be taken into consideration. The states and the localities must at least match the federal allotments with equal contributions of their own. The combined funds may be spent for "locating crippled children, and for providing medical, surgical, corrective and other services and care and facilities for diagnosis, hospitalization and after-care, for children who are crippled."

[1] 74th Congress, 1st Session, Senate Report No. 628, Calendar No. 661, p. 19.

There are the usual requirements of financial participation by the states, with either central administration or supervision by a state agency, while the state agencies must also report to the Children's Bureau and cooperate with other bodies working locally for the same ends, etc.

Child Welfare Services

Annual subventions of $1,500,000 are to be made to the states to aid homeless and neglected children. These also include children who either are or should be in institutions or foster homes and those who either actually are, or are in danger of becoming, delinquent. It is estimated that there are at present not far from 300,000 children who are in either institutions or foster homes; and that about 200,000 children annually come before the courts as delinquents.[1] Services have been developed to a very considerable extent in cities to care for such children but they are unfortunately largely lacking in the rural regions. The grant in question is to be used primarily for these rural regions and it does not have to be matched in any degree by the states and localities. Each state is to receive a minimum of $10,000 a year and the remainder is to be allotted primarily according to the proportion which the rural population of a given state forms of the total rural population for the country as a whole. The work is to be carried on or directed in the states

[1] *Ibid.*, p. 19.

by the various public welfare agencies under the general supervision of the Children's Bureau.

Vocational Rehabilitation

The federal government has granted aid to the states for vocational rehabilitation ever since 1920. A dispassionate survey which was made some ten years ago indicated that this work was in general not very efficiently done and that in many states it had fallen into purely political hands.[1] The present act adds for each of the fiscal years of 1936 and 1937 $841,000 to the existing appropriations and adds $1,938,000 for subsequent years. These sums are to be allotted among the states according to the methods now used and must be matched by the states and their political subdivisions. The new grants, like the present ones, are to be administered by the Office of Education, which is in the Department of the Interior.

Aid for the Needy Blind

The 1930 census listed approximately 63,500 people as being blind. This figure is, however, probably an underestimate and the total number whose vision is virtually useless is in all probability not far from 100,000.[2] According to the census statistics, 45 per cent of the blind were over sixty-

[1] R. D. Cahn, "Federal Aid for Vocational Rehabilitation," *Journal of Political Economy*, Vol. XXXII. In some states such as New York, the work was on a much higher level.
[2] 74th Congress, 1st Session, Senate Report No. 628, Calendar No. 661, p. 22.

five years of age, although only 5.4 per cent of the population were in this age group. Approximately 70 per cent of the blind are indeed above forty-five years of age.

Comparatively few of the blind are able to earn a living, and twenty-two states in order to help meet this situation now have pensions for this group. Returns from eighteen of these states for 1934 showed 22,861 blind persons receiving pensions which totaled $5,177,000 and which averaged $18.25 a month.[1] The costs of these pensions were shared about equally between the states and the counties with the latter paying slightly more than half. If the four states which did not report were included, the total number of pensioners would probably closely approximate 25,000. This would be about 40 per cent of the number of the blind listed by the census and about one-quarter of the total number in the country as a whole.

Title X of the act appropriates $3,000,000 for the fiscal year of 1935–1936 for this purpose and provides that such later sums will be granted as may be needed. These amounts are to be granted to the states for pensions to the blind who are needy but who are not in public institutions.[2] The allotments must be matched by the states or localities and virtually the same rules apply in the case of the blind as in the case of the aged. Thus the federal

[1] Senate Report No. 628, Calendar No. 661, 74th Congress, 1st Session, pp. 23–24.
[2] A further grant of 5 per cent is added for administration.

aid is not to exceed $15 a month for any one person and the residence requirements of the states are not to exceed five years within the preceding nine and no citizenship requirement shall bar persons who are citizens. The states must provide either a centralized administration or state supervision and the states must make the pensions mandatory throughout their political subdivisions and contribute financially themselves. No one can receive both a pension for the blind and an old age pension at the same time. These grants, like those for old age pensions, are to be administered by the Social Security Board.

Public Health

Title VI of the act appropriates $10,000,000 a year for public health purposes. The Public Health Service is itself directly granted $2,000,000 a year with which to carry on research, while the remaining $8,000,000 is to be allotted to the states for the purpose of aiding in the development of public health work. The Public Health Service is given broad powers in helping to aid and stimulate these state and local efforts, but one of the types of work which is almost certain to be aided is the wider establishment of county health officers and departments. This $8,000,000 is to be allotted as between the states according to their population, their health problems and their financial needs, and the federal grants need not be matched by either the states or the localities.

[205]

Chapter VIII

ADMINISTRATION

THE Social Security Act will naturally create very real problems of administration. The important new functions which are provided for will require the development of new and improved techniques to carry them through. New agencies are being set up within the national government and some realignment of functions as between federal departments will become necessary. But the administrative readjustments will not stop here. In addition new agencies must be created within the states and counties and here also there will be need for a closer articulation of the various services. Out of the system will undoubtedly come increasingly developed agencies which will specialize functionally in: (1) old age insurance; (2) employment and unemployment compensation; (3) welfare, including old age pensions, mother's aid, aid to the blind; (4) health work, etc. This functional division of labor will not only develop to an increasing degree within the state governments, but it will also lead to new administrative developments within the counties.

The Social Security Board

The new federal agency set up by the act (Title VII) is the Social Security Board. This is outside the Department of Labor. It is given the direct administration of mandatory old age insurance. In addition, it will exercise loose general supervision over the grants by and to the states for old age pensions and pensions for the blind and over the administration of the state unemployment insurance systems and of mother's pensions. It will also pass on the unemployment insurance laws themselves and in addition it is given general powers of planning in the field of social security.

The board is composed of three members, each of whom receives a salary of $10,000 a year. Not more than two are to be members of the same political party and during their term of office they are not to engage in any other business, vocation or employment. They are to serve for six years, except that in order to obtain overlapping terms, one of the first three appointees is to serve for two and another for four years. The board does not elect its own chairman; he is appointed by the President. The board will organize its staff and fix the necessary salaries. Attorneys and experts can be appointed by it without regard to the civil service laws.

Let us first consider the problems which will arise in those lines of work which will be administered by the state and local authorities but over which the board will exercise loose general supervision. These lines are state old age pensions, unemployment insurance and its administration, mother's aid or pensions, and the pensions for the blind. In all these cases the board will have to pass upon the state laws to see if they come up to the minimum standards which are required by the national act and which have previously been described. The board will also have to carry on some supervisory work over the administration of these plans to make sure that they are in practice conforming to the principles of the act. It can also through its requirement of reports check and audit expenditures and can help to work out a more or less standardized series of records. The board is, however, severely crippled in all these lines of work because of its being deprived of all power over appointments, tenure and the salaries of the state and local employees in these services. While the board should probably not be given specific powers of appointment in these services within the states, it would be helpful if it were given the power of working out the general qualifications which the occupants of these posts should possess; of giving the civil service examinations required and of developing the rules of tenure and promotion which would operate in the direction of advancing the efficient workers, thus eliminating the unfit and safeguarding the personnel from political raids made against them by various state and local factions. But under the present law all this will be impossible.

For its expenses in administering the system of state old age pensions during the first year, the board was given by the act $250,000. It is granted an equal sum to administer the subventions for mother's pensions, and $30,000 more for the administration of the pensions to the blind. The costs of directly administering the mandatory old age insurance features and of supervising unemployment insurance are ostensibly to be borne from taxes. In reality the costs of the former can be met from the differences between the amounts paid in the form of taxes by employers and employees and the amounts paid out in annuities. This is, of course, the way in which the administrative costs of private companies are met. Judging from experience the governmental costs in such matters should be a smaller percentage than would be the case if the insurance were handled by competing private companies. For the government, because of the mandatory feature of the act, will free itself from competitive soliciting and selling costs. It is understood that the actuaries, in making their estimates as to the size of the annuities which could be paid from the contributions, allowed a 5 per cent loading for administrative costs. If the costs can in practice be held down to this figure it will represent a real triumph for social insurance. The costs of supervising unemployment insurance will be comparatively insignificant and can in turn be met from that proportion of the one-tenth of the payroll tax retained by the federal government which is not returned to the states for their administration of unemployment insurance.

Since the federal government will furnish the states with the entire amount which they will spend for administering unemployment insurance, its control over this type of work will necessarily be greater than it will be in the case of old age pensions, mother's pensions and pensions for the blind. For in these instances the federal government will only furnish from one-half to one-third of the total amounts needed and the state and local governments will have to provide the remainder.

A special problem will arise in the administration of unemployment insurance because of the fact that the direction of the federal-state employment system under the Wagner-Peyser Act of 1933 is lodged in the Department of Labor. The only way to administer unemployment insurance is, of course, through these employment offices, which need to be extended and enlarged. The overwhelming proportion of the funds for the conduct of these offices will not come from the appropriations made under the Wagner-Peyser Act but rather from the larger grants which will be made under the Social Security Act. There will be great danger, therefore, of duplicate and conflicting administrative control over the employment offices of the country. On the one side, the Department of Labor through the United States Employment Service will tend to exert its claims under the Wagner-Peyser Act. The Social Security Board, on the other hand, will almost inevitably try to exercise some control through the large sums which it will allot for administration. The sums expended by the state agencies for placement work under the earlier act can hardly be differentiated with any accuracy from the amounts designed for the administration of unemployment insurance since the two types of work are inextricably interwoven.

Whether the board or the Department of Labor will succeed in exercising the supervisory control over the state employment offices will largely depend on whether the larger sums at the disposal of the board will outweigh the superior political influence of the department. The department may, moreover, be able to obtain a "sphere of influence" over the board because of the share which the Secretary of Labor had in helping the President to select the members of the board. It should also be remembered that the United States Employment Service is able through the Wagner-Peyser Act to exercise much greater control over the personnel standards of the state employment services than the Social Security Board is given under the Social Security Act.[1] It is possible, therefore, that there may be great administrative difficulties connected with this dualism of control. The obvious remedy would be to put the federal supervision of the employment offices in one set of hands. This would either mean that the United States Employment Service should be transferred from the Department

---

[1] By the spring of 1934, eighteen of the twenty-four states which were then affiliated with the United States Employment Service had accepted the merit system of examinations for their personnel, which had been worked out by the federal employment services. See William H. Stead, "How Ready is the Employment Service to Administer Unemployment Insurance?" *Social Security* (1935), p. 189.

of Labor to the Social Security Board, or that the board should be placed, as was originally proposed, and as the Senate voted, in the Department of Labor. The latter would seem from the standpoint of strict logic to be preferable since desirable administrative cohesiveness is not obtained by distributing very similar functions among a large number of organizations which report directly to the President.[1]

As has been stated, the treasury will keep and manage the idle reserves of the state unemployment insurance funds and the latter can draw upon these funds to meet the claims for benefit. The treasury has certain possibilities of lessening depressions and stabilizing business through its use of these funds. During periods of undue expansion, it can deposit these funds with the Federal Reserve Banks and thus in the fashion which has been explained draw down the reserves of the member banks in the system and put increased pressure upon them to rediscount commercial paper and bankers' acceptances in order to build up these reserves. This will give the Federal Reserve System some opportunity of checking the undesired expansion by raising the rediscount rate. While the effect of this raising of the rate has been overstressed, as I have shown elsewhere,[2] it can be used to at least some effect. During periods of depres-

---

[1] The case is different with the National Labor Relations Board. This body is to perform essentially judicial rather than administrative functions and should probably be out from underneath departmental control, which might frequently be political in nature.

[2] See my *Controlling Depressions*, pp. 99–122.

sion, on the other hand, the treasury can use these funds to buy bonds on the open market, thus giving the member banks more cash reserves.[1] This may give the banks some stimulus to expand loans to business and hence to increase production and employment. But this stimulus will largely be held back by the reluctance of business to borrow during a depression and also by the reluctance of banks to lend. If such a policy were used in the early stages of a depression, however, it would have much more effect than if it were delayed until the depression was severe. It will be necessary, however, on this point, as on many others, to coordinate and harmonize the policies of the reserve banks and the reserve system with those of the treasury so that the two will not work at cross purposes. The case for the unified direction of both of these agencies is, therefore, strengthened. The most important influence which unemployment insurance will exercise in lessening depressions will tend to be, however, through the sustained spending on the part of those who actually receive benefits.

The hardest administrative task of the board will be that of handling the mandatory insurance system. It will have to maintain individual records for each of the some twenty-six million persons who will be insured under it. This record will have to show the total earnings received by the worker during his insured lifetime in order that annuities at the age of sixty-five may be computed or death

---

[1] It will, however, be hampered in doing this by the necessity of using the funds for the unemployment benefits and by the decrease in the reserve.

benefits paid. This will necessarily involve keeping track of a given worker as he moves from job to job and state to state. There will be so many persons with identical names that in order to differentiate between them and to credit the earnings to the proper persons it may well be necessary to give out numbers to the workers which they may take about with them and retain throughout their lifetime. This would insure that the contributions made by and for a given worker would be credited to his account and to no other. There is, of course, in all this an element of danger. The numbers might be used by employers' associations as the basis for a blacklist. This should, of course, be made illegal, but it may be difficult to check.

There will also be need for accurate administration in the payment of death benefits and the annuities.[1] Not only will the fact of death have to be established, but the proper heirs will have to be certified. In the case of those who reach the age of sixty-five and become eligible for the benefits, certain very necessary safeguards will have to be observed. Thus, it will be necessary to determine whether the claimant is in fact sixty-five years of age. Since birth registration is a comparatively recent requirement in most of our states only a minority of the present working force can produce

---

[1] The board is to certify to the Treasury the name and address of each person entitled to benefit, together with the amount of payment. The Treasury is then to make out the necessary checks and disburse the amounts prior to audit by the general accounting office (Title III, Section 207).

irrefutable proof of the date of their birth. It is understood that a special census may be taken this year which will have as one of its purposes the establishment of the real ages of the various members of the working force. This material, if properly collected, can be used to fill out the personal records of the workers and to lessen the possibility of persons claiming benefit before they are in fact sixty-five. In addition the individual census records for the year 1900, when both the month and day of birth were recorded, are being tabulated and put on cards so that an adequate check will be obtained for those born before that date.

Another task will be that of determining whether the person who claims the benefit is in fact the one for and by whom the contributions have been paid. Where payments are made by local agencies to those who have worked for a long span of time in a given locality, this task, if honestly carried out, is relatively simple. To the degree, however, to which the workers move from locality to locality and to the degree to which the control over the payment of the benefits is centralized, the difficulty of administration is in this respect increased. Some records of identification will need to be developed, but under no conditions should these be used to develop a secret police or an espionage system over the workers, such as some American fascist groups now seem to demand.

Two final administrative jobs will be to check up on the deaths of annuitants so that unearned monthly benefits will not continue to be paid after the death of the annuitant and to see that an annuitant does not continue in regular employment after the age of sixty-five.

It will be obvious in all these matters which deal with payments that there will be a great need for the Social Security Board to have local branches which can investigate and handle these cases. The local employment offices, which will have a continuous contact with the workers both from the standpoint of placement work and from that of the payment of unemployment insurance benefits, would seem by all odds to be the most logical agencies for this work of administration. These local offices can also be of assistance in finding the ages of those entering industry and in carrying on the needed local investigations. All this will mean that the officials of these offices should be commissioned by the Social Security Board, so that they may serve as federal representatives as well as state officers. This strengthens the necessity for unifying the administration of the board and the United States Employment Service.

The Effect of the Social Security Act upon State Administration

The act will very greatly increase the sums of money collected and disbursed by the states and will necessitate many administrative changes.

The following brief tabulation will show the purposes for which federal aid is granted to the states, the amounts to be allotted for the first year, and the conditions as to matching.

TABLE XI
FEDERAL GRANTS TO THE STATES UNDER THE SOCIAL SECURITY ACT

Purpose	Amount of total grant, 1935–1936	Requirements as to matching by states	Federal supervisory body
1. Administration of unemployment insurance	$ 4,000,000[1]	No matching	Social Security Board
2. Old age pensions.......	49,750,000	50 per cent of total, except 5 per cent for administration	Social Security Board
3. Mother's aid (mother's pensions).	24,750,000	66⅔ per cent of total	Social Security Board
4. Aid to blind..........	3,000,000	50 per cent of total	Social Security Board
5. Maternal and child health.	3,800,000	50 per cent of total, except for $980,000 allotted on basis of need	Children's Bureau
6. Crippled children......	2,850,000	50 per cent of total	Children's Bureau
7. Child welfare..........	1,500,000	No matching	Children's Bureau
8. Public health..........	8,000,000	No matching	Public Health Service
9. Vocational rehabilitation.	841,000[2]	50 per cent of total	Office of Education
Total.................	$98,491,000		

[1] For the year 1936–1937, the authorized appropriation is $49,000,000.

[2] For 1937–1938, the authorized appropriation is $1,938,000. For 1936–1937, the same sum is authorized, as for 1935–1936, or $841,000.

It will thus be seen that the act aimed to make available for the states during the current fiscal year approximately 98.5 millions of dollars. In order to utilize this money, the states and the localities would on their part have to spend an additional total of approximately 107.7 millions of dollars more. This would have made a total maximum of approximately 206 millions. While only a fraction of these sums will now be expended before June 30, 1936, we may expect the succeeding years to see the total expenditures for this purpose increase. In the first place, the grants for the administration of unemployment insurance are specifically increased to $49,000,000 a year for the year 1936–1937. Similarly, for 1937–1938 the grants for vocational rehabilitation are raised by approximately a million dollars. Secondly, it should be noted that for succeeding years, no precise restrictions have been placed on the maximum amounts of the total federal grants for old age pensions, mother's aid or mother's pensions, and pensions to the blind. The phrase governing future appropriations for these purposes is that the sums shall be "sufficient to carry out the purposes," of the act. This means that unless the act is later amended, the states will be left free not only to spend more than the sums initially authorized by the federal government but also to have the federal government meet its share of the cost of these additional expenditures. In the case of old age pensions at least and perhaps also in the case of mother's pensions, the states are likely to expend in later years very much more than during the opening year.

If one examines these functions and activities it will be seen that they group themselves into three classes: (1) welfare; (2) employment and unemployment insurance; (3) health.

Let us take the welfare functions first. These include old age pensions, mother's pensions, the pensions for the blind and the care of dependent and delinquent children. An urgent need will be

created for state departments of public welfare and
those states which now do not have such bodies will
have to create them. In those states where welfare
and other functions are carried on within the same
department, it will be well to revise the administrative set-up so that one department can handle
all the welfare work. There will certainly be enough
for such a department to do in virtually every
state. Under such a plan the state welfare departments would, therefore, be charged not only with
the administration of charitable institutions but
also with the administration or supervision of these
specified grants to people in their own homes.

It would, on the whole, be highly unfortunate to
split up these various functions so that they would
be administered by two or more sets of state
authorities. The local work in these fields should be
carried out, as we shall see, by a unified single
agency. It would be poor administrative policy to
make these local agencies responsible to more than
one state body. It would, furthermore, be an error
to separate the state administration of these functions from the body which is also administering
such state institutions as hospitals, convalescent
homes, etc. For some of the old people and some of
the blind will need hospital, clinical and domiciliary
care. So at times will the children who have lost one
of their parents. There should, therefore, be close
coordination between the grants for support within
the home and the management of the state institutions, and this can be furthered if they are brought

under one central control. Since the state welfare departments are generally given charge over the types of state institutions mentioned, they should be placed in charge of the administration or supervision of the grants in question.

The administration of unemployment insurance should be combined with the conduct of the various state employment offices. In fact, it will be impossible to handle the claims for benefit except through the employment offices. For it will be necessary to have offices to which the unemployed workers should go after they have lost their jobs and where they can, at stated periods, sign the register of the unemployed. This office must be one which is handling the applications for jobs so that it may impose a work test upon the applicants for benefit by referring them to the jobs for which they are fitted. Indeed, it is one of the great superiorities of the insurance system over relief that such a constant and intimate check-up on the willingness of the applicant to work can be made. The employment offices in their turn will be aided by the fact that virtually all the unemployed will be registered there, and the offices will, therefore, have a wide range of eligible workers whom they can furnish at the call of employers to fill vacant positions. If the offices could also receive notice of all the help desired by employers, they would be able to pool the demand for labor as well as the labor supply, and thus reduce the wastes of a disorganized labor market.

If it is granted that the administration of the employment offices should be combined with that of unemployment insurance, the question remains whether both of these functions should be performed by the present state departments of labor or by separate bodies. On the one hand is the fact that the level of administration in most of the state departments of labor is, except for certain honorable exceptions, not particularly high and that a new body might be enabled to start fresh without some of the encumbrances which might well surround the work if it were lodged in the existing departments. On the other side, however, is the danger of scattering somewhat similar functions among a wide variety of uncoordinated departments. The statistical services of most state departments of labor could and should be coordinated with those of the unemployment insurance system and not separated from them. Similarly, the state departments of labor through their inspection services will have the addresses, size, etc., of most factories, mines and in some cases, stores. These will be of the utmost aid to the insurance system in seeing that all eligible employers conform to the state act.

Of the nine laws that have been passed, five, in Alabama, New York, Wisconsin, New Hampshire and Utah, lodge the administration of unemployment insurance in the hands of the existing state body that handles labor matters, while the laws of Washington and California create separate commissions to administer the system.[1] In many states a happy solution of this administrative dilemma would be to create an independent commission inside the existing department of labor, somewhat in the same manner as is provided for in the Massachusetts law. Such a body would have the advantages of separateness with the power to build up its work without too great interference from existing authorities, and at the same time obtain the associated advantages which the other branches of the department of labor might be able to offer.

The administrative tasks involved in unemployment insurance are, of course, great. In the first place, the number of employment offices will have to be increased and their premises enlarged. For by the spring of 1935 the existing state employment offices, according to William H. Stead, served only about 25 per cent of the territorial area of the country and about 45 per cent of its population.[2] Not only will new offices have to be set up in the uncovered territory but many more offices will have to be established in cities where the state services now have only one or at the most a few.

These offices will of course have to build up work records of each man with a listing of his previous positions and the workers will have to be classified

---

[1] The law for the District of Columbia provides a separate board with the Chairman of the Commissioners as Chairman of the District Unemployment Compensation Board and the other commissioners as members ex officio.

[2] William H. Stead, "How Ready Is the Employment Service to Administer Unemployment Insurance?" *Social Security*, p. 188.

as regards their trades, etc. Those who are unemployed should sign the register during working
hours on at least three days a week, including that
on which they are paid benefits. These times for
signing should come at staggered intervals during
each day. By paying benefits both on Friday and
on Saturday, or alternatively on Monday and Tuesday for the preceding week, it will be possible to
divide the unemployed into two main groups,
namely, those signing the register on Monday,
Wednesday and Friday, and those signing on
Tuesday, Thursday and Saturday. Within each of
these days, groups would, of course, sign at different
hours. In this way the work of handling these
records would be diffused in a systematic fashion
throughout the week, instead of creating alternate
peaks and valleys. The time of the unemployed
would also be saved.

It will also probably be desirable to adopt the
English method of cards, one of which each workman will have and which will be in the possession
of the employer while the workmen are employed
and which will be lodged by the workers with the
employment office when they lose their jobs.
These cards will, of course, remain in the employment offices as long as the workman is unemployed but should be transferred to the next
employer when work is found. There should, of
course, be a central office for each state where
individual records will be kept for each worker,
covering such subjects as the total weeks of em-

ployment, the worker's wages and the total number of weeks of benefit which he has received. There will be need for a uniformity of these records as between states.

State departments of health will also need to be set up in those states where they do not now exist and strengthened where they do. For these agencies will administer or supervise the grants for maternal and child health and will help the Public Health Service in the creation of local or county health units. They will also have a large if not a predominant share in the carrying out of the work for crippled children.

County Administration

While unemployment insurance should be directly administered by the states, the other forms are likely to be predominantly administered by the counties.[1] Except in the smaller states, old age pensions, mother's pensions, pensions for the blind and the grants for maternal and child welfare will probably be administered primarily by these units. So will the grants for public health work. There is an excellent opportunity for the states to set up unified agencies within the counties instead of having these functions diffused locally over a wide variety of groups.

---

[1] The county is in general an unsatisfactory unit of administration. Most states have undoubtedly too many and a consolidation into larger local areas is much needed. As this is done, the possibility of functional development advocated above will increase.

At present old age pensions are generally administered by the county commissioners although in some cases the county judges are in general charge. Mother's pensions, on the other hand, are commonly handled by the juvenile and county courts, although other bodies also participate in the administration. The pensions to the blind are often supervised by still a third set of officials.

It is highly desirable that counties of appreciable size should establish departments of welfare which will handle all these functions. Such departments are now in existence in most of our large urban counties and throughout a few states. The most notable state which has set up such a basic system of public welfare administration is North Carolina, which has led the way in this movement. The vast majority of the counties in the country however lack such units and the increased volume of welfare work which the Security Act will create necessitates some such form of organization.

The development in the field of educational administration furnishes an interesting parallel in this respect. Up until a quarter of a century ago the primary unit of educational administration was the town or city. This led to the predominance of untrained local boards and to a rather low standard of efficiency, particularly in the smaller towns and the countryside. During the last twenty-five years, however, county departments of education headed by full-time salaried superintendents have rapidly developed and these departments have materially raised the level of teaching and of education. A similar beneficial result should follow from the creation of county welfare bureaus. Professionally trained workers can be largely substituted for the ineffective "local supervisors of the poor," and the whole work can be placed on a much more efficient and self-respecting basis. Where the counties are of sufficient size, a specialized staff can be built up to handle the various functions administered. Such a change would, of course, also go far to improve the present localized administration of the poor law, which before the depression was little short of a diffused national disgrace.

In the larger towns and of course in the cities paid workers can directly administer these functions with the aid of representative advisory boards. In the smaller towns the unpaid boards might still function directly but they would be checked up and supervised by the county welfare officer.

The major purpose of Title VI is to create similar functioning units for public health work in the counties and localities. This should be of great aid in the rural regions and smaller towns and cities where reduction in mortality in recent years has lagged behind the progress which has been made in the cities.

If, therefore, we look five or ten years into the future, we shall probably see our counties generally equipped with specialized departments of health and welfare as well as of education. Counties which are themselves too small to provide such services may, of course, combine with others to obtain them.

The fact that the state boards of health are entrusted, so far as the states are concerned, with the administration or supervision of the work in the field of maternal and child health will mean that in the main these activities will be administered locally by the county or local health authorities. In some cases, however, the welfare authorities may be used; while in others coopera- tive arrangements may be made with private agencies. A similar provision is likely to develop in the case of the grants for crippled children.

The Appointment of the Security Board and the Filibuster on the Appropriations Bill

As Chairman of the Social Security Board the President has appointed John G. Winant, the Republican ex-Governor of New Hampshire, who served as chairman of the board to settle the textile strike of 1934 and who at the time of his appoint- ment was Assistant Director of the International Labor Office in Geneva. Mr. Winant has an ex- cellent record as a progressive administrator and his appointment is a distinctly distinguished one. For the four-year term Arthur J. Altmeyer of Wisconsin was appointed. At the time of his appointment, Mr. Altmeyer was Second Assist- ant Secretary of Labor and prior to that had been Secretary of the Wisconsin Industrial Commission. As the third member the President appointed V. M. Miles of Arkansas, a former Democratic national committeeman from that state.

The work of the board and the immediate possibilities of granting federal subventions for the specified purposes were, however, embarrassed by the five-hour filibuster conducted by the late Senator Long of Louisiana during the closing hours of the session. This filibuster prevented the deficiency appropriations bill from being passed and the administration then announced that it had shut off the possibility of immediate funds for these purposes.

Part Three

THE PROBLEMS OF SOCIAL SECURITY IMMEDIATELY AFTER THE PASSAGE OF THE ACT

CHAPTER IX

SOME NEEDED NEXT STEPS

THE Social Security Act should not be viewed as the triumphant and perfect conclusion to the struggle to obtain greater security. It is on the contrary full of weaknesses and is strikingly incomplete. If we are to progress, the act should instead be regarded as merely a first step which must soon be followed by others. It is therefore appropriate to consider what these next steps should be.

1. The Social Security Board should be given the power to see that adequate old age pensions are paid by the states. Under the present form of the act, the states can pay as low old age pensions as they wish without any control by the Security Board. This, as has been indicated, may lead some states merely to continue their present low scale of pensions and thus cause the federal subventions to be an aid to their treasuries rather than to their old people. It may also induce the states without pensions to pay totally inadequate sums.

This danger cannot adequately be guarded against by prescribing in the federal act statutory minima which must be paid. For the circumstances of individual applicants will vary and there will be some who will need only small grants to eke out their private resources and those of their children. The best way of handling the matter is therefore to give administrative discretion to the Security Board to prescribe the minimum amounts which should be paid. The Board can then fix slightly different minima for various sections of the country and for localities of differing sizes and prescribe that the pensions must be such that, when combined with the private income of the applicants, their total income will at least be brought up to these amounts.

2. The amount of the federal subventions for old age pensions should be raised from $15 to at least $20 a month. While a pension of $30 a month may be enough for an aged person in the rural areas of the country and in the smaller towns, it is certainly not adequate for maintenance in the larger cities. And yet under the present act, if such persons are paid more than $30 a month, the entire amount of this extra allowance must be borne by the states and localities. In order to provide more adequately for the aged persons in cities and in high cost areas the amount of the federal grant should therefore be raised by at least $5 a month. With a corresponding grant from the state and locality, this would make possible pensions amounting to $40 a month.

3. The Security Board should be given a considerable sum of money to grant as outright aid for pensions to states which are particularly poor. The requirement that the states and localities must

match each dollar of federal subventions will put
the poorer states under a heavy strain and in many
cases, because of their poverty, will prevent adequate pensions from being paid. In order to insure
that at least minimum pensions are paid, there
should be placed at the disposal of the board a sum
of money which it can grant to the states which
are really hard pressed without any requirement
for matching upon their part. This sum could be
set initially at approximately twenty millions of
dollars. It should of course be apportioned according to definite rules in order to lessen any temptа-
tion to use it for political purposes. It is suggested
that it should be given to those states where the
average amount of assessed property per person
over the age of sixty-five is below the average for
the country as a whole. It could for example be
apportioned according to the degree to which these
state averages, when weighted by their aged
population, fall below the average for the nation
as a whole.

4. The present provision under old age insurance that the young workers and their employers
should pay for the unearned annuities of the older
workers should be modified and at least a portion
of this cost should be lodged against the government itself. As we have seen, one of the most dubious features of the present act is the high rate of
contributions which are required by and on behalf
of the younger workers so that the older workers
may receive the minimum annuities which are

guaranteed. This requirement will also necessitate the building up of an excessively high reserve with all the attendant dangers of unduly diminishing the sums available for the purchase of consumers goods and of stimulating the construction of uneconomic public works. Instead of saddling all these costs upon the young workers, it is proper that the government should meet a portion of them. It is recommended therefore that the total contributions from employers and employees should not exceed a maximum of 5 or at the most 5½ per cent instead of the 6 per cent provided in the act. This maximum, instead of being reached in 1949, as is now provided, could also be postponed until 1953 or 1954. This would not only shift a portion of an excessive burden but it would also reduce the maximum size of the reserve with attendant benefits to all.

5. The requirement that an aged person must withdraw from a gainful occupation in order to secure an annuity should ultimately be withdrawn. As we have seen, the requirement that the annuities will be paid only to those who, after they have reached the age of sixty-five, have left gainful employment is an unjust confusion of the idea of relief with that of insurance. The workers themselves will have paid, whether directly or indirectly, for their benefits. To say that in addition they must leave industry in order to get their money back is certainly unjust. This requirement should therefore in general be waived. It might however be

retained up until 1950 or 1955 because of the predominance of unearned over earned annuities up until that time.

6. Even if the tax offset method of financing unemployment insurance is retained, additional federal funds should be obtained and used for aiding states with high unemployment rates to maintain minimum benefits and to provide benefits for workers who migrate from state to state.

It has been pointed out that one of the great weaknesses of the present act is the fact that the states where unemployment is high will not be able to insure even a decent minimum of benefits to their unemployed. This will be unfair to these workers since they will not be responsible for the fact of their unemployment and should not be penalized for what is outside their control.

As long as the unemployment insurance is conducted on a state basis, the only effective way to meet this situation is to set up a special federal fund which will then be distributed to those states where unemployment is appreciably above the average and which will enable them to pay benefits for at least a minimum period of sixteen weeks but preferably for twenty weeks. It is probable that an amount equal to 1 per cent of the payroll, or approximately 200 million dollars a year, would be enough to guarantee a minimum of sixteen weeks' benefit. This might even be done with a smaller amount, amounting to three-quarters of one per cent of the payroll or to approximately 150 millions a year. Unless some such program as this is carried through, we shall have, as has been pointed out, great irregularities in benefits as between states and gross inadequacies in some.

If the states fail to provide sufficient reciprocal provisions to care for workers who after acquiring eligibility in one state become unemployed in another before acquiring eligibility there, then the federal government should create a fund to provide for these cases of transfer.

7. If the constitutionality of the national system of old age insurance is upheld, then the tax offset system of providing for unemployment insurance should be transformed into a national system. Such a national system would provide for a much needed uniformity of eligibility rules and benefits for the country as a whole.[1] Even if the constitutionality of both the national system of old age insurance and the tax offset method are denied, it would probably still be possible to establish a federal-state system of unemployment insurance based upon a 100 per cent grant-in-aid to the states. This system could then rather easily be developed to provide a uniformity of benefits as between states. Unfortunately such a change will now require a rather widespread amendment of the existing state laws.

8. A second line of defense should speedily be built up behind the system of unemployment

---

[1] The constitutional case for a national system of unemployment insurance is stronger than for old age pensions since it can be used to lessen depressions and hence protect the integrity of commerce as a whole.

insurance. Whether it be sooner or later, the standard benefits under unemployment insurance will sometime be exhausted. What then will be the fate of the unemployed? It is desirable to lay a foundation now for meeting this emergency and not to wait until the pressure of immediate circumstances forces action. It is suggested that the best way for coping with this situation is to provide emergency benefits for those who are in need when they can no longer claim standard benefits but to graduate these allowances according to a means test conducted under more or less uniform standards. In return for these grants, the recipients of emergency benefits should be asked to perform work of a public nature or to receive training. The funds for these emergency benefits would in turn be furnished by the federal and state governments and the payments could be handled through the employment rather than the relief offices.

9. The federal grants in behalf of mothers' pensions should be increased to meet half of the total costs instead of as at present only one-third. As has been observed, it is not clear why the federal government should meet half the cost of pensions for the aged but only one-third of the grants for children who have lost the support of their fathers. The children are at the least as important as the old people and there is no good reason why the federal government should not bear as large a share of their allowances as it does in the case of the old people.

[237]

10. The federal administrative authorities should be given the power to lay down minimum standards for the selection, tenure and promotion of those state and local officials who will be involved in the administration of various sections of this act. The present lack of control is likely to lead in the states to the appointment of political workers to administer the system and to have disastrous consequences. Since federal monies will be received for some of these services and offsets against federal taxes granted for the remainder, it is very proper that the federal government should be given some voice in the fixation of personnel standards. The state governments may, of course, make the formal appointments and promotions but the general standards under which these are to be done should be worked out by the federal administrative authorities. These could for example require civil service examinations and determine the respective weights to be given to experience and other qualifications. They could also set the examinations and help grade the papers, etc.

11. As rapidly as possible, a system of health insurance should be instituted which will provide a more even distribution of the costs of medical care and also a cash benefit to compensate in part for the loss of earnings. The nation can afford to give good medical attention to all, but the major difficulty lies in the uneven distribution of sickness costs. What could be borne, if distributed evenly over the group as a whole, falls therefore with

crushing weight upon the small minority who, at any one time, are ill. Health insurance is the best way, so far as the employed workers are concerned, of distributing this burden over a large number and thus reducing the individual sacrifices involved.

In drawing up a program of health insurance the following points need to be followed: (*a*) So far as possible medical care should be provided for the families of the insured workers and not merely for these workers themselves. (*b*) The medical care provided should include the services of specialists, dentists, etc., and not merely those of a general practitioner. (*c*) The patient should be given the free choice of a doctor. (*d*) The unskilled and semiskilled workers will have great difficulty in meeting their proportionate share of the cost and this will be especially true in view of the contributions which they will have to make for insurance against old age and unemployment. Some public grants are therefore needed to help meet the cost of providing medical care for this group. (*e*) Emphasis should be placed upon preventive medicine, and annual physical examinations, etc., should be required. (*f*) The medical profession should be encouraged to assume professional responsibility for the service given and to exercise, within limits, the general rights of self-government.

12. The previous recommendations have called for the lifting of a portion of the costs of social insurance from the backs of workers and consumers and for their assumption by the federal

government. Nothing will be gained however if these funds are then derived from taxes on consumption. In order that these costs may be borne with the least sacrifice, they should be met from taxes on excess profits and on the upper brackets of personal incomes. For the workers are already severely burdened both by the present system of financing social insurance and by the numerous state sales taxes.

13. Social insurance at its best merely enables those workers who, for one reason or another, are unable to be employed to live more nearly on the level which would be theirs if they had a job. But even this level is far too low for an extremely large section of the population. The unskilled laborer who receives 40 cents an hour for forty to fifty hours of work a week and whose weekly earnings are therefore only $16 to $20 does not receive enough, even when fully employed, to care for a family with children. There are similarly large groups of semiskilled workers whose full-time earnings are grossly inadequate to meet the costs of a health and decency level of living. If we are to give real social security to the employed population, it is therefore not enough merely to provide social insurance for the interruptions of working-class incomes. It is equally necessary to raise the levels of those incomes to an adequate amount.

Moreover, unless this is done, there will be a constant and indeed an increasing pressure to make the insurance system operate at cross purposes from the wage system. For if the experience of the last twenty years is any guide, the working class is likely to demand in an increasing measure from the government that social insurance should provide them with adequate maintenance during those periods in which, through no fault of their own, they cannot find employment. If however, the wages of these men when employed are inadequate in terms of generally recognized needs, this will lead, as under the Lundeen bill, to a demand for a scale of benefits which will be in excess of the wage level for a large class. This would certainly not be insurance, which merely aims to compensate for losses suffered and not to give one a premium for losing his job.

In short, there is likely to be a sharp conflict between the demand by the workers that the government guarantee their maintenance when out of work and the failure of privately owned industry to provide adequate maintenance to large sections of the workers when they have a job. This conflict will be particularly acute in view of the fact that social insurance, under our existing economic set-up, will customarily pay in benefits appreciably less than what the worker would earn if he had been employed. This is of course done to discourage malingering. But the forces of discontent will not be stilled when men who are out of work are paid only a fraction of an already insufficient amount.

[241]

The best way of meeting this situation, as long as we retain the capitalistic system, is to increase the level of wages itself. This can be done by an increase in the technical efficiency of industry, by a greater growth in the quantity of capital than of labor with a consequent increase in the marginal productivity of the latter, and also by a decrease in the power of monopolies and of all impediments in the way of price competition which cause labor to be paid less than its net social productivity.

14. The experience of Germany has shown us that genuine social security is not obtained merely by a system of social insurance which necessarily includes the employed workers but which provides no reciprocal protection for the self-employed. For Germany, of all European countries, had the most extensive system of social insurance. Old age pensions and health insurance were launched there in the eighties and early nineties while unemployment insurance was initiated in 1927 under the Weimar Republic. But the shop-keepers, the small peasants, and the independent professional workers felt omitted from all this and it was these groups, together with the clerks, which furnished the main membership of the Hitler movement. If we are to prevent a similar movement from developing here, we must not confine our efforts at security to the wage-earners and lower-salaried workers alone but we should include the self-employed as well.

It is true of course that this group will indirectly benefit from the greater stabilization of wage-

[242]

earners' incomes which social insurance will effect. Unemployment insurance and old age benefits will enable rents to be paid, grocery bills to be met and doctors to be engaged to a far greater degree than at present. Health insurance will moreover sweep a much larger proportion of the population into the ranks of paying patients than is at present the case. Despite the opposition of the official leaders of the medical profession it would be of real economic benefit to the rank and file of practitioners. Then too the system of old age pensions will directly protect the self-employed from indigent old age. It is also desirable to enable the self-employed to buy annuities for their old age at as low a cost as possible. For this reason, the original provision that the federal government should sell voluntary policies providing old age insurance to those not covered by the compulsory features of the act should be restored.

But more than this is needed. Perhaps one answer is the development of a system of public health and of public medical services which will be available for the self-employed, just as health insurance will provide medical care for the employed population. A widespread system of cooperative credit and marketing which will permit the small producers to acquire fixed and working capital on easier terms and to market their products more effectively will also be of real help.

15. Behind all these attempts to attain security within our present system lies the question as to

whether our social and political structure will itself prove secure. It is menaced today by business depressions and by war. If it is not able to prevent these twin scourges from assuming virulent form, it will inevitably be changed and transformed. But in the intervening period, life is likely to be extraordinarily insecure. The real struggle for security may therefore be carried through upon a larger stage than that which has been sketched in this book. But in that larger struggle of mankind this smaller one will have its part.

Chapter X

PRIVATE PENSION PLANS AND THE CLARK AMENDMENT

WHETHER private pension plans are to be exempted from the national old age insurance system is still an open issue. The act as such does not exempt them. It is understood that there is a gentleman's agreement for the appointment of an interim congressional committee to investigate this question and that this committee is to report to the next session of Congress where the issue will again be fought out. Since the taxes for mandatory old age insurance do not go into effect until 1937, it will be possible for Congress to amend the act during the 1936 session if it so desires. The question of the exemption of private plans is therefore the most immediately pressing issue of policy before Congress and the country, and a somewhat full discussion of the issues involved is appropriate.

Existing Private Pension Plans

It is fortunate that an exhaustive and careful study of private pension plans has been recently published by the Industrial Relations Counselors under the direction of Murray W. Latimer.[1] This study showed that in 1930 there were about 420 such voluntary plans in firms employing approximately 3,500,000 workmen or about 15 per cent of the number covered by the act. Most of the plans were in effect in giant companies rather than in small concerns. A quarter of all of these employees were in companies employing over 100,000 workers, while 70 per cent were in concerns which had over 25,000. Only 2 per cent were in firms with fewer than 2,000 employees. When classified by industry, around 40 per cent were found to be on the railways, 18 per cent in other public utilities, 11 per cent in the iron and steel industry and 7 per cent in the field of chemicals. This left 24 per cent, or about one-quarter of the total, in all other lines of industry.

These pension plans were instituted for a variety of reasons. A genuine desire to care for superannuated employees was beyond question one factor. Perhaps even more powerful, however, was the fact that a pension system enabled a company to clear its working force of its older employees without arousing bitterness on the part of its workers or the general public. To drop, without compensation, old men who had been long in the employ of a company would injure it in the opinion of its staff and in those of the consuming and voting

[1] Murray W. Latimer, *Industrial Pension Plans* (1933), 2 vols. See also an earlier and able study by Luther Conant, *A Critical Analysis of Industrial Pension Systems* (1922). For union plans see Latimer, *Trade Union Pension Plans* (1933).

public. This would be particularly true if the company were of such a size as to attract attention and be in the public eye. A pension system offered to these concerns a dignified way of getting rid of their superannuated employees. There were also other reasons. By paying pensions, the workers would be emotionally and economically attached to their employers and would be less likely to join unions. Moreover, if they did join a union or if they went out on strike, then, because of conditions which were frequently attached to the pensions, they could often be penalized by being deprived of their pension rights. This consequently served as a further deterrent to active unionism as was manifested by the way in which the older workers were reluctant to join the shopmen's strike of 1922.

Of necessity, the private plans could give pensions only to those who had been in their employ for a long period of years. This was generally set at twenty or twenty-five years. The pensions were customarily computed at a rate of 1 per cent or 1½ per cent of the average wage during a given period for each year worked. Thus if a worker had been employed for twenty-five years he would receive each month from 25 to 37½ per cent of his basic wage. The period chosen for computing the basic wage was generally the last five or ten years of employment. This choice of years worked adversely in the case of manual workers, whose earnings tended to decrease during the twilight of their activity, but worked favorably for executives, whose earnings tended to increase during this period.

The earlier pension plans had tended almost exclusively to be noncontributory. But beginning in the twenties, there was an increasing movement toward putting them upon a contributory basis so that the workers might meet at least a portion of the costs. This movement was caused by the increasing expense of the plans and by the realization that a large proportion of the systems were actuarially unsound. To reduce expenses for the companies, the basis of contributions was therefore widened. The insurance companies also increasingly came to carry some of the reserves instead of their being exclusively in the possession of the companies themselves.

It should, of course, be realized that the protection which was thus offered to the workers inside these companies was rather sharply limited and that there was little surety that the hoped-for pensions would in fact be received. Thus if a worker left a company before he reached the pensionable age he almost invariably lost all claim to a pension. In a similar fashion he lost his claim if he were dropped for personal inefficiency, for a decline in production or for changes in technique. If the concern failed, then, unless the reserves were set up independently in an insurance company, the workers also lost out. Even if a worker once began to receive a pension there was no surety that it would continue. In some cases he could be dropped from the pension rolls by the company, if, in their opinion, he was acting in a fashion prejudicial to their interest. Moreover, should the company find itself to be financially embarassed or if it thought the expense to be too great, it could discontinue paying its share of the pensions. This was done for example in the celebrated Morris case in Illinois when that packing concern was taken over by the Armour Company.

In short, the established legal theory was and is that a private pension is a gratuity which since it is given can be taken away at will by the donor. The courts have refused to regard it as a deferred wage or as something earned by the workers. They have held to this position in the face of evidence which was produced in the Morris case that many of the recipients had refused better paid jobs elsewhere because of the prospect of a pension if they stayed with the Morris Company and despite the fact that in some cases workers had apparently actually been urged by officials of that company to refuse these other offers on the ground that if they stayed they would be entitled to a pension. This legal view that the pensions are a gratuity is certainly in conflict with the general economic tendency for special privileges to be absorbed into the basic wage by lessening the necessity for increases, etc., and to help hold men in such periods of rising wage rates as we experienced prior to the great depression. But it was the legal view and not the economic facts which prevailed.

For all these reasons the proportion of the workers who actually receive private pensions is relatively small. Mr. Latimer estimated that in 1927 the total number of pensioners was approximately 90,000, while similar estimates for 1931 and 1935 fix the numbers at 140,000 and 165,000 respectively. But since there are in the country approximately seven million persons over the age of sixty-five, even the latter figure would not include more than 2½ per cent of the total number of aged persons. Some idea of the large proportion who for one reason or another are eliminated can be obtained from the fact that, while perhaps four million different workers have been employed by the railroads, yet nevertheless the total number who have received pensions from these relatively long-established plans has been not far from 120,000.

The existence of these pension plans also affected the hiring policies of many companies and the firing policies of some. Where a concern paid its premiums to an insurance company instead of carrying its own reserve, the costs would be much greater for older than for younger workers and there was therefore a direct incentive for it to discriminate against older applicants for jobs. Even where a firm administered its own system it was naturally reluctant to hire workers over 40 or 45 years of age. For although these workers, if hired, would not be able to satisfy the requirement for twenty or twenty-five years of continuous employment and consequently would not be legally eligible for a pension at the age of 65 or thereabouts, it would still be difficult for the firm to drop them when they became superannuated without making some provision for them. One result, therefore, of the private pension plans was to make it more difficult for the older workers to obtain fresh employment once they lost a former job.[1]

In addition, there have been many charges that some firms at least who were administering their own funds have reduced their costs by discharging most of their older workers as they neared the pensionable age. It is difficult, of course, to determine definitely whether or not these accusations are correct and if so how widespread has been the practice. For if such a policy existed, it would necessarily be carried out surreptitiously and would never openly be stated. There is, however, a considerable body of testimony to indicate that some companies have in fact carried out such an antisocial program.

During the depression a number of the private plans have been given up. A large number of smaller companies have however recently established systems which may have been put into effect in the hope that they would enable the concerns in question to contract out from the mandatory features of old age insurance. Instead therefore of 420 plans as in 1930, it is estimated that there are now (1935) not far from 750 different systems.

---

[1] Workmen's compensation and group insurance operate in the same direction.

But, despite the increase in the number of plans, it is probable that the total number of workers covered is no greater and may indeed be less than it was five years ago. For the companies which have dropped their plans have in general been large concerns while the new ones which have come in have on the whole been small.

The average amount paid as a pension under the private plans was about $50 per month in 1927, $61 in 1931 and $58 in 1933. The pensions therefore, even when carried through, are not on any markedly munificent scale, and this is a fact which becomes all the more important in view of the arguments advanced by certain Senators and newspapers that the private plans should be continued because they are in so many cases much more liberal than any amounts which could be paid under the Social Security Act.

The Arguments in Favor of the Clark Amendment and the Exemption of Private Plans

It was argued by Senator Clark and his followers that if private plans were not exempted the employers would be compelled to drop them. For while they might afford the contributions to one system whether public or private, they could not afford contributions to both. With the discontinuance of the private plans would go the superior advantages which many were presumed to possess over the projected public system.

[252]

This claim is however greatly weakened by two factors. First, the benefits provided by the existing private plans are, in the great majority of instances, inferior rather than superior to those promised under the present act. Even if the private plans were discontinued the workers would benefit on the whole from coming under the governmental system. As a matter of fact, the subsequent additions which Senator Clark made to his amendment and which were designed to guarantee equal benefits to the workers under the private plans would have required an extensive upward revision of all but a few of these systems.

Secondly, even though under the act the basic protection for future old age is to be provided by the public system, there is nothing to prevent an employer from maintaining a private system to give additional and supplementary benefits. The general minimum could therefore be handled by the governmental system and the private plans could then be used to give such further protection as the employers might desire to provide. This is what has happened in Great Britain in connection with compulsory unemployment insurance, where some years ago Miss Mary Gilson found that there were more workers covered under supplementary private plans than there were in this country, where the entire field of unemployment compensation was free for voluntary insurance and for nothing else. It cannot therefore be said that a failure to exempt the private plans need result in any large lowering of rights already provided. On the contrary the general tendency, even for those now under the private systems, would have been precisely the opposite.

It is probable, however, that a certain number of the older workers under the private plans might have suffered. For if upon the failure to exempt, employers were completely to discontinue their former plans, then some of those already receiving such pensions might be dropped from the pension rolls while others who are nearing the retirement age would lose the future benefits to which they would have looked forward. Since these older workers, if over 60 years of age, will be completely disqualified from the public system and if only a few years under this age will receive low benefits, some will undoubtedly to their own loss fall between the two stools. While the more socially-minded employers would probably make some provision for these workers even if they wound up their private plans, there is no surety that this would be the case with most employers. There is therefore something in the contention advanced by the proponents of private plans but very much less than is claimed.

Another reason why many concerns want to retain their own plans is that they have built up some good-will among their workers by instituting them. If they are largely forced to discontinue these plans so that the workers receive benefits as a right from the compulsory system then this good-will will largely be lost. Unionization and a more aggresive policy by the employees is therefore more likely. It should of course be added that this was one of the most important reasons why the American Federation of Labor has opposed the exemption of the private plans.

The other main argument in favor of exempting the private systems is the contention that private enterprise because of its alleged superiority should be the rule and governmental activity the exception. Why, it was asked, should private plans be blotted out if they can do the work as well? Closely allied with this is the query which Senator Clark raised with great effect on the floor of the Senate. What possible harm could be done, by exempting the company plans, he asked, if they were required to provide equal benefits and if adequate safeguards were thrown around them?

This query seemed to receive substantial support by the apparent safeguards which Senator Clark attached to his amendment when he proposed it on the floor of the Senate.[1] Thus he provided that in order for a private plan to be certified for exemption, it had to be submitted to the Social Security Board and be approved by it. It was expressly stated that the benefits provided by every approved private plan must be at least equal to those provided under the act by the public system. This applied in the case of both the old age annuities and the death benefits to the heirs of the

[1] See *The Congressional Record*, 74th Congress, 1st session (1935), p. 9912.

insured person. In order to provide a greater degree
of safety and of separation of funds than has in the
past characterized many private plans, it was
stated that the reserves must be kept in and the
insurance consequently handled either by a private
insurance company or by a trustee. While any
private plan had to be open to all employed
workers in the concern who wished to join, they
were not compelled to do so. On the contrary they
could elect not to join. Another later qualification
which was attached to the Clark amendment
provided that an employer must not in any way
coerce or restrain a worker from deciding whether
or not he wished to join such a plan or to withdraw
from it even though he had previously joined. This
last clause was indeed closely parallel in structure
to the provisions which, in Section 7A of the
National Recovery Act and in the Wagner Industrial Disputes Act, attempted to prevent the
imposition by employers of "yellow-dog" contracts.

If a worker who was previously insured in a
private plan left it and came under the public
system because his employment with that firm was
terminated, or because he had voluntarily resigned
from the private plan though continuing to be
employed, then the private plan was required to
turn over to the public system the equivalent
amounts which would have been credited to the
account of the worker had he previously been
entirely under the public system.

Again, as if to remove any last doubt, it was
provided that both employer and workers must

make contributions to the private plans which must be at least equal to those required under the act. These were the required sums plus compound interest, which would be transferred to the federal account if the worker moved out of the private plan.

In view of all these safeguards it seemed to the majority of the Senate and to a goodly section of the public that there was really no legitimate objection against granting such an exemption.

One final shrewd argument for exemption was advanced in the Senate by Senator George of Georgia. If the private plans were not exempted, most of them would be abandoned in the earlier stages of the act. Then if the mandatory old age insurance provisions were later declared to be unconstitutional, those at present under the private plans would have had this protection destroyed without any permanent substitute having been provided for it.

The Exemption of Private Plans and the Adverse Selection of Risks

The most fundamental objection to an outright exemption of the private plans from the mandatory insurance system is that it would result in an adverse selection of risks for the public plan. This follows from two facts namely: (1) that the premiums under any private plan would be much higher for the older workers than for the younger; and (2) that an employer would be free either to bring all his employees under such a plan or not to do so. It should also be remembered that the consent of the individual workman would also be required before he could be included under a private plan of his employer.

All these forces would operate in the direction of having the private plans primarily include the younger workers, so that the governmental system would be unduly weighted down with the older workers. The result would be that the promised benefits could not be paid from the prescribed rates of contribution. Unless government subsidies were therefore advanced to make up the deficit either the benefits would have to be reduced or the contributions increased.

Let us take up each of these points in turn and follow through its implications.

In the first place, there are marked differences between the annual premiums which are needed at various ages in order to insure a given monthly annuity to the survivor at the age of sixty-five. This is shown by the relative cost at different ages of buying with a lump-sum payment an annuity of $100 per annum to begin at the age of sixty-five.

Age at Which Annuity Is Bought	Lump-sum Payment Required to Yield an Annual Annuity of $100 at Age of 65
22	$186.20
27	218.27
47	427.10
57	647.57

It will thus be seen that the required rate at the age of forty-seven is almost twice that required at the age of twenty-seven and that it is two and a quarter times the amount needed at the age of twenty-two. The rate required at the age of fifty-seven is indeed virtually three times the rate for those twenty-seven years old and almost four times that required at the age of twenty-two. The chief reason for these differences is, of course, that the payments for the younger men have a much longer time in which the principle of compound interest upon a payment can accumulate.

It is therefore apparent that firms whose employees are of less than the average age would ordinarily wish to set up a private plan if they were free to do so. For they could furnish the same protection as guaranteed under the federal act at an appreciably smaller cost. On the other hand, firms with a working force whose ages were above the average would not wish to set up separate plans. For if they were to provide the accepted scale of benefits, they would have to pay a much higher rate of contributions than would be the case if they went under the government system. The firms would therefore tend to arrange themselves in such a way as would reduce their outlay to a minimum. This would result in an adverse selection to the government, with the younger workers tending to be outside the government system and the older workers within it.

[259]

Nor is this all. The choices made by the workers would operate to strengthen the same adverse tendency. The private plans would tend to be overwhelmingly upon a contributory basis. The younger workers would therefore not need to contribute as much as the law called for in order to receive the same protection, while the older workers would have to contribute more. Even where a firm with an age composition of its workers which was lower than the average should therefore elect to put in a private plan, the workers whose ages were above the average would tend to elect the public scheme if their premiums were graduated according to their age. Even if the contributions of the workers under a private plan were to be uniform for all ages, the employers who would have to pay higher premiums for the older workers would naturally want them to be under the public plan rather than their own. They would therefore naturally seek to influence their choice and any legal restraint upon their actions would be even less effective than was Section 7A. For the aged workers would not lose by choosing the public plan and hence would tend not to resist any such influence upon the part of the employers nor protest against it. Moreover the younger workers would want to have the older workers under the public plan so that they themselves could get higher benefits for their contributions.

Finally, there would also be a tendency for the firms with private plans to rid themselves of the older workers in order not to pay the higher premiums and in hiring new workers to give decided preference to the younger applicants. The exemption of the private plans would therefore make it more difficult for the older workers to find and retain jobs. It would also lead to the present generation of young workers being employed as long as they continued young but being weeded out rather rigidly as they passed into the upper age groups.

But it will be objected that all this reasoning has been based upon the assumption that while the benefits under the private plans were to be kept at an equality with those of public schemes their contributions might however be less. Could not all this be checked, however, if the private plans were required, as they were under the proposed Clark amendment, to pay in contributions sums at least equal to those required under the public system? If this were done, what incentive would there then be for firms and individuals to range themselves in such an adverse form of selection? Such a provision would, of course, be a desirable safeguard. But even though the firms were to pay the same contributions as under the government plan they would be able, if they had a young group of workers, to promise to them a larger scale of benefits than that provided under the act. The offer of these large benefits would in turn serve to build up good-will on the part of the workers for the company. Since added benefits which are given by a firm tend to become embedded in its basic wage rate, the result would generally be that the firms with the younger workers and the private plans would be able to pay less than the prevailing rate and hence make their savings in this way.

The firms which had an older than average group of workers would, moreover, still not wish to establish private plans since this would cost more than would membership in the government system. Firms which, because of the low average age of their employees, had established private plans, would not wish their older workers to be included and would discourage them from joining. They would also find it to be somewhat to their advantage to discharge the insured workers when they become older since these workers would cost the firms more than the given minimum rate of contributions.

This tendency would be powerfully reinforced by the unearned annuities which those in the upper age groups will for some years receive. If a private firm were to retain these workers until they reached the age of sixty-five, it would have to pay them not only the earned but the unearned annuities as well. For the private plans would then be forced under the Clark amendment to pay equal benefits to those provided in the government system. But if they could get rid of these workers before they reached the age of sixty-five, they would then only have to turn over to the government the actual contributions made by and for those workers. These companies would thus be able to free themselves from paying the unearned annuities. There would be a distinct tendency therefore for the firms with private plans either to put pressure upon the older workers to elect the public system or to discharge them before they reached the age of sixty-five and thus throw the older workers either upon the public plan or upon relief.

It will therefore be seen that the exemption of the private plans would heavily load the public system with the older workers, even with the supposed safeguards which Senator Clark proposed. It would throw the public system out of equilibrium and require a raising of the contribution rate in order to maintain the promised scale of benefits. This would put further pressure upon additional firms to get out of the public system.

Inequality of Treatment and the Disposition of Liquidated Plans

The Clark amendment would also create decided inequalities as between the recipients of pensions. If a worker were first attached to a private plan and then came into the public system, the earlier required payments made by him and by his employer would be taken over by the treasury and he would receive one pension at the specified annuity rates. If however he were first employed under the public plan and later came under a private scheme, he would receive two pensions—one from the government and one from his employer. Since the benefits under the public system are higher on the first blocks of income received than on the latter, the result would be that the second group would receive larger pensions than the first even though their total earnings were identical.

In addition there is a possibility that when a private plan is terminated, there will be a surplus left after the legal contributions plus accumulated interest is turned over to the government. This surplus would presumably belong to the employers in question and it might therefore be to the interest of private concerns to close out their plans when this surplus was at an approximate maximum.

The Question of Constitutionality

The exemption of the private plans would also distinctly weaken the constitutionality of the old age insurance program. For in respect to federal taxation, it would divide employees into two sharply distinguished classes. The group which did not have private plans would have to pay their taxes into the federal treasury while those with private plans would not. Since the constitution requires federal taxes to be uniform throughout the country, it might well be decided that this would be a violation of the taxing power and lead to a rejection of this section of the act.[1]

[1] The constitutional difficulties would be greater in this case than when private firms were allowed to set up their own unemployment insurance funds. For these latter private systems would be technically under state and

Summary

For all these reasons it is evident that private plans should not be exempted from the public system. For to do so would introduce an adverse selection into the public system which might wreck it and which in any event would be a grave source of weakness. The policy of exemptions would also create inequalities and still further endanger the constitutionality of the plan. If Congress is therefore alert to the real issues involved it will not saddle the system with the Clark amendment. The primary groups which would benefit from such a policy would be the insurance companies, insurance brokers[1] and salesmen, and certain private companies whose policies would be largely antisocial. The main mass of the workers would lose by it. And it is this group with which we should primarily be concerned.

---

not federal laws and it could be argued that the uniformity provision would not apply here. The exemptions from the old age insurance plan would however be from a federal tax.

[1] It was in fact a firm of insurance brokers which seemed to furnish the major driving force behind the Clark amendment.

CHAPTER XI

CONSTITUTIONAL PROSPECTS AS THEY APPEARED IN 1935[1]

NO one can predict with complete certainty what the decision of the United States Supreme Court will be upon the various constitutional issues which are raised by the Social Security Act. Economically the country is a unit with a predominantly national market. It follows as Professor Gulick has well observed that "nothing effective can be done in the regulation or stabilization of economic affairs unless the area of planning and control has the same boundaries as the economic structure."[2] There is imperative need therefore for a system of national legislation which will at once regulate and set the terms under which business and industry are, in the main, to be carried on. But this economic and political necessity finds itself confronted with the judicial review by the Supreme Court of congressional and indeed of state acts. When the propertied classes have wished to check federal action which might be

---

[1] This chapter was written some eighteen months before the decisions of the Supreme Court in the Social Security cases. These are discussed in Chapter XIV.

[2] Professor C. A. Gulick, quoted in Corwin, *The Twilight of the Supreme Court*, pp. 45–46.

adverse to their interests, they have found able attorneys who have assured both them and the courts that these laws were in areas which were exclusively reserved to the states and hence were not properly the subject for federal legislation. Similarly, when the states have passed laws aiming to regulate industry or to protect the weak either from the insecurity of their position or from the cumulative bargaining advantages which the strong possess, these same attorneys or others of their kind have immediately declared these acts also to be unconstitutional because they took "liberty and property without due process of law" and hence violated the Fourteenth Amendment to the Constitution.

In short, the common attitude of the propertied classes and of their attorneys has been that virtually all regulatory and protective legislation should be declared unconstitutional. If Congress passes such legislation, it is declared to be within the province of the states. If the states take action, then it is said to be a violation of due process. And what the leaders of the bar have seductively argued, the court has at least partially proclaimed. The net result was that for nearly twenty-five years, or roughly between 1884 and 1909, the decisions of the Supreme Court were designed to exalt the theory of laissez faire and to prevent governmental action in the field of economic life.

At the same time there was a tendency for the courts to throw out an anchor to windward by recognizing the doctrine of police power for the states and in not checking the spending powers of Congress. In short, the courts left themselves free to choose one side or the other of the question of federal or state action and this ambivalent possibility has continued to the present. It was therefore a sage comment upon the part of our present learned Chief Justice of the Supreme Court when he declared, as Governor of New York, "We are under a Constitution but the Constitution is what the judges say it is."

Such being the case now as then, it is impossible to speak as definitely as do many subtle advocates of what will inevitably be the constitutional fate of the various features of the Security Act. About all that can be done is to indicate the main issues involved, to show where the weight of constitutional precedents lies, and to point out lines of logic which the judges might use if they wished to decide in a given way.

We may perhaps divide the constitutional features of the act into three parts, namely, (1) the federal aid sections of the bill, covering the subventions to the states for old age pensions, mothers' pensions, the care of dependent, delinquent and crippled children, maternity and infancy care, public health, etc., (2) the tax offset features of the bill, which deal with unemployment insurance, (3) the national system of old age insurance, and then (4) to discuss in addition the constitutionality of state unemployment insurance laws.

The Constitutionality of the Federal Aid Provision

While nothing is absolutely certain in the field of constitutional law, the constitutionality of federal aid would seem to be as firmly established as any practice could be. In the first place, it is long rooted in usage. Outright federal grants have been given to the states to create and maintain state agricultural colleges and to develop the national guard. Numerous subventions have also been given by the national government to stimulate research. Grants calling for a matching of the federal funds have been made for agricultural extension work, the construction of highways, vocational education, venereal disease prevention, the protection of forests from fires, vocational rehabilitation, and maternity and infancy care. In no case has the constitutionality of this device been overthrown.

Furthermore in the case of *Massachusetts* v. *Mellon* and *Frothingham* v. *Mellon*, the Supreme Court explicitly and by a unanimous vote refused to declare a federal aid measure of the ordinary type to be unconstitutional.[1] This case arose out of the complaint of the state of Massachusetts and of Frothingham, a local taxpayer, that the national government by granting federal aid to the states for the health care of mothers and children was: (1) spending money for purposes other than those permitted in the Constitution and therefore invading fields of action which should be the exclusive

[1] *Massachusetts* v. *Mellon; Frothingham* v. *Mellon*, 262 U.S. 447.

province of the states, (2) taking the money of taxpayers to spend on objects not constitutionally permitted to it and (3) coercing the states on penalty of suffering a financial loss if they did not agree to carry out certain functions and conform to a set of rules and regulations laid down by the federal government in matters which were not a part of its legitimate concern.

One of the fundamental issues involved was whether Congress could appropriate money for purposes which it regarded as for the "general welfare" and therefore as coming under the constitution but which were not specifically enumerated in that document. Certainly if Congress were limited to the latter interpretation a large portion of the public expenditures of the last two decades would have had to be canceled. The court in a unanimous opinion refused to give any such interpretation. It declared that "in the last analysis, the complaint of the plaintiff is brought to the naked contention that Congress has usurped the reserved powers of the several States by the mere enactment of the statute, though nothing has been done and nothing is to be done without their consent; and it is plain that that question, as it is thus presented, is political and not judicial in character, and therefore is not a matter which admits of the exercise of the judicial power."

In refusing to enjoin the Secretary of the Treasury from paying out funds for this purpose upon complaint of the state of Massachusetts the court also said: "It cannot be conceded that a state as *parens patria* may institute judicial proceedings to protect citizens of the United States from the operation of the statutes thereof." It was on the contrary the federal government which bore this relationship to its citizens.

Nor was the interest of a given taxpayer sufficient to justify him in launching such a suit. "His interest," declared the court, "in the moneys of the Treasury—partly realized from taxation and partly from other sources—is shared with millions of others; is comparatively minute and indeterminable, and the effect upon future taxation, of any payment out of funds so remote, fluctuating and uncertain that no basis is afforded to the preventive powers of a court of equity." The moral of this refusal to enjoin appropriations for what Congress regarded as the general welfare, in the words of Professor Corwin,[1] seems to be "that so long as Congress has the prudence to lay and collect taxes without specifying the purposes to which the proceeds from any particular tax are to be devoted, it may continue to appropriate the national funds without judicial let or hindrance."

In dealing with the contention that the system of federal aid required the states to give up their sovereignty, the court, through the opinion of Justice Sutherland, observed sapiently: "Nor does the statute require the states to do or to yield anything. If Congress enacted it with the ulterior purpose of tempting them to yield, that purpose

[1] *The Twilight of the Supreme Court*, p. 176.

[271]

may be effectively frustrated by the simple expedient of not yielding." In other words the states were free to accept the federal aid if they wished, or to refuse it. If they accepted it, they must spend it for such purposes as the federal government specified.

This would certainly seem to be a direct and positive affirmation of the constitutionality of federal aid. There are well-supported rumors however that it is the intention of certain interests to attack even the federal aid features of the act. One judicial loophole which seems to be left to this group and indeed to the court, if it wishes to reverse its position, may lie in a curious sentence in the opinion of the court in *Massachusetts* v. *Mellon*.[1] This was Justice Sutherland's declaration that "we have reached the conclusion that the cases must be disposed of for want of jurisdiction without considering the merits of the constitutional questions." It is indeed difficult to determine what the court was doing in the sections of the opinion which have been quoted unless it was discussing the constitutional issues. But the way may technically have been cleared by this sentence for a later court to go into what it considers to be "the constitutional issues" and, if it so desires, to distinguish the case at hand from that of *Massachusetts* v. *Mellon* and to declare federal aid to be unconstitutional. This will be a difficult position to take but the

---

[1] There is a further possibility that the court would recognize a suit brought by the Executive department against a federal-aid law passed by a previous administration.

Supreme Court has shown itself in the past capable of making such an about face.[1] Unless however some such striking reversal of judicial opinion occurs, we may expect with some confidence that the federal aid features of the Social Security Act will be upheld.

The Constitutionality of the Tax Offset Provisions

We come now to less certain ground. The offset provision in connection with one portion of the payroll tax will undoubtedly be attacked on the ground that the taxing powers are here not being used to obtain revenue but to compel the states to enact unemployment insurance laws. It will therefore be alleged that it is regulatory and coercive in its nature and that according to the precedent laid down in the second Child Labor Case[2] it should be declared unconstitutional.[3]

The power of Congress however to levy payroll taxes would seem to be unquestioned. The court declared in *Bailey* v. *Drexel Furniture Co.* that a tax must have some revenue features and could not be exclusively regulatory in its nature. It did not rule that an act could not combine regulatory features with revenue purposes. Had it done so it would have been compelled to reverse the approval

---

[1] Thus, see the way *Holden* v. *Hardy*, 169 U.S. 366, was later reversed by *Lochner* v. *New York*, 198 U.S. 45.

[2] *Bailey* v. *Drexel Furniture Co.*, 259 U.S. 20. See also *Hill* v. *Wallace*, 259 U.S. 44.

[3] See testimony of James A. Emery, attorney for the National Manufacturers Association. *Hearings before Committee on Ways and Means*, House of Representatives, 74th Congress, 1st session, on H.R. 4120, pp. 1020–1036.

it had previously given to the oleomargarine tax and to outlaw the protective tariff. In the oleo case, for example, a tax of 10 cents a pound was levied on yellow oleo while the tax was but one-fourth of a cent on white oleo. In order, therefore, to protect the American cow from the competition of vegetable products, the tax was made 40 times greater on oleo that resembled butter than on oleo which did not. The revenue purpose might therefore be placed at 2½ per cent and the regulatory purpose at 97½ per cent. And yet the 2½ per cent was apparently enough to save the constitutionality of the remaining 97½ per cent.[1]

If such be the minimum Volstead revenue contents which are needed to ensure constitutionality, it can be claimed that Title IX more than meets this test. For even if every state passes an unemployment insurance law, the federal government will retain one-tenth of the tax for its own purposes. It is true that in another title (III) grants are made to the states for the purpose of administering their unemployment insurance acts. There is in fact, as we have pointed out, an economic connection between the two titles but there is no formal and avowed legal connection and it can therefore be argued that the funds derived from Title IX are merged in the federal treasury before the amounts appropriated by Title III are disbursed from it. The amounts distributed as grants

[1] *McCray* v. *U.S.*, 195 U.S. 27. See also the comments of Chief Justice Taft in the Drexel Furniture Co. case.

for the administration of unemployment insurance may not indeed exhaust the 10 per cent of the payroll tax retained by the federal government.

All this should be sufficient to justify this portion of Titles IX and III, if the courts have a disposition to do so.

So far as the alleged coercive nature of the offset provision is concerned, it can be answered that the states are free not to pass unemployment insurance laws if they do not approve of this policy. And the case of *Florida* v. *Mellon*[1] in which the Supreme Court unanimously upheld the offset features of the federal inheritance tax is a powerful precedent in favor of the offset features of the present act. In that decision Justice Sutherland again speaking, as in *Massachusetts* v. *Mellon*, for a united court declared: "The contention that the federal tax is not uniform because other states impose inheritance taxes while Florida does not is without merit. Congress cannot accommodate its legislation to the conflicting or dissimilar laws of the several states nor control the diverse conditions to be found in the various states which necessarily work unlike results from the enforcement of the same tax. All the Constitution requires is that the law shall be uniform in the sense that its liability shall be alike in all parts of the United States."

There is one dissimilarity however between the circumstances under which the Federal Inheritance Tax Act was passed and those under which the

[1] *Florida* v. *Mellon*, 273 U.S. 12.

present law was enacted. At the time of the former law all but three states had inheritance taxes. The federal act was therefore designed to prevent the "cut-throat" competition of Florida, in striving to obtain the residence of the wealthy, from compelling other states to give up the tax systems which they had previously put into effect. In the case of the Social Security Act, there was only one state with an unemployment insurance law when the federal bill was proposed and only seven when it became a law. It can thus be alleged that the purpose of the federal inheritance tax was to conserve existing state systems while the purpose of the Security Act is to coerce the states into taking action which otherwise they would not.

But despite all this the two laws are similar in that the federal government used the tax offset feature in both cases to encourage lines of action in the states which it wished to foster. The primary purpose in both cases was to restrain undue competition between the states. The fact that the inheritance tax has been declared constitutional without a dissenting voice should therefore count heavily in favor of Title IX of the present act.

Will State Unemployment Insurance Laws Be Declared Constitutional?

The questions involved in this issue are of a different nature. They do not deal with the division of power between the national government and the states but whether the contributions required from employers, and possibly workers, constitute the taking of property without "due process of law."

It will undoubtedly be claimed: (1) that employers should not be made responsible for a risk of industry which they cannot control and (2) that, in particular, the contributions of employers should not be merged into a general fund for the relief of other workers than their own. In support of this latter contention, the adverse decision of the Supreme Court about the pooling method in the railway retirement case will, of course, be cited. The opinion of the minority may however be able to win some acceptance on this issue.

There are three rather powerful sets of precedents in opposition to these contentions and in favor of the constitutionality of such state laws.

The first deal with the taxes imposed by numerous states upon the owners of all dogs, the proceeds from which were then used as funds with which to indemnify the owners of all sheep killed by dogs. The courts uniformly upheld these laws and declared that the owners of every dog were obligated to pay such a tax even though their dogs might have been completely innocent. The fact of the loss and the inability to locate specific responsibility led the courts therefore to approve the assessments upon poodles as well as St. Bernards and upon Pekingese as well as blood-

[277]

hounds.[1] What has been declared constitutional in the case of sheep may possibly therefore be appropriate, in the eyes of the courts, in the case of men.

Secondly, in the case of state laws guaranteeing bank deposits, taxes levied upon all banks including the strong have been pooled to indemnify depositors in weaker banks which fail. And yet on two occasions the Supreme Court has declared such a pooling provision to be constitutional.[2]

The decisions in the workmen's compensation cases are of a more recent vintage. In four important cases the United States Supreme Court upheld the constitutionality of such laws.[3] In the Washington case, it affirmed a law which established a state fund and prescribed different rates for various occupational groups according to the relative degree of hazard. Certain of the statements of the court in this case are equally appropriate to the question of unemployment insurance. "The authority of the states to enact such laws as reasonably are deemed to be necessary to promote the health, safety and general welfare of their people carries with it, a wide judgment and

[1] See *Morey* v. *Brown*, 42 N.H. 373; *Tenney* v. *Lenz*, 16 Wis. 589; *Mitchell* v. *Williams*, 27 Ind. 62; *Van Horn* v. *People*, 46 Mich. 183; *Longyear* v. *Buck*, 83 Mich. 236; *Cole* v. *Hall*, 103 Ill. 30; *Holst* v. *Roe*, 39 Ohio St. 340; *McGlone* v. *Womack*, 129 Ky. 274, 283.

[2] *Noble State Bank* v. *Haskell*, 219 U.S. 104; *Abie State Bank* v. *Bryan*, 282 U.S. 765.

[3] See *New York Central* v. *White*, 243 U.S. 188; *Hawkins* v. *Bleakly*, 243 U.S. 210; *Mountain Timber Co.* v. *Washington*, 243 U.S. 219; *Arizona Copper Co.* v. *Hammer*, 250 U.S. 400.

[278]

discretion as to what matters are of sufficiently general importance to be subjected to state regulation and administration. . . .

"It is said that the compensation or pension under this law is not confined to those who are left without means of support. This is true. But is the state powerless to succor the wounded except they be reduced to the last extremity? Is it debarred from compensating an injured man until his own resources are first exhausted?"

The court then went on to deal with the argument that the entire cost of compensation should not be imposed on industry and that firms with low accident rates should not contribute to the compensation of injured workers in plants with higher rates.

"We are unable to discern any ground in natural justice or fundamental right that prevents the State from imposing the entire burden upon the industries that occasion the losses. . . .

"To the criticism that carefully managed plants are in effect required to contribute to make good the losses arising through the negligence of their competitors, it is sufficient to say that the act recognizes that no management however careful can afford immunity from personal injuries to employees. . . . Taking the fact that accidental injuries are inevitable . . . we deem the State acted within its power in declaring that no employer should conduct such an industry without making stated and fairly apportioned contributions

[279]

adequate to maintain a public fund for indemnifying injured employees and dependents of those killed, irrespective of the particular plant in which the accident might happen to occur. In short it cannot be deemed arbitrary or unreasonable for the State . . . to impose the burden upon the industry through a system of occupation taxes limited to the actual losses occurring in the respective classes of occupation."

If there is any consistency in the opinions of the court, then in the light of this decision and that in the Arizona case which followed it, the constitutionality of state unemployment insurance acts would seem to be fairly assured. For if the states can spend money on relief they would certainly seem to be authorized to take steps so that these persons may be cared for before they are forced to go on relief.

The Constitutionality of Mandatory Old Age Pensions

Perhaps the weakest section of the Security Act from a constitutional standpoint is that which provides for mandatory old age insurance. While Title VIII which levies the taxes upon employers and employees is formally distinct from Title II which prescribes the scale of benefits to those over the age of sixty-five and to the heirs of the deceased, there is in fact a close and immediate connection between them. The individual benefits to be paid are computed upon the basis of the contributions or taxes levied and upon nothing else. It will undoubtedly be charged that these titles of the act in effect therefore prescribe the specific purpose for which the tax is levied and that they are consequently unconstitutional since they launch the federal government into the performance of functions not specifically delegated to it by the constitution. There is certainly very real danger that such may indeed be the fate of this feature of the act.

A good case can however be made for such a provision by simply interpreting the "general welfare" clause in a literal fashion. If Congress can further the general welfare by its system of taxation and appropriations why, it may be asked, must the two be separated from each other in order to gain the approval of the courts? Why cannot this be done by levying a tax for a specific purpose if that purpose can, in the minds of reasonable men, be thought to promote the general welfare? Even if this feature is declared unconstitutional it may perhaps be revised in the same manner as was the Railway Pension Act. This would be done through passing two separate and distinct acts. One of these would levy the taxes while the other would grant the benefits. This would have at least a better chance of being declared constitutional than the inclusion of the two branches of the system as different titles of the same act.

A Word in Conclusion

The lines of reasoning which have been suggested above have been framed in terms of customary constitutional reasoning. But more is needed if we are to give to our society the plasticity which it needs. Ours is a changing society and if our political organization is to grapple with these changing and expanding issues it must be given the opportunity to adapt itself to the times. It has been extremely fortunate for America that under John Marshall the powers of the federal government were sufficiently expanded to enable it to meet the westward growth of the country, and that under Abraham Lincoln the narrowing interpretations of Taney and Buchanan were replaced with a program which enabled it to prevent the dissolution of the union and the continuation of slavery. There is equal need today for the constitution to grow with the times and to permit a peaceful adaptation to the problems of change. If this can be effected through legislation and judicial interpretation, peaceful change will be facilitated but if this is impossible then a constitutional amendment will become a necessity. In any event, those who would confine us to the straitjacket of narrow powers do a disservice to the country and to the constitution which they profess to honor. For the troubles of our economic life will still continue but the agency adapted for control and alleviation will be stripped of its powers to act. Our national life cannot be chopped into forty-eight separate sections. If this happens and if the states are also prevented from acting, then no one knows where the blind forces of change will carry us. Only one surmise can safely be hazarded and that is that it will be to a very different state from that envisaged by the founding fathers.

Part Four

DEVELOPMENTS UNDER THE ACT

CHAPTER XII

THE RESPONSE OF THE STATES IN 1935

SINCE only old age insurance is to be administered directly by the national government, state action is necessary to make the other features of the act effective. The purpose of the present chapter is to analyze the progress which has been made thus far by the various states in the field of old age pensions and unemployment insurance and to indicate the further steps which seem desirable in each of these lines.

The Present Status of Old Age Pensions

By July, 1935, thirty-one states and two territories had mandatory old age insurance laws, while four states had optional acts. The table on pages 232 and 233 prepared by Abraham Epstein shows the main features of these laws.[1]

From an examination of this table, it is fairly evident that state legislation needs to develop along the following lines.

1. The twelve states without any such legislation need to fall in line at the earliest possible moment. In the south the states where such action is required are Virginia, North Carolina, South

---

[1] Taken from *Social Security*, 1935, p. 236.

TABLE XII

SUMMARY OF OLD AGE INSURANCE LAWS, JULY, 1935

State	Year adopted	Pension age	Maximum pension	Years of citizenship	Years in state	Source of funds state or county
State-wide mandatory systems:						
Alabama	1935	65	$30 per month[9]	5	5	⅓ state, ⅓ county, ½ federal
Alaska: men	1915	65	$35 per month	Citizenship	25	Territory
women		60	$45 per month			
Arizona	1933	70	$30 per month	Citizenship	35	67% state, 33% county
Arkansas	1935	65[1]	$30 per month	Not required	5	State
California	1929-1935	65[2]	$35 maximum $20 minimum	Citizenship	5[3]	⅓ state, ⅓ county
Colorado	1933-1935	65	$1 per day	15	15	State
Connecticut	1935	65	$7 per week	Citizenship[4]	5	State
Delaware	1931	65	$25 per month	Not required	5	State
District of Columbia	1935	65	No maximum	Citizenship	5	District
Florida	1935	65[5]	$35 maximum $10 minimum $60 per family	Citizenship	10	State and county
Hawaii	1933	65	$15 per month	30	15	County
Idaho	1931	65	$25 per month	15	10	County
Illinois	1935	65	$1 per day	Citizenship	5	State
Indiana	1933	70	$15 per month	15	15	½ state, ½ county
Iowa	1934-1935	65	$25 per month	Citizenship	5	State
Maine[6]	1933	65	$1 per day	Citizenship	15	½ state, ½ county
Maryland	1927-1935	65	$1 per day	15	5	⅔ state, ⅓ county
Massachusetts	1930	70	No maximum	Citizenship	20	⅓ state, ⅔ local
Michigan	1933-1935	65[1,2]	$30 per month	Citizenship	10[7]	State
Minnesota	1929	70	$1 per day	15	15	County
Mississippi	1935	65	Reasonable subsistence	Citizenship	5	State
Missouri	1935	70	$30 single $45 couple	Citizenship	5	State

[288]

Montana	1923–1935	65[2]	No maximum	Citizenship	5	¾ state, ¼ county
Nebraska	1933–1935	65	$30 single / $50 couple	Citizenship	5	State
New Hampshire[3]	1931–1935	70	$30 per month	Citizenship	5	5% state, rest county and federal
New Jersey	1931	70	$1 per day	Citizenship	15	¾ state, ¼ county
New York	1930	70	No maximum	Citizenship	10	½ state, ½ county
North Dakota	1933	68	$150 per year	Citizenship	20	State
Ohio	1933	65	$25 per month	Citizenship	5	State
Oklahoma	1935	65	$30 per month	Citizenship	5	State
Oregon	1933–1935	65	$30 per month	Citizenship	5	State[8]
Pennsylvania	1934	70	$30 single / $45 couple	15	15	State
Rhode Island	1935	65	$30 per month	Citizenship or 20 years residence in United States	5	State
Texas	1935	60 for men 55 for women	$30 per month	Citizenship	5	State
Vermont	1935	65	$30 single / $45 couple	Citizenship	5	State
Washington	1933–1935	65	$30 per month	Citizenship	5	State
Wisconsin	1925–1935	70	$1 per day	15	15	State
Wyoming	1929–1935	65	$30 per month	Citizenship	5	½ state, ½ county
County optional systems:						
Kentucky[6]	1926	70	$250 per year	15	10	County
Nevada[6]	1925	65	$1 per day	15	10	County
Utah[6]	1929	65	$25 per month	15	15	County
West Virginia[6]	1931	65	$1 per day	15	10	County

1 May be age seventy until January 1, 1940.
2 Reduced from age seventy in 1935.
3 Only while federal aid is available; otherwise fifteen years.
4 If federal law allows aid to noncitizens the state will grant them pensions.
5 Also allows pensions to infirm persons regardless of age.
6 No pensions ever paid.
7 To be reduced to five if federal law requires.
8 Law does not go into effect until federal funds are available.
9 $50 to Civil War veterans.

Carolina, Georgia, Alabama, Mississippi, Louisiana and Texas. In the southwest Oklahoma and New Mexico are at the time of writing still without laws, as are Kansas and South Dakota in the middle west.[1] Some southern states will have to amend their constitutions before they take action. This was done in Texas by a big vote on August 24.

2. The four states with optional laws should make them mandatory. These are West Virginia and Kentucky in the south, Nevada and Utah in the west.[2]

3. The residence requirements will need to be reduced by many states. While a number of state legislatures have recently reduced this to five out of the last ten years, there are still a number of states where the requirements are very much higher than the maximum requirement which is permitted under the federal law. Thus Arizona requires no less than thirty-five years of residence as a prerequisite, while Alaska requires twenty-five years. In North Dakota the requirement is twenty years, while there are no less than six states and one territory where the period for eligibility is fifteen years. These are Colorado, Hawaii, Indiana, Maine, Minnesota, New Jersey and Pennsylvania. Incidentally, among the states with optional systems, Utah also imposes a fifteen-year residence rule. Three of the mandatory states need to reduce their residence period from ten to five years. These are Florida, Idaho and New York. The remaining three

[1] Since then Alabama, Mississippi, Oklahoma and Texas passed laws.

[2] Kentucky has since approved a constitutional amendment permitting passage of an old age pension law.

optional states, namely, Kentucky, Nevada and West Virginia, also have a ten-year provision, which needs to be revised.

4. The scale of the pensions needs to be raised in many states. Thus, in Indiana the maximum pension which can be granted amounts to only $15 a month, while in North Dakota the yearly maximum is but $150, which in turn amounts to the extremely low monthly maximum of $12.50. In Kentucky the legal upper limit is $250 a year or a little over $20 a month. There are five states which have monthly limits of only $25, namely, Delaware, Idaho, Iowa, Ohio and Utah. Nor would there appear to be any adequate reason for limiting, as do a number of states, the amounts which can be paid to a couple to the low monthly figure of $45. It would seem as though the legal maximum for virtually all the states should not be less than $30 a maximum for a single individual and let us say $50 or $52.50 for a couple. In states which are in a comparatively better financial position, it would indeed be desirable to remove the upper limit entirely as New York, Massachusetts, Montana and the District of Columbia have done. This will certainly make it possible to give more adequate treatment to aged persons who may have special needs because of sickness, injuries, etc.[1] In all probability the pressure of public opinion for raising the legal maximum to at least as high as $30 will be very

[1] See Francis Bardwell, "Adequate Assistance vs. an Inflexible Maximum," *Social Security*, 1935, pp. 12-18.

strong in virtually all the states, although it may be less effective politically in some of the states of the deep south. This public pressure is likely, therefore, to establish the $30 point as the prevailing upper limit.

5. The granting of adequate pensions will not, however, be ensured merely by fixing an adequate maximum limit. For it will still be possible for the local administrative authorities to dole out very small pensions and to use the federal grants to help their own treasuries rather than the old people themselves. Thus the present scale of pensions in most states is still shockingly low, as is indicated by the table on page 237 giving the average pensions which were paid in various states in December 1934.[1]

In no less than fifteen of these twenty-three states, the average pension was under $15 a month while in six the average was less than $10. There were indeed only five states where the average pension was over $20 a month. Such low averages cannot be fully accounted for by the presence of private resources on the part of the pensioners. The primary reason for their lowness is the desire of the administrative authorities to economize because of the scantiness of state and local funds. Many applicants who need the full pension are therefore only given a fraction of this amount and all too frequently the pensions are administered on bare relief standards or worse. The desire to

[1] *Social Security* (1935), p. 237.

economize also leads in many places to a distinct limitation upon the total number of persons who are to be granted pensions. The coming of the federal grants, by bringing additional funds, will make possible more adequate pensions. But, in nearly half of the states which now have pension laws, more money will be needed from the states and localities themselves if decent pensions are to be paid.

TABLE XIII

AVERAGE MONTHLY PENSIONS BY STATES, DECEMBER, 1934

State	Average monthly pension	State	Average monthly pension
Arizona	$23.75	Nebraska	3.88
California	20.00	New Hampshire	19.06
Colorado	10.81	New Jersey	15.19
Delaware	9.95	New York	21.06
Idaho	8.83	North Dakota	6.19
Indiana	7.26	Ohio	14.44
Iowa	13.25	Oregon	10.54
Maryland	22.08	Utah	9.83
Massachusetts	24.35	Washington	12.80
Michigan	10.00	Wisconsin	19.95
Minnesota	12.24	Wyoming	12.12
Montana	12.41		
		Average	16.16

There is great danger, however, that some states will try to keep down the average pension in order either that the federal grant may bring financial relief to the states or that the increased costs, if any, may be lightened. Thus a state paying pensions which now average $10 a month might use the federal subvention to increase the average pension to only $14. In this case $7 would be met by the state and localities. The federal subvention would therefore have reduced the average state outlay by 30 per cent. It would in fact be possible for the state to pay out no more in pensions than before and thus pocket all of the federal funds for itself. In this case we would have federal aid for the states but not for the aged.

The desire to economize may also lead many states which do increase their outlays to do so in as small a degree as possible so that even with the federal matched sums the total will be inadequate.

Under the present act, the Security Board has no power to force the scale of benefits upward. Aside from the inducement of the federal grants the only protection which the aged have is the pressure of public opinion. There is need therefore for some federal control in fixing the minimum pensions to be paid, but in the meantime there is a moral obligation upon the states to be generous in respect to the size and the number of pensions granted. An alert and informed public opinion is therefore needed to see that the pension system really protects the aged needy in an adequate manner.

6. The age of eligibility should be reduced as speedily as possible to sixty-five years. While the states have until 1940 to reach this point, it is desirable that they approach it voluntarily before then. Eleven states, however, namely, Arizona, Indiana, Kentucky, Massachusetts, Minnesota,

Missouri, New Hampshire, New Jersey, New York, Oregon and Pennsylvania, do not now grant eligibility until the age of seventy is reached, while North Dakota fixes sixty-eight as its pensionable age.[1] While the reduction of the age of eligibility to sixty-five would greatly increase the number of pensioners and the total financial outlays in these states, it should nevertheless be remembered that the federal government will be paying for virtually half of the total cost. This might well mean that the total outlay of the state governments would be no greater than before. If, indeed, the state governments concerned do not lower their age of eligibility and do not loosen their other regulations, so that the total number of their pensioners will not increase, then, as has been pointed out, the immediate effect of the federal grants will be to give aid to the treasuries of the states rather than to the aged. Such was not the purpose of the national act. There is great need, therefore, for the states with well-established pension systems to increase the number pensioned as well as the average grant per person, so that the aged may benefit.

There are also two states, Arkansas and Michigan, which though they fix sixty-five years as the pensionable age provide that this provision is not to go into effect until 1940 and that in the meantime seventy is to be the age of eligibility. These laws, therefore, are pitched on as low a level in this respect as is possible to obtain the federal grant.

[1] Oregon has since reduced the pensionable age to sixty-five.

There is always of course a temptation for states to act in this fashion, but it is most certainly desirable that they should voluntarily rise above the minimum.

7. There is need for the states to permit aged persons to own a certain amount of property without disqualifying themselves for pensions. A number of the states have introduced such provisions into their laws which are eminently sensible. If an aged couple own their own home but have little or no cash income, it would be at once cruel and foolish to compel them to sell their house and then exhaust the proceeds before they can receive relief. In the first place, it might well be impossible to make such a sale within any given period of time, and in the meantime the aged person would be in need of food, clothing, and possibly medical attention. Secondly, in many cases the personal attachment to the home is so great that when it is lost the aged person will feel that a great deal has been taken out of his life and that it is a cruel system which will strip him of the objects to which he is accustomed and for which he has an affection before it will grant him relief. Finally, once the home is sold and the aged person is placed on relief, then an allowance will have to be given him to provide him with shelter in order to take the place of that which has been taken away from him. Is it not, therefore, better to permit him to own and occupy his home in the first place and merely to deduct its rental value from the amounts which otherwise would be given to him?

[296]

The same principle, though to a somewhat lesser degree, applies also in the case of other property than homes. If an aged person owns some additional real estate, it may be impossible to realize upon it at the moment. It is, furthermore, a very harsh policy to insist that a person must be compelled to give up his savings and be ground down into a state of complete destitution before aid is given. Many persons who need a pension as a transitional aid to tide them over a difficult period will later be relatively able to do without it because of an improvement in family circumstances or a turn for the better in their own affairs. If they are compelled to sacrifice a small business, a farm, or some other form of property before they can get any aid, they may be permanently injured and indeed prevented from later improving their condition. It is, therefore, sensible to provide that persons who are in need should be permitted to own up to approximately $5,000 of property, but that they should be credited as having an income of 5 per cent upon these holdings so that this amount can be deducted from the sums which would otherwise be granted to them. To make this situation more flexible and to encourage individual savings, the total income permitted from all sources should be more than the maximum pension itself. Thus, it might be provided that the total yearly income including the pension should not exceed $540. Then if the pension were limited to $30 a month, it would be possible for the applicant to have $180 a year income from other sources and still receive, (if in the opinion of the administrator it was needed) the full pension of $360. If, however, he owned a house worth $3,000 and other property worth $2,000 and made $50 a year himself, his total income from outside sources would be reckoned as $300 (i.e., 5 per cent on $5,000 plus $50). If he needed the full amount of $540 to maintain him, then the pension would amount to only $240 a year, or $20 a month. If it developed that $360 would protect him, then the pension would only be for the balance of $60 or a monthly figure of $5.

But if the government provides these grants to prevent small property owners from being stripped of their holdings during their lifetimes, it is only proper that it should be repaid for its advances out of the estates of these persons after they die. The state laws should, therefore, provide for the recapture of these pensions to the degree that sufficient assets are left upon decease. Nor should gifts made by aged pensioners in anticipation of death be permitted to defeat this purpose. To the degree to which such collections are effected by the states, the Security Act provides that the net proceeds be shared equally with the federal government so that it may also be reimbursed.[1]

---

[1] There is a defect in this provision which was absent from the Senate draft. If a state pays a pension of more than $30 and thus bears a larger share than the federal government, there is no good reason why the federal government should obtain half of any sums which are thus recaptured. The Senate draft provided that the federal share should only be "in proportion to the part of the old age assistance which represents the payments made by the United States."

8. In the administration of the pension system the laws providing for the legal responsibility of relatives must be recognized but should not be too inflexibly enforced. As has been pointed out, the American pension system differs from the European in providing aid only if relatives obligated under the law to care for aged dependents are not in fact able to do so in any adequate manner. This fact combined with the test of the personal resources of the aged themselves necessarily imparts a major admixture of relief into our pension system. Whatever may be the wisdom of this as a social policy there can be no doubt that it will remain for a long time. Two steps can, however, be taken to lessen the onerousness of such provisions: (*a*) Collateral relatives can be freed to a greater degree from the legal obligation to support aged dependents. While it is proper that one should help to support one's parents and grandparents and perhaps one's brothers and sisters, the obligation in the case of uncles and aunts is, for example, certainly far less. (*b*) Those legally responsible should not themselves be forced down to a submarginal standard of living in order to support their older relatives. This is especially important where there are young children in the family who would suffer from such an impairment of the minimum standard of living. Just what this standard of living is that should be protected will of course have to be worked out. It would be much better to define it as a minimum of health and decency rather than merely as a minimum of

physical subsistence. Certainly in no case should it be as low as the so-called "poverty" level.

9. Pensions should not be denied to those in private institutions for the aged or in public nursing homes or infirmaries. One of the primary purposes of old age pensions has been to enable the old people to stay in their homes and with their relatives instead of being forced into poorhouses. The fundamental principle behind this agitation has of course been correct. By the addition of small sums it is frequently made possible for sons, daughters, etc., to maintain parents and other aged relatives in their homes when this could not be done without such grants. The pensions also frequently make it possible for aged persons who so desire to live by themselves. By thus sparing old people from the humiliations attendant upon entering a poor farm the old age pensions have done and will do great good. Nor is this all. Since it is notorious that many poor farms have been run primarily for the profit of the politically influential superintendents rather than for the benefit of the aged, the old age pensions help to remove thousands of peculiarly defenseless people from the attendant tyranny, exploitation and neglect. It is natural and perhaps proper therefore that virtually all state laws should prohibit the pensions from being paid to those who are in a public institution.

The dislike for institutional care has, however, commonly been carried too far, so that there is a movement to prevent the pensions from being paid to those who are in any private institutions for the aged or who may be receiving treatment in a state hospital, etc. The truth of the matter is of course that while a large proportion of the aged ought not to be in an institution, there is nevertheless a large group who need the skilled and specialized care which only an institution can present. A great many of the old people are ill or crippled and need specialized nursing and medical care. This can commonly be furnished more effectively in a home for the aged or an infirmary than in the private home or lodgings of the aged person. There are also many who prefer the congregate life of an institution to the lonely life of a lodging house or living by themselves. There are also somewhat psychopathic persons who are far better off in an institution than outside. If such a person then enters a place where he can be taken care of better than otherwise, it certainly seems inconsistent to deny the person a pension with which he might pay for this better care. Three safeguards should, however, be attached to any such permission. The first is that the pensions should be paid only to those who are in private homes which are approved as adequate and efficient by the state welfare department which administers the act. The second proviso should be that the pension should be paid to the individual and not to the institution. Finally, the approval of the welfare workers should be required for either the entrance or the continuance of an aged person in such a private home or institution.

There is also no sufficient reason as a state develops competent nursing homes, infirmaries, hospitals, etc., why persons needing treatment there should not receive a pension while residents of them. Before the days of federal action, this could have been opposed on the ground that it was unnecessary since the state would be paying for them anyway as patients and to furnish pensions would merely mean taking money out of one pocket and putting it into another. The same objection no longer holds with the coming of federal aid for old age pensions. The cost of maintaining the state or county institutions is borne by these governments and they are not federally aided. Aged persons in need of institutional treatment who are sent to such places will, when they are taken off the pension rolls, increase the expenditures of the state and decrease the aid given by the federal government. It is certainly unfair to penalize a state for thus giving superior treatment to its aged. But under no conditions should the old and discredited poorhouse system be brought back under another name.

A primary purpose of pensions is to abolish the need of forcing individuals to enter institutions because of their poverty. It will of course need skillful administration to prevent the old abuses from coming back and to lead to such an integration of institutional and home care for the aged as will best serve the purpose. As the administration improves it will, therefore, be well to remove the present absolute prohibition upon federal aid being given for pensions to those in public institutions and to qualify this in such a fashion as will permit institutional care to be utilized for the ill and infirm as needed.

10. The financing of the proportion of the cost of old age pensions which is to be borne by the states and localities should be done upon progressive rather than regressive lines. There will be a temptation for many of the states to bear their share of the cost by either installing a sales tax or by adding to the sales tax which they already have. This has been the most common method which the states have used to finance relief during the depression, and it is also being used by a number of states to bear the cost of old age pensions.

But a sales tax is about the most unjust form of taxation which can be devised. It is not even a proportional form of taxation, but is instead grossly regressive since it makes the poorer families actually pay a larger proportion of their income than the well-to-do and wealthy. For the expenditures of the wealthy for personal services are not taxed, nor are their investments. It follows, therefore, that a sales tax takes a smaller percentage from them than it does from the poor and the lower income groups in general.

There is a real need, therefore, for more state taxes on income and corporation profits and for higher rates of progression than now prevail. The need for such a policy is also increased by the fact

[303]

that, as Robert H. Jackson of the Treasury Department has shown, the proportion of federal revenues realized from the regressive excise taxes and customs duties has increased during the depression while the proportion obtained from taxes on the well-to-do have decreased.[1]

It is certainly desirable to get as far away as possible from this situation where the costs of taking care of the poorest are lodged upon the shoulders of the poor. There is too much of this in the federal program itself and it is necessary to avoid it in the working out of the state taxation programs for the support of old age pensions, mothers' aid and the other parts of the security program which call for state funds. This need for income and corporation taxes is increased by the fact that real estate is still in a difficult situation and can by no means bear as large a share of taxes as in the past.[2]

If the income levies do not raise enough money and it is necessary to levy some kind of a sales tax then at the very least it is essential that expenditures for food and for clothing of moderate price should be exempted from the tax.

Unemployment Insurance

As has been stated, eight states and the District of Columbia at the time of writing (September, 1935)

[1] See R. H. Jackson, "The Rich Get Richer," *New Republic*, Vol. LXXXIV (August 28, 1935), p. 68.

[2] If one is a single-taxer, one will of course welcome the opportunity to increase the taxes on bare land values as distinguished from improvements.

have passed unemployment insurance laws. These are Wisconsin, New York, New Hampshire, Utah, Washington, California, Alabama and Massachusetts. In addition, the North Carolina legislature has empowered the Executive Council of that state to enact the type of law which it deems best.

The main features of these acts are shown in Table XIV on pages 250 and 251.

It will thus be seen that seven of the acts, District of Columbia, California, New Hampshire, New York, Washington, Alabama and Massachusetts have pooled funds; and two, Utah and Wisconsin, plant reserves. The Alabama, California, District of Columbia and New Hampshire laws provide for merit rating beginning in 1941. Five of the six states with pooled funds, namely, California, Massachusetts, Alabama, New Hampshire and Washington, require contributions from the workers. Except in Massachusetts the workers' contributions are not to exceed 1 per cent of wages, although California and New Hampshire make the workers' assessment for the first year only one-half of 1 per cent. Ultimately the workers' contributions in Massachusetts are to be 1½ per cent.

There is a pronounced tendency for the acts to grant a longer period of benefits to those who have previously been employed for longer periods of time without drawing benefits. This is particularly seen in the laws of California, Massachusetts,

[305]

TABLE XIV

SUMMARY OF UNEMPLOYMENT INSURANCE LAWS[1]

State and year	Pooled or company funds	Coverage	Contributions	Waiting period	Benefits			Administration
					Conditions	Amount per week	Duration	
Alabama 1935	Pooled	Employees in firms of 8 or more workers	Employers 0.9% of payroll, 1936 1.8% of payroll, 1937 2.7% of payroll, 1938[3] Workers 1% from 1936 on	3 weeks	26 weeks in 1 year or 40 weeks in 2 years	50% of wages; maximum $15	16 weeks, plus 1 week for each 20 weeks of work in last 260 weeks	Unemployment Compensation Commission
California[2] 1935	Pooled	Employees in firms covered by national act	Employers 0.9% f payroll, 1936 1.8% of payroll, 1937 2.7% of payroll, 1938 Workers ½% of wages, 1936 1% of wages, 1937	4 weeks first 2 years, then 3 weeks	26 weeks' work in last year or 1-year residence	50% of wages; maximum $15, minimum $7	13 weeks for 103 weeks of contribution, 20 weeks for more	Unemployment Reserves Commission
District of Columbia[8] 1935	Pooled	All employees	Employers 1% of payroll, 1936 2% of payroll, 1937 3% of payroll, 1938[3] Workers None	3 weeks	13 weeks in previous year	65% of wages; maximum $15, plus dependents' allowances	16 weeks, plus 1 week for each 20 weeks of work in last 260 weeks	Unemployment Compensation Board
Massachusetts[2] 1935	Pooled	Employees in firms of 8 or more earning less than $2,500 yearly	Employers 1% of payroll, 1936[3] 2% of payroll, 1937[3] 3% of payroll, 1938[3,4] Workers 1% of wages, 1937 ½% of employers' rate from 1938 on	4 weeks	90 days' work in 1 year or 130 in 2 years	50% of wages; maximum $15, minimum $5	16 weeks plus 1 week for each 18 weeks of contribution in last 6 years, plus 1 week for each previous 26 weeks	Unemployment Insurance Commission in State Department of Labor and Industries.
New Hampshire[2] 1935	Pooled	All manual workers; nonmanuals earning no more than $2,500 a year; in firms of 4 or more workers	Employers 1% of payroll, 1936 2% of payroll, 1937 3% of payroll, 1938[3] Workers ½% of wages, 1936 1% of wages, 1937	3 weeks	60 days' work in previous year	50% of wages; maximum $15. 70% of $10 or less; but not more than $5	16 weeks plus maximum of 10 additional weeks based on previous employment	Department of Labor

TABLE XIV. (Continued)

State and year	Pooled or company funds	Coverage	Contributions	Waiting period	Benefits			Administration
					Conditions	Amount per week	Duration	
New York 1935	Pooled	All manual workers; nonmanuals earning no more than $50 a week; in firms of 4 or more workers	Employers 1% of payroll, 1936 2% of payroll, 1937 3% of payroll, 1938 Workers None	3 weeks	90 days in 1 year or 130 in 2 years	50% of wages; maximum $15, minimum $5	16 weeks	Department of Labor
North Carolina 1935	Governor and council empowered to put a system into effect if federal law is passed. No details specified.							
Utah[4] 1935	Company funds	All manual workers; nonmanuals earning no more than $2,000 a yr.; in firms of 4 or more workers	Employers 3% of payroll[5] Workers May contribute voluntarily	2 weeks	20 weeks in 1 year	50% of wages; maximum $18, minimum $6	16 weeks	Industrial Commission
Washington[4] 1935	Pooled	Employees in firms of 4 or more workers	Employers 1% or 2%, 1936[6] 1% or 2%, 1937[6] 3%, 1938 Workers 1% from 1936 on	6 weeks	26 weeks in 1 year or 40 in 2 years	50% of wages; maximum $15	15 weeks plus 1 week for each 16 weeks of work in last 260 weeks	Unemployment Insurance Commission
Wisconsin 1923-1935	Company funds	Employees in firms of 8 or more earning less than $250 per month[10]	Employers[9] 2% of payrolls[8] Workers May contribute voluntarily	3 weeks	....	50% of wages; maximum $15,[7] minimum $5	8⅔ to 13 weeks	Industrial Commission

[307]

1 Taken primarily from *Social Security*, p. 238.
2 Goes into effect when federal law is enacted. Becomes inoperative if federal law is invalidated.
3 Merit rating provided.
4 Becomes effective after federal law is enacted.
5 After two years in system, employers' contribution reduced to 1 per cent if the reserve per employee is $75, and discontinued if reserve is $100 or more.
6 According to index of production.
7 Reduced if reserve is low.
8 Contributions by the district: 1936, $100,000; 1937, $125,000; 1938, $175,000.
9 Contributions must average 2.7% after 1938 so long as federal law is valid.
10 So long as the federal law is held valid, all employees are included.

New Hampshire and Washington. It is not provided for in the New York and Utah acts. The basic benefit period is sixteen weeks in Massachusetts, New Hampshire, New York, and Utah; it is fifteen weeks in Washington and thirteen in California. It is lower still in Wisconsin.

It is interesting to note that the California, New Hampshire, and Massachusetts laws provide that they are to be discontinued if the federal act is invalidated. If this qualification becomes general, one of the arguments for the tax offset method will disappear. For one of the alleged superiorities advanced for that device was that, even if the federal law were later to be declared unconstitutional, it would meanwhile have served its purpose by geting the states to pass laws which would be constitutional. Under the provision which has been adopted by these three states, however, if and when the federal tax offset system is declared unconstitutional, the corresponding state acts will automatically disappear.

In view of the fact that so many of the states will take action in the near future on the type of employment insurance which they are to enact, the following recommendations may be pertinent.[1]

1. The state systems should provide pooled funds rather than individual company reserves. The reasons for this position have been rather thoroughly discussed in the preceding chapters.

[1] For a fuller treatment of some of these points, see my *Standards of Unemployment Insurance.*

Individual company reserves will result in a great inequality of benefits because there will be great differences in the volume of unemployment between enterprises.[1] This inequality will in many cases carry with it gross inadequacies as well and will inevitably arouse strong opposition from the general rank and file of the workers. Nor will these differences between firms in the relative amount of unemployment reflect in any significant degree the differences in their business ability. For unemployment, unlike accidents, is primarily caused by forces outside the individual concern.[2]

The drift of legislative opinion is very clearly toward the pooled fund and away from the Wisconsin system of plant reserves. It will be remembered that during the legislative sessions of 1931 the Wisconsin system almost had the field to itself, but that by 1933 the pooled reserve was on virtually even terms as measured by the number of bills. For the sessions of 1935, out of sixty-nine bills which have been studied from a large number of states, no less than forty provided for pooled funds. Of these, twenty-four had no provision for merit rating, while sixteen did. On the other hand,

---

[1] The only way to guarantee equality of treatment under the Wisconsin plan would be to provide fixed benefits and then make individual employers pay these benefits regardless of how much it cost them. This would mean removing any maximum from the contributions of the employers. The Wisconsin plan is, however, careful to fix such a maximum and, therefore, must scale down benefits in those firms where unemployment is relatively high.

[2] It seems extraordinary that the proponents of the Wisconsin idea, after six years of a world-wide depression, should still cling so strongly to their idea of almost exclusive individual responsibility.

only ten bills provided for separate employers' reserves, while six called for industry reserves.[1] The rest of the proposals were either introduced only by title or were unusual variants. The pooled fund proposals were, therefore, outnumbering the proposals for separate reserves at a rate of two and one-half to one. This tendency is reflected in the fact that seven out of the eight laws which have thus far been passed this year (1935) are of this model.

There is likely, however, to be a movement in favor of plant reserves by certain large groups of employers. These will wish to encourage the workers to think in terms of the individual plant rather than the industry or all business and to associate their interests with those of the firm. On the other hand, organized labor will oppose the system of plant reserves not merely on actuarial grounds but also because they believe it will foster the spirit of separatism and company unionism which in the eyes of many employers is its merit.[2]

[1] See Donald M. Smith, *A Comparison of Unemployment Insurance Bills in American State Legislatures* (M.A. thesis, University of Chicago), p. 6.

[2] Thus see the statement by President William Green of the A.F. of L., *House Hearings, op. cit.,* p. 395. "There is a serious menace to organized labor in the individual company reserve. Employers who are strongly opposed to the free and independent organization of trade unions will be able to use their company or industry reserve as a weapon . . . against unionization of their employees. They might offer slightly higher benefits, or pay benefits for a little longer period, upon the understanding that their employees remained unorganized; they could use their unemployment reserves around which to build a company union, and thus prevent the growth of bona fide trade unions. Speaking for the American Federation of Labor . . . I protest most emphatically against any provision which permits a State to set up unemployment reserves on the basis of company or of industry."

Virtually all the legitimate purposes and none of the attendant disadvantages of the company reserve plan would be conserved by a system of merit rating inside the pooled fund. After an initial period in which to accumulate experience, the rates might be varied somewhat from plant to plant or industry to industry to take account of and to reward such real accomplishments in the field of stabilization as might have occurred. But care will have to be used not to give personal credit to a firm for what is merely an industrial trend. Thus, from 1921 to 1926 the manufacturers of silk stockings gave full employment, but this was primarily caused by the great growth in demand rather than by individual good management. Similarly, it should be realized that one industry may have little unemployment itself but cause great unemployment elsewhere. Thus, the radio and the phonograph have struck body blows at the piano industry and similarly the rise of silk and rayon injured cotton manufacturing. The problem of merit rating is, therefore, not so simple as is sometimes argued.

2. Should the workers contribute towards the support of the state systems?

It should be realized that the 3 per cent assessment upon employers provided by the federal act will not give a very appreciable amount of protection. If a three weeks' waiting period is used, the average which can be promised for the country as a whole will probably not exceed fourteen or fifteen weeks of benefit per year. In the states with low unemployment rates such as South Dakota this can of course be increased, but in states with high unemployment such as Michigan, even less than this can be given. Such provisions are of course grossly inadequate and it is desirable to extend the benefit period to at least twenty weeks and if possible to twenty-six weeks. But to do so will require additional funds in all except the states with extremely low unemployment rates. Where states can provide these additional revenues through income and corporation taxes, it is of course highly desirable that they should do so. Where this cannot be done, it is better, however, for the workers to make a small direct contribution in order to insure more adequate benefits. For the essence of insurance is that less suffering is caused by the many making small contributions than for a minority to suffer great losses.

There are certain other advantages besides more adequate benefits which may be obtained by direct contributions on the part of the workers. They will make it more certain that the workers will have an equal share with the employers in the administration of the act and this is particularly important in the matter of defining what are "just grounds" for leaving work, and what is "suitable" employment. They will also probably help to enlist the interest of the rank and file more effectively in preventing malingering. Many labor leaders are coming to see that since the employers' contributions will largely be borne by labor in an indirect fashion, there is something to be gained by labor's making a direct contribution in order to have a voice in the conduct of the system. While the leading officials of the American Federation of Labor itself oppose contributions by the workers, it is significant that the labor movement in Illinois, New Hampshire, Massachusetts and Ohio has supported bills which call for such payments. But if the workers do make contributions, these should not be large and should not exceed 1 per cent at a maximum. Since the employer's contributions will be only 1 per cent and 2 per cent during the first two years, the contributions of labor should either be omitted entirely for the first year or started at only one-half of 1 per cent. The provision of this additional 1 per cent should furnish, on the average, approximately five weeks of additional benefit.

3. Should the states themselves contribute?

This question has already been answered. Wherever the states can raise appreciable sums of money through progressive income and corporation taxes, it is highly desirable that this should be done. It is probable that an adequate unemployment insurance system will cost at least 5 per cent of the payroll, and there is, therefore, a need for contributions from the more well-to-do.

4. What should be the scale of benefits?

In all probability, a benefit scale amounting to approximately 50 per cent of current full-time earnings is the best which can be given at this time.

From an administrative standpoint it is important that checks of not too many different amounts should be issued. The drafters of some of the existing state laws have not fully considered these difficulties since they generally provide for benefits equal to one-half of each person's full-time wage, subject of course to a maximum provision. This will mean in practice that since the weekly wages will vary greatly literally hundreds of different sized checks will have to be made out for benefits. This will not only involve an immense amount of added administrative work but will give an opportunity for frauds and mistakes.

In order to avoid this difficulty it would be well to provide either separate wage categories with one basic benefit for all those within the category or to pay benefits to the nearest full dollar to the 50 per cent figure. It is also desirable to fix a minimum and maximum figure for weekly benefits. These should be either $4.00 or $5.00 for the bottom, and approximately $15.00 for the top.

5. What salary limits, if any, should be imposed in the state law?

The federal act will collect taxes against which offsets may be made on all wages and salaries paid without regard to amount. It would seem wise, therefore, for the state unemployment insurance systems to include not only all wage-earners but all salaried workers as well. The limitation of benefits to $15 a week will, however, prevent the upper-salaried group from receiving an undue amount of protection; and indeed will result in their giving indirect aid to the lower-salaried workers.

In order to avoid offending the upper-salaried employees, it will, however, be wise if the workers are not asked to make any payments on that portion of their wages and salaries which is above $30 a week or the approximate amount which would be insured under a 50 per cent benefit scale.

6. How long a benefit period should be provided?

The answer to this question is largely suggested by the discussion in this and previous chapters. It will necessarily depend on the total rate of assessment or the amount of funds and upon the state. For the average state, an assessment of 3 per cent should give from fourteen to fifteen weeks of benefit subject to a four-week waiting period. A 4 per cent assessment should give twenty weeks of benefit and a 5 per cent rate from twenty-six to thirty weeks. In states like Michigan, the corresponding number of weeks would be nearer ten, fifteen and twenty respectively. In South Dakota or Georgia the weeks might be twenty, thirty and forty.

7. How long a waiting period should be required?

It is desirable to prevent the funds from being consumed by paying benefits to those who are unemployed for only short periods of time, thus diverting aid from those who are unemployed for long periods and who consequently will need assistance the most. For this reason, the waiting period should be appreciably longer than the six days required under the English act and should be at least three weeks. In states with high unemployment, a waiting period of four weeks may be necessary in order to conserve the funds for those who will need them most.

8. What should be the eligibility requirements as regards previous periods of employment?

It is proper to confine the benefits to those who are customarily a part of the effective labor supply and to exclude those who merely enter industry to meet seasonal peaks and then retire to family or student life. For this reason the requirement that, in order to be eligible for benefits, a worker must have been employed in an insured occupation for at least thirty-six weeks in the two preceding insurance years or twenty weeks in the last year is reasonable in periods of stable employment.

To impose such a standard in the midst of a depression would be perhaps unduly severe and this ruling might be modified to a total of thirty-two weeks in the two preceding insurance years or seventeen in the immediately preceding year.

9. Should extra weeks of benefit be granted to those with longer periods of employment?

It is in general desirable to reward those who have long records of employment with longer than average periods of benefit. This will be especially important if the workers themselves make contributions. This purpose can be carried out by providing that, within limits, more than the standard weeks of benefit will be granted to an unemployed worker for every given block of weeks above a certain number during which he was employed in an insurable occupation during the two preceding years. Thus, it could be provided that one additional week of benefits would be given for every four weeks of employment in these two preceding years above a total of seventy-two or of eighty weeks. This would permit the worker who had been employed steadily during this time to draw from six to eight weeks of additional benefits.

It will be noted, however, that this arrangement would not provide any additional weeks of benefit for those who were employed more than the minimum number of thirty-two or thirty-six weeks during the two preceding years but less than the seventy-two or eighty weeks set out above. While it would complicate the situation, this difficulty might be met: (*a*) By lowering the maximum benefit period to those who had been employed for thirty-six or twenty weeks by from five to six weeks a year. This would mean that a ten-week benefit period would be given instead of a fifteen-week period and so on. Then it could be provided that for each five weeks worked in excess of this minimum an added week of benefits would be paid. This would give a more even graduation of benefits to employment, but it would hurt those who for one reason or another, and perhaps largely through no fault of their own, had been unable to obtain much more than the minimum number of weeks of work required to qualify. This possibility is, therefore, merely advanced as a suggestion but is not advocated by the author at this time.

Some further allowance should also be made for those who in the future will have stable employment records covering more than the two preceding years.

10. What special provision if any should be made to cover seasonal employment?

Unless the unemployment insurance systems are carefully framed, there will be danger that the funds will be largely devoted to paying benefits for the seasonally unemployed, whose needs are least, at the expense of curtailing benefits to the unemployed who lose their jobs because of business depressions and whose needs (along with the technologically unemployed) are greatest. The relative volume of unemployment is very high in the industries such as clothing and the building trades where each year brings its dull seasons. The workers in these trades are already generally paid a higher hourly rate to compensate them for the less than the average number of hours which they are able to work. To pay them full insurance benefits for virtually all the time which they do not work within a year would, therefore, be in effect to pay them twice for the same thing. While the provision of unemployment insurance in this fashion would probably ultimately operate to reduce the hourly differential, this would take time and at best might be incomplete. Much needed funds would, therefore, be given to persons who were already largely protected against the very risk for which payment was being made.

In addition, since this type of unemployment is more or less regular in its incidence from year to year and largely predictable in its amount, the workers have in large measure the possibility of making sufficient savings during the busy seasons to carry them through the idle months. Insurance is not, therefore, so much needed in these cases in order to help equalize personal incomes through time. In the case of technological and cyclical unemployment, however, both the incidence and the duration of unemployment are far less predictable, with the result that some form of insurance is greatly needed.

It is, therefore, desirable to exclude a very large proportion of chronic seasonal unemployment from compensation. The best way to do this is not to impose for all industries as long a waiting period as eight weeks, as Professor A. H. Hansen once proposed, but instead to permit the administrative authorities to increase the waiting period in industries with pronounced seasonal unemployment. Thus, in coal mining and the building and clothing trades, a waiting period of ten weeks might be required, while in others it might be eight, six or fewer weeks. Some such program as this is most certainly needed if the funds are to be conserved for the most severe and most unexpected varieties of unemployment.

11. What provision should be made in the case of part-time employment?

Workers may suffer from an insufficient volume of current employment as well as from complete unemployment. Where workers are employed only one, two or even three days a week, their earnings are severely reduced because of lost time, and they should be given some protection. On the other hand, if every bit of lost time were counted as unemployment and compensated for, then the insurance funds would be unduly dissipated on small scraps of time instead of being saved for the large blocks which are lost through outright unemployment.

Perhaps the best way of meeting this situation would be to provide that no compensation be paid as long as the days of work offered did not fall below four. In this way the decrease from a six- or a five-day week would be borne by the workers. Then each day less than four a week which was worked would be counted as unemployed time. After eighteen of these days (i.e., three weeks) had been accumulated within an insurance year, then compensation would begin under the usual terms. Only full days of unemployment would, however, be counted and the loss of half-days or odd hours because of administrative reasons would not be tallied.

12. What penalties should be imposed upon those who leave their work without just cause, or who will not accept suitable employment?

Unemployed persons who have left their jobs without "just cause" should not of course receive benefits on the same terms as those who have lost them through no fault of their own. Nor should those who refuse "suitable employment." There are, however, two vital questions which necessarily arise in this connection, namely, how should "just cause" and "suitable employment" be defined and should the guilty person be completely barred from all benefits or should he merely be disqualified for an added period of time?

The precise meaning of these terms will have to be primarily worked out by the administrative authorities, as in Great Britain, where the decisions on these points fill a number of volumes. A codification of the British decisions on these points would in fact be one of the most useful pieces of research which could be undertaken and would be of great aid to American administrative authorities. Certain criteria can, however, be fairly clearly indicated. Where a worker has been dropped because of lack of work he is entitled to benefit. Where he is discharged for gross insubordination or inefficiency, then if these charges are confirmed and there are no sufficiently mitigating circumstances, he cannot be said to have left for a "just cause." If his insubordination were caused by previous abuse on the part of employer or foreman then this can serve as an excuse. Where the worker voluntarily throws up a "good" job, he should suffer some penalty. If the job is unhealthful, or in the case of juveniles or women has undue moral hazards, then a worker is justified in quitting it.

Whether a worker can claim "just cause" for leaving a job which is conducted under nonunion conditions, or where he has to sign a yellow-dog contract or where the wages and hours are substantially less favorable than those prevailing for similar work in the locality is uncertain. The federal act merely lays down these criteria for new jobs; it does not explicitly apply them to jobs which a worker is already holding. One can easily foresee that the unions will urge that these same standards should be applied to all types of work and that the employers' associations will try to prevent this definition from being enlarged. Which will win will depend not only upon the good sense of the administrators, but also upon the economic and political balance of power which prevails.

It should of course be understood that, if a worker leaves his job because he is sick or injured and hence is unable to work, he will not be eligible for unemployment benefits. Unemployment insurance is designed to protect those who though able and willing to work are yet unable to find suitable employment. Such persons as these should be protected by workmen's compensation and by health insurance, but these should not be confused with unemployment insurance.

Some of the points in connection with suitable employment have already been mentioned in the discussion of the national act. If a strike or lock-out is in progress in the plant it is not "suitable" employment, and a worker may refuse it without penalty. If he is required to sign a yellow-dog contract, it is not suitable work and he also may refuse without loss of rights. If the wages, hours and conditions of work are "substantially less favorable" than those prevailing for similar work in the locality, the worker may properly regard the job as "unsuitable" and refuse it without loss of rights. As has been indicated, the state laws may use a more rigid definition and insist on a precise equality with the prevailing rate, although this prevailing rate is sometimes difficult to ascertain. If the state laws use the same phrase of "substantially less favorable" which is embodied in the national act, then there will be, as stated, an administrative problem of determining just how much wages and conditions must be below the prevailing standard before the differences become "substantial."

Work of an excessively dangerous or unhealthful character will in all probability be regarded as unsuitable, as will work which presents moral dangers for juveniles and women.

Two important questions which are certain to arise are the degree to which workers should be permitted to refuse other work than that to which they are accustomed or trained as "unsuitable" and the degree to which they may refuse work away

from their home locality. A skilled worker in a die-
ing craft cannot be allowed perpetually to refuse
other work and to receive unemployment benefits,
for this would create an idle pool of labor and prevent much needed fluidity. On the other hand, he
should not be forced immediately to take other
work for this might mean a serious impairment of
his economic position. He should be given, in short,
some time in which to adjust himself and find work,
if he can, in the jobs for which he is best adapted.
But the question as to how much time should be
allowed him is one upon which no a priori pro-
nouncement can be made and which will have to
be worked out from the experience of administration. Unskilled and semiskilled workers will
present a less difficult problem since they can be
switched from job to job and industry to industry
with much greater ease.

The case is similar as regards geographical shifts.
All workers should be allowed some time to find
work in their own locality. If this is not available,
then after a period single men can be asked to take
positions elsewhere if they are available and, in
other respects, suitable. But such pressure should
be much more sparingly applied to men with
families, particularly to married men who own their
homes, for such a transfer might mean a disruption
of family ties and an economic loss which should be
avoided if at all possible.

Once it is, however, adjudged that a worker has
left his job without "just cause" or has refused
"suitable employment," the question will arise as

to how severely he should be punished. Unlike the former issue, this should be primarily settled by the laws themselves rather than by administrative interpretations. The Wisconsin act is particularly severe in this respect, and completely disqualifies a man. The New Hampshire act, on the other hand, disqualifies him for three weeks in addition to the usual waiting period.

Since the benefits which the worker receives will in all probability be approximately only half his customary wage, it is perhaps unnecessary to impose complete disqualification as a deterrent. On the other hand, it may be wise to make the penalty somewhat heavier than that provided under the New Hampshire law. A provision that the added period of disqualification is not to exceed six weeks nor be less than four with discretion given to the administrative authorities to graduate the amounts between these upper and lower limits may well prove to be the wisest.

13. What special administrative safeguards should be set up?

We have already spoken of the fact that while conditions will differ from state to state, it seems generally desirable to confide the administration of the system to commissions located inside the state departments of labor. These commissions should include representatives of employers' organizations and accredited organizations of labor.

In addition, it will be advisable to create two sets of advisory boards. The first will be for the state as a whole and should have at least three accredited representatives of employers' organizations, three from corresponding organizations of labor, and three who are chosen to represent the general public. Such a body if well selected can do a great deal in protecting administrative posts from the spoilsmen and in enlisting the support of the various groups in the state for the measure. Similarly, local committees can assist the insurance offices and at times provide a lay court before whom the questions of "just cause" and "suitable employment" can be tried. Ultimate appeal can of course be made to the state administrative body.

Since the summarization of state legislation was written Oregon has been added to the growing list of states with pooled fund plans. The law also provides for plant reserves and guaranteed employment accounts and some confusion exists as to the importance of the pooled fund. Coverage in the Oregon law is extended to employers of four or more and excluded employments are identical with those in the federal law. Contributions are required from employers at the regular rate of 2.7 per cent and from employees at the regular rate of 1 per cent. The qualification period is 26 weeks employment within 52 weeks or 40 within 104. Benefits are payable at the rate of 50 per cent of weekly wages with a maximum of $15 and a minimum of $7. The waiting period is three weeks total unemployment or its equivalent partial unemployment. Administration is by a state unemployment compensation commission.

CHAPTER XIII

DEVELOPMENTS IN 1936

1. *The Progress of Old Age Pensions*

BY the middle of September, 1936, the old age
pension laws in thirty-nine states and territories[1] had been approved by the Social
Security Board as coming up to the minimum
standards set by the act. Four more laws (i.e., those
of Nevada, South Dakota, Florida and West Virginia) were before the board for approval and laws
existed in three other jurisdictions which were not
before the board for action.[1] Only five states had
failed to pass such laws. These were Tennessee,
Georgia, South Carolina, North Carolina and Virginia. It is probable that most of these remaining
five states will pass old age pension laws in the near
future and that the system will shortly be uni-
versalized in this country. By July of 1936, 710,000
aged persons were receiving pensions under the
approved pension laws and it was estimated that
the number in these states would be at least 800,000
by September. Since there were other states, such
as Pennsylvania, where pensions were being paid,
which were not included in the above totals, the

[1] Including Hawaii and the District of Columbia.
[2] I.e., Arizona, Kansas and Alaska.

total number in receipt of such grants was somewhat larger. It was indeed probable that by December 1, 1936, approximately 1,000,000 aged persons would be on the pension rolls. Since the total number who are sixty-five years and over is approximately 7.7 millions, this would mean about 13 per cent of this group.

The following statistics on the relative proportion of those eligible to receive pensions who were being

State	Number of recipients of old age pensions per 1,000 estimated population over 65 years of age	State	Number of recipients of old age pensions per 1,000 estimated population over 65 years of age
Oklahoma......	367	Vermont............	115
Colorado.......	304	California...........	107
Idaho..........	263	Michigan............	103
Wyoming.......	224	Maryland...........	93
Nebraska.......	221	Massachusetts.......	91
Minnesota......	205	Connecticut.........	72
Ohio..........	187	Alabama...........	71
Mississippi.....	175	New Jersey..........	67
Utah..........	173	North Dakota.......	67
Washington....	150	New Hampshire.....	54
Iowa..........	142	Missouri...........	53
Wisconsin......	141	New Mexico.........	45
Arkansas.......	137	Rhode Island........	39
Delaware.......	120	District of Columbia.	13
Oregon.........	120	Maine..............	13
Indiana........	115		

paid them in June, 1936, are of interest in showing the wide variations which existed between states at that time.

The average monthly pensions amounted in June to the following sums in the various states.

State	Average monthly grant	State	Average monthly grant
Alabama	$10.71	Missouri	$ 8.95
Arkansas	5.54	Nebraska	15.33
California	23.24	New Hampshire	20.82
Colorado	19.07	New Jersey	15.88
Connecticut	22.32	New Mexico	14.48
Delaware	10.29	New York	20.59
District of Columbia	25.26	North Dakota	15.32
Hawaii	11.40	Ohio	15.10
Idaho	21.12	Oklahoma	7.92
Indiana	8.00	Oregon	20.49
Iowa	14.54	Rhode Island	17.47
Maine	19.75	Texas	16.00
Maryland	12.75	Utah	18.51
Massachusetts	23.51	Vermont	11.16
Michigan	16.39	Washington	20.46
Minnesota	18.53	Wisconsin	17.74
Mississippi	3.62	Wyoming	21.01
		Average for 34 states.	$16.02

An examination of this table, together with those which have gone before, indicates the following:

1. That the average pensions are still very low in many states. Thus, there were five states in which this average was less than $10 a month. These were Arkansas, Indiana, Mississippi, Missouri and Oklahoma. The Mississippi average was, indeed, only $3.62. Oklahoma, with the third lowest average pension in the country, was the state with by far the highest proportion of pen-

sioners, since the previous table showed that no less than 36.7 per cent of those 65 years and over were on the roles. This state was, then, clearly following the policy of granting pensions to as many persons as possible instead of bringing the pension itself up to an adequate amount.

2. In most states, the added federal monies had been used to increase the number of aged persons receiving assistance rather than to raise the average amount of assistance given. Thus, of twenty-three states for which statistics are available of the average monthly pension paid in December, 1935, and June, 1936, there were seventeen where the average was either less in the latter than the former month or not more than $2.50 greater.[1]

3. In some states, however, the average size of the pension had been markedly increased under the federal grants. This was true, for example, of Idaho, Michigan, Minnesota, Oregon, Utah and Wyoming.

Whether some states are not using part of the federal aid to give relief to their own budgets rather than using the full amount for old age assistance is still uncertain. There are indications, however, that this is being practiced by some states.

Another tendency which is very marked is that for the states to bear a predominant share of the cost of matching the federal monies. Thus, in no

---

[1] See *Social Security* 1936, p. 167, published by the American Association for Social Security, and *Public Assistance*, Vol. I, No. 6, p. 2, published by Social Security Board.

less than seventeen jurisdictions the state provides all the needed local funds. These are Arkansas, Connecticut, Delaware, Illinois, Iowa, Kentucky, Michigan, Mississippi, Missouri, Oregon, Pennsylvania, Rhode Island, Texas, Vermont, Washington, West Virginia and Alaska. In two more, New Jersey and Wisconsin, the state pays from 75 to 87½ per cent of the local costs. In four states, Arizona, Maryland, Massachusetts and Minnesota, two-thirds of the costs are so met. Indiana contributes 60 per cent, and Nebraska 57½ per cent. In seven states, i.e., Alabama, California, Colorado, Maine, Montana, New York and Wyoming, the costs are shared equally between the local governments and the states, while in New Hampshire the state pays only 5 per cent, or one-twentieth of the local costs.[1] Since the states which bear the entire cost are in general those which have recently passed old age pension laws, while the 50–50 laws were in the main passed during the years prior to 1933, it will be seen that there has been a progressive tendency to have the states bear an increasing proportion of the expense.

Three types of administrative systems have developed. (1) The first and most numerous is that in which the county or locality is given the task of investigating and passing upon the claims for assistance and making the payments, with reimbursement by the state for its share of both federal

[1] See "Digest of Old Age Assistance Laws of Several States and Territories as of Sept. 1, 1936," Works Progress Administration.

and state grants. There seem to be twenty states with this system, of which California, Massachusetts, New York, New Jersey, Pennsylvania and Wisconsin are the most important. (2) The second type is that of outright state administration, where a state agency makes the investigations, passes on claims and disburses the grants. There are ten states which use this method, namely, Connecticut, Delaware, Florida, Rhode Island, Texas, Vermont, Washington, West Virginia, Wyoming and Alaska. (3) Finally, there is a hybrid type, where the local authorities receive and investigate claims and make recommendations to the state agency, which finally passes upon them and which disburses the money. There are eight states in this group, namely, Alabama, Illinois, Iowa, Michigan, Mississippi, Missouri, Nebraska and Ohio. It will thus be seen that most, though not all, of the states in the last two categories also provide all the funds to match the federal grants. This is another illustration of the general rule that the authority which foots the bills will generally demand and obtain the administrative control.

2. *The Development in the Fields of Mothers' Pensions, Assistance to the Blind, Health Care of Mothers and Infants, etc.*

By the middle of September, 1936, the laws of twenty-two states relating to aid for dependent children, or mothers' pensions, had been approved by the Security Board.[1] There were eight more laws which were before it for consideration,[2] and sixteen other states with legislation in this field which had not submitted their plans to the board for approval.[3] There were two states, South Carolina and Georgia, without any such legislation. In July, there were 70,000 families in nineteen states with approved plans which were being aided in this fashion, and these families included 178,000 children for whom grants were being given.

The remaining states which were not yet receiving federal aid were also granting assistance to a very considerable added number of families and children. In the nineteen states mentioned above, the total payments for July were $1,606,000, or an average monthly grant per child of $9.04. This average of course varied from state to state. It was low in such southern states as Alabama, Arkansas and Oklahoma, where the averages were less than $4 per month. In twelve states, however, the average was over $10 a month, and in California it was $13.52.

So far as the needy blind are concerned, the plans of twenty-two states had been approved by

[1] I.e., Maine, Vermont, New Hampshire, New Jersey, Delaware, Maryland, Alabama, Arkansas, Louisiana, Oklahoma, Indiana, Michigan, Wisconsin, Nebraska, New Mexico, Arizona, Utah, Colorado, Wyoming, Idaho, Washington and California.

[2] I.e., Massachusetts, Rhode Island, Connecticut, Pennsylvania, West Virginia, Virginia, Ohio and Minnesota.

[3] I.e., New York, North Carolina, Florida, Tennessee, Kentucky, Mississippi, Texas, Kansas, Missouri, Illinois, Iowa, South Dakota, North Dakota, Montana, Nevada and Oregon.

September 15, and five plans were before the board for action, while there were thirteen more states with laws which had not yet submitted their programs. In July, 22,000 individuals were receiving such pensions in the twenty states for which the board had then approved plans and the total amounts thus paid out in that month were $586,000 or an average of $26.24.[1]

Real progress was also being made with the grants for maternity and child health and public health.

3. Unemployment Insurance

By November of 1936, there were seventeen states that had passed unemployment insurance laws. In addition to the ten states mentioned in Chapter XII, namely, Alabama, California, District of Columbia, Massachusetts, New Hampshire, New York, Oregon, Utah, Washington and Wisconsin, seven more states passed such laws prior to the 1936 elections. These were Idaho, Indiana, Louisiana, Mississippi, South Carolina, Rhode Island and Texas. On the basis of the 1930 *Census of Occupations*, it would appear that, had there been no unemployment, these laws would have covered approximately 9.0 millions of workers, or 40 per cent of the 22.3 millions in the country who would have been included under the revenue section (Title IX) of the act. While the number who

[1] "Monthly Statistics for the United States," *Public Assistance*, Vol. I, No. 7.

would have actually fallen under these acts at their time of passage was considerably less than this, owing to the large percentage of unemployment, it is probable that the ratio of the included workers within these states to those who are eligible in the country as a whole was not greatly different.

After the presidential election of 1936, a large number of states hurried to pass unemployment insurance laws during special sessions of their legislatures. The general popular approval of the Social Security Act as a whole was a partial stimulant to this action. It was accelerated, however, by the statement of the Social Security Board that unless the states passed acts of their own before the end of the year, it would not recommend that taxes collected in 1936 under Title IX be credited to these states but that these sums would instead revert to the federal government. While this penalty was later lifted by Congress, the possibility of losing this money stirred many states to action; and in the closing six weeks of the year, no less than twenty states fell into line and passed such laws. These were Arizona, Connecticut, Colorado, Kentucky, Iowa, Maine, Maryland, Michigan, Minnesota, New Jersey, New Mexico, North Carolina, Ohio, Oklahoma, Pennsylvania, South Dakota, Tennessee, Vermont, Virginia and West Virginia. These laws were passed somewhat hastily, and in some cases only a day or two intervened between the time when the bill was introduced and, after having been passed by both houses of the legislature, signed by the governor. In order to avoid the charge of retroactive taxation, the payrolls in the last quarter or month of the year were frequently used as the basis for taxation in 1936. The Social Security Board cooperated in the drafting of most of these measures, and a change which it made in December in computing benefits and determining benefits and eligibility distinguished the later acts from those which had gone before.

Thus far the tide of legislation had turned strongly in favor of the pooled fund and away from that of the plant reserve. Since Utah repealed its former plant reserve system and replaced it with a pooled fund, Wisconsin was left as the only purely employer reserve state. By November 1, 1936, fourteen of the states had outright pooled funds, while Indiana had a hybrid system in which five-sixths of the contributions were kept in company reserves, and the remaining one-sixth was pooled. This latter compromise system was copied in December by Kentucky and South Dakota; while Vermont passed an optional act permitting employers to set up a separate reserve or to insure in the state fund. Aside from these states, the others all adopted pooled funds.

But the issue was not yet fully settled. Most of the organized employing interests of the country apparently preferred the Wisconsin system and by now had become its most forceful advocates. There were three reasons for this. (1) In the so-called "light" industries and in retailing, utilities, etc., the relative unemployment is less than for industry as a whole. These industries in many cases therefore would not have to pay out so much under a system of plant reserves as under a state-pooled fund. (2) Employers tend to believe that separate plant reserves would bind the workers more closely to them and lead them to think of themselves more in their relationship to their plant or company than as members of the general working class. In this way many employers believe that the plant reserve system could be used to reinforce the company union. (3) This last tendency would be strengthened if the employers were to secure from the Security Board permission to pay out unemployment benefits from their own offices rather than from the public employment bureaus. It will be remembered that the act specifies that benefits are to be paid "through public employment offices . . . or such other agencies as the Board may approve." Many employers are hoping that the board will approve their paying out benefits directly to their workers. This would of course strengthen their position since many workers would feel that the benefits were in part gratuities and would also fear that the employers might discriminate against them should they be active in organizational activities.

Severe struggles on this point have already occurred in the legislatures of Illinois and Ohio, and it is probable that they will recur in these and other states during the forth-coming legislative sessions. It is not unfair to state that the tactics of many employers' associations seem to be to delay action as long as possible, and then, if it is found that public sentiment demands the passage of some legislation, to try to substitute the plant reserve system for the state-pooled fund. The Social Security Board is itself preserving a strict neutrality on this issue.

Most of the states with pooled funds provide that a separate account shall be kept of the receipts from each employer and the disbursements to his unemployed workers. In eight states this is to be done for future merit rating. These are Alabama, California, the District of Columbia, Louisiana, New Hampshire, Oregon, South Carolina and Washington. In Massachusetts, Mississippi and Rhode Island, these are to be kept for bookkeeping purposes only and no explicit promise is made about future merit rating. In New York no separate accounts are to be kept.

Virtually all the state acts provide that they shall cease to be effective should the federal act be declared unconstitutional or inoperative. This is what many students of the question foresaw when the federal act was under consideration. It will be remembered that the framers of that act believed that, even if the tax-offset feature were ultimately declared unconstitutional, it would have served its purpose in getting the states to pass laws which, they thought, would continue even though the federal act were to disappear. The scaffold, they reasoned, could be torn down, but the house would remain. In practice, however, the tearing down of the federal scaffold would sweep away most of the state laws as well. The New York and Wisconsin laws would not, however, automatically disappear, and would continue unless specifically repealed by the state legislatures.

While the coverage of most of the state acts is virtually identical with the federal act, this is not invariably true. The New York, New Hampshire, Oregon, Rhode Island, Utah and Washington laws include firms employing four or more workers, while that for the District of Columbia includes all establishments with one or more workers. Ten states require contributions from the workers. These are Alabama, California, Idaho, Indiana, Louisiana, Massachusetts, New Hampshire, Rhode Island, Utah and Washington. These contributions generally have 1 per cent as their maximum but in Massachusetts and Rhode Island this will be 1½ per cent.

The length of the waiting period varies between the states. In Indiana, Mississippi and South Carolina, it is but two weeks. In most other states it is three, but in Massachusetts it is four and in Washington six weeks. The scale of benefits is almost uniformly 50 per cent of normal earnings subject to a maximum benefit of $15 a week, and with minimum benefits, where stated, ranging between $5 and $7 a week. Qualifying periods of prior employment are required in all states, varying from thirteen to twenty-six weeks during the preceding year.

The duration of ordinary benefits has customarily a double limitation. (1) The weeks of benefit must not exceed a given ratio to the previous weeks of employment within the two preceding years in insured occupations. This is 1 to 3 in the District of Columbia and New York, and 1 to 4 in Alabama, California, Indiana, Louisiana, Massachusetts, Mississippi, New Hampshire, Oregon, Rhode Island and South Carolina. Wisconsin has a curious system of requiring a 1 to 4 ratio when the benefit is less than $10 a week, and 1 to 5 and 1 to 6 ratios when the benefits range between $10 and $12.50 and $12.50 and $15, respectively. (2) There is also a maximum number of weeks of ordinary benefits which can be paid in any one year. This ranges from twelve weeks as in Mississippi and South Carolina to thirteen weeks in California, fifteen weeks in Indiana, Louisiana, Oregon and Washington, sixteen weeks in Alabama, the District of Columbia, Massachusetts, New Hampshire and New York. Rhode Island has the most liberal provision, with a twenty weeks' period.

In addition to the ordinary benefits, however, a certain number of added weeks of benefit will be granted in most states to those workers who have had a high previous record of employment during the preceding two years. In other words, the benefit period is to be decreased for those who have not been employed steadily during the preceding period and is to be increased for those who have. This will reduce the costs of maintaining some of the less efficient workers and will give corresponding added protection to some of the more efficient. To the degree, however, that the preceding lack of employment was due to industrial rather than to personal causes, it will work injustice.

A study of the probable cost of the various state systems indicates that, where the funds are exclusively derived from the contributions of the employers and hence do not exceed 2.7 or 3.0 per cent, it will be very doubtful whether the scale and duration of benefits promised can be furnished in most of these states from the funds available, if unemployment in the future comes up to the average for the twelve years from 1922 to 1933 inclusive. If the benefits are to be maintained, and most certainly if they are to be increased in these states, additional funds will have to be obtained.

Most states do not completely disqualify an unemployed worker from benefit if he is discharged for cause or if he refuses to accept suitable employment. He is instead customarily disqualified for an added period of weeks in addition to the ordinary waiting period.

Wisconsin is the only state where the payment of benefits has actually begun. In the other states, owing to the requirement that contributions must continue for two years before payments are made, the benefits could not commence until 1938 and even in some cases until 1939. Since over two-thirds of the jurisdictions still lack such legislation, then, even if they had passed laws at the 1937 sessions of their legislatures, benefits could not commence until well into 1938 and in some cases 1939. It will, therefore, have taken at least ten years from the outbreak of the great depression in 1929 to make any effective provision for the unemployed through insurance. This means that those who are unemployed in the meantime will have to be protected by other methods and that, if they are not able to obtain sufficient employment to qualify for benefit under the insurance acts, that these other methods will have to be continued.

Various administrative problems are developing which need to be carefully worked out.

1. One question is as to the proper procedure in investigating the earnings and past employment of a claimant for benefits. In Wisconsin, following the precedent of workmen's compensation, these past earnings and the employment record are investigated only after the workman has been dropped from his job and claims benefit. This is called the separation or severance method. In New Hampshire and New York, on the other hand, the current employment and earnings records are furnished by employers from their payrolls, and individual cards are made out for the workers under the system and will be ready in advance of the actual application for benefit. This is called the payroll method.

On the whole, it would seem that the Wisconsin group has miscalculated the relative volume of cases under workmen's compensation and unemployment insurance. The proportion of workers who are injured is very much less than those thrown out of work. Consequently, while the separations method is adequate in cases of workmen's compensation, it promises to break down when it is faced with a volume of unemployment of 10 per cent or more.

The payroll method would seem to be better, since it will assemble information by which a speedy payment of claims can be made. But this, in turn, could probably be simplified if the employers would submit one payroll a year or one each half year and then file only changes in the payroll.

2. The question of partial unemployment is causing a great deal of trouble, as the author expected that it would. It would seem better to include only half-days or full days lost and to obtain the record for this by having the partially employed worker sign the roll at the public employment office instead of throwing the burden of reporting upon the employers.

3. If benefits are continued at approximately onehalf the normal wages, great administrative difficulties will be created by making out weekly benefits payments of so many different amounts. Thus, with a minimum weekly benefit of $5 and a maximum of $15, there would be no less than 1,000 different amounts of benefits, and in a large state most, if not all, of these would have to be paid. Even with modern check-writing machines, this would be difficult to do weekly. It would seem, therefore, wise to reduce the benefits to not

more than ten and preferably seven or eight different denominations. This could be done (*a*) by paying the percentage of benefits to the nearest dollar, (*b*) by grouping the workers into the given number of wage categories and fixing a benefit rate for each.

4. In computing normal earnings it will be wise to use full-time weekly wages instead of actual weekly earnings[1] since the latter will very frequently include undertime and overtime in its total.

The most important developments as regards the constitutionality of the state unemployment laws is the New York case. The New York Court of Appeals in April held the law of that state to be constitutional by a 5 to 2 decision.[2] This decision was appealed and the case is now before the U. S. Supreme Court. The unemployment insurance provisions of the federal act are being challenged by the Newark (N. J.) Milk Co. before Federal Judge Fake and the New Jersey Social Security Commission has recommended to the state government that it fight in the courts the collection of federal taxes for this purpose.

The Republican candidate for the Presidency, Governor Alfred M. Landon of Kansas, in his

---

[1] For an explanation of these terms, see the first chapter of my *Real Wages in the United States* 1890–1926.

[2] The Washington act has been declared unconstitutional on a technicality by a 5 to 4 opinion of the Supreme Court of that state. The Court held that the act, which was passed before the Wagner-Doughton bill was finally approved, had never become effective because of subsequent changes in the federal act.

Milwaukee speech urged the scrapping of the tax-offset features of the federal act and the returning of the problem of legislation to the states. It was pointed out by many students of the question, including ex-Governor Winant, that this would make state legislation largely impossible because of the fear of interstate competition.

4. *Old Age Insurance*

The Social Security Board has been somewhat slow in registering the workers who will come under the old age insurance features of the act and in developing plans for recording information about their earnings, etc. It is now understood, however, that registration will start in early November and that the workers will receive numbers through the post offices.[1] In order to prevent the possibility that employers may use these numbers to identify workers for black-listing purposes on future jobs, the board will permit workers to change their numbers upon request when the latter suspect that they may be black-listed.

In the last weeks of the Presidential campaign a violent campaign was launched by opponents of President Roosevelt against the act in an effort to detach the wage-earners from his support. Slips were placed in the pay envelopes of workers and articles appeared in the more violent of the

---

[1] It is also understood that these identical numbers will be used in most of the state unemployment insurance systems.

anti-administration newspapers, which in many cases indulged in half-truths and in some cases downright misrepresentations about the contributions the workers were to make. (1) The fact that the employers were to make equal contributions was frequently not mentioned and the impression conveyed in these cases was that the workers were to pay the whole bill. (2) In many cases the impression was also conveyed that the workers either were not to receive anything in return for their contributions or that, if they did, this would be much less than it should be. No mention was made by these opponents of the fact that the average monthly annuities to be received by the workmen would be much greater than they could obtain with similar payments from any private insurance company. (3) The charge was frequently made that the funds would be dissipated by Congress and that, if this were done, the insured persons would receive little or nothing in return. The fact that the monies must be invested in government securities, and hence would presumably be the safest of all investments, was not mentioned.

While these implications were resented by informed friends of social security, there was a growing agreement that the reserves to be accumulated under the act were excessive and that the rate of contributions might be decreased. Governor Landon, in his Milwaukee speech, however, did not content himself with proposing amendments, but instead declared himself in favor of repealing this section of the act.

During the closing days of the campaign, certain new papers which were opposing the Roosevelt administration also sponsored the "dog-tag" scare in which they photographed workers with metal disks about their necks which they said the Social Security Board planned to put there as a means of identification. This was completely false.

One effect of the attempt by employers and the Republican Party to turn the workers against the Roosevelt administration by stressing the amount of taxes or contributions which they would have to pay has been to lessen the possibility of having the workers assume as much of this burden in the future. After the employers' campaign, it will be difficult for them to convince the workers or the state legislatures that the employees should also contribute to the unemployment insurance funds. Moreover, if the total amount of the old age insurance tax is reduced, as now seems probable, it will tend to be lowered more for the workers' share than for the employers'. While the employers will undoubtedly object to this, they will have to blame the action of a large part of their own number for it.

Chapter XIV

DEVELOPMENTS IN 1937 AND EARLY 1938

DURING the last year and a half, six sets of developments have occurred in the field of social security. (1) The Supreme Court upheld the constitutionality of the Social Security Act as regards both old age insurance and unemployment compensation and approved the constitutionality of the various state unemployment insurance laws. (2) Old age pension or assistance laws had been enacted by all of the states, and such pensions were being paid to over a million and a half aged persons. Weaknesses in the system and, in some states, abuses of administration were, however, developing. (3) The collection of contributions under the compulsory old age insurance system was begun, and widespread discussion developed over the proper financing of such a system. (4) Unemployment insurance or compensation laws had been passed in every state; and on January 1, 1938, twenty-two states moved into the period when they began to pay out benefits to the qualified unemployed. (5) Distinct progress was made in the welfare features of the act in so far as children, the blind, and public health were

[348]

concerned. (6) Various administrative problems were developing. Each of these developments will be discussed in turn.

1. The Decisions of the Supreme Court

All of the features of the Social Security Act whose constitutionality was questioned were upheld by the United States Supreme Court in a series of decisions which were handed down on May 24, 1937. The unemployment compensation sections were affirmed in the case of the *Steward Machine Co. v. Davis* by a five to four decision.[1] The chief points at issue were: (1) Whether federal taxes could be levied on employment and wages and whether the exemptions granted did not make the law class legislation in that it applied to some groups but not to others. (2) Whether the federal government, by the use of its taxing powers, had coerced the states into dealing with unemployment compensation which, it was argued by the opponents, should be the exclusive concern of the states. (3) Whether the federal government was seeking revenue for the treasury or providing a program for dealing with unemployment. (4) Whether the standards to which the state laws were required to conform in order that the 90 per cent offset be granted constituted an invasion of the rights of the states.

Justice Cardozo wrote the majority opinion, in which he was joined by Justices Brandeis, Stone

[1] *Steward Machine Co. v. Davis*, 301 U.S. 548.

and Roberts and by Chief Justice Hughes. The opinion ruled that it was as proper for the federal government to tax employment as it was for it to tax property and incomes and cited historical precedents to justify this ruling. The uniformity of the tax, it was stated, need be only geographical, not occupational. The exemptions granted had practical and theoretical justification and hence could not be condemned as arbitrary. Justice Cardozo then went on to say that the depression had shown that relief to the unemployed was a legitimate national function. " . . . the states," he declared, "were unable to give the requisite relief. The problem had become national in area and dimensions. There was need of help from the nation if the people were not to starve. It is too late today for the argument to be heard with tolerance that in a crisis so extreme the use of the moneys of the nation to relieve the unemployed and their dependents is a use for any purpose narrower than the promotion of the general welfare."

The court pointed out that the institution of unemployment insurance would care for a large fraction of those who would otherwise have to be granted relief and hence would diminish the relief load upon both the nation and the individual states. It was difficult for the states individually to pass such laws because of their fear of interstate competition, and this failure to act caused "a disproportionate burden, and a mountainous one" to be "laid upon the resources of the Government of the nation." It was, therefore, legitimate for Congress to "attempt to find a method by which all these public agencies may work together to a common end."

The principle of the offset was justified by the court on the ground that if "the general welfare would better be promoted by relief through local units than by the system then in vogue, the cooperating localities ought not in all fairness to pay a second time." While the use of the offset was admittedly an "inducement" to the states to pass such legislation, it was not, in the opinion of the court, "coercion." "Till now," stated the court, "the law has been guided by a robust common sense which assumes the freedom of the will as a working hypothesis in the solution of its problems. . . . We cannot say that she [Alabama] was acting, not of her unfettered will, but under the strain of a persuasion equivalent to undue influence, when she chose to have relief administered under laws of her own making, by agents of her own selection, instead of under federal laws, administered by federal officers, with all the ensuing evils, at least to many minds, of federal patronage and power." Justice Cardozo went on to say that this did not mean that such tax devices were constitutional if levied for purposes which were not distinctly national, but that wherever the outermost line might be drawn, the security act was within it.

The standards to which the state laws must conform did not call for the surrender by the states of their quasi-sovereign powers. The states were instead given a wide range of choice as to the type of laws that they might pass. And the standards required were designed to make the laws effective in serving their basic assigned purpose, namely, to help the unemployed. Even the requirement that the state moneys must be deposited in the federal treasury is justifiable, since it is designed both to assure the safety of the funds and to promote the stability of business.

The four so-called "conservative" justices dissented. Justices McReynolds and Butler did so because they believed the offset features of the law coerced the states into giving up their sovereign powers. While Justices Sutherland and Van Devanter did not primarily object on this score, they declared that requiring the states to deposit their receipts with the federal treasury was an unconstitutional invasion of the rights of the states.

On the same day the court, by another five to four decision, upheld the constitutionality of state unemployment insurance laws of the pooled type in the case of *Carmichael* v. *Southern Coal Co.*,[1] which involved the Alabama law. Justice Stone, in handing down the majority opinion, stated that: " . . . expenditures for the relief of the unemployed, conditioned on unemployment alone, without proof of indigence of recipients of the benefits,

[1] 301 U.S. 495.

is a permissible use of state funds." Unemployment insurance would reduce the need for relief being given on the basis of indigence by helping to protect the income of workers who had lost their jobs. The fact that the contributions or taxes were pooled, and that hence some employers were assessed to pay benefits to workers who had been employed by others, did not invalidate the law. For, as the court observed, "A tax is not an assessment of benefits. It is, as we have said, a means of distributing the burden of the cost of government. The only benefit to which the taxpayer is constitutionally entitled is that derived from his enjoyment of the privileges of living in an organized society, established and safeguarded by the devotion of taxes to public purposes. . . . A corporation cannot object to the use of the taxes which it pays for the maintenance of schools because it has no children. . . .

"Many believe that the responsibility for the business cycle, the chief cause of unemployment, cannot be apportioned to individual employers in accordance with their employment experience; that a business may be least responsible for the depression from which it suffers the most.

"The Alabama legislature may have proceeded upon the view, for which there is abundant authority, that the causes of unemployment are too complex to admit of a meticulous appraisal of employer responsibility. It may have concluded that unemployment is an inseparable incident of modern industry, with its most serious manifestations in industrial production, that employees will be best protected, and that the cost of the remedy, at least until more accurate and complete data are available, may best be distributed by imposing the tax evenly upon all industrial production, and in such form that it will be added to labor costs which are ultimately absorbed by the public in the prices which it pays for consumers goods.

"If the question were ours to decide, we could not say that the legislature, in accepting the present scheme rather than another, had no basis for its choice, or was arbitrary or unreasonable in its action. But, as the state is free to distribute the burden of a tax without regard to the particular purpose for which it is to be used, there is no warrant in the constitution for setting the tax aside because a court thinks that it could have drawn a better statute or could have distributed the burden more wisely. Those are functions reserved for the legislature.

The exemptions granted in the Alabama law, which approximately conformed to those embodied in the federal act, were also declared not to be unreasonable or arbitrary. The relatively high administrative costs of collecting taxes from small employers was held to justify the exemptions granted on the basis of numbers employed. The exemptions for particular classes of employment were upheld on the grounds that "the state is free to select a particular class as a subject

[354]

for taxation" and that for administrative or other valid reasons it may exclude certain groups. "A legislature," the court declared, "is not bound to tax every member of a class or none. It may make distinctions of degree having a rational basis, and when subjected to judicial scrutiny they must be presumed to rest on that basis if there is any conceivable state of facts which would support it."

The same four justices dissented in this case as in the *Steward Machine Co.* case. Justices Sutherland, Van Devanter and Butler joined in a minority opinion which declared that while the Wisconsin system of separate employer reserves was "fair, reasonable, and just," the pooled fund plan of Alabama was "so arbitrary as to result in a denial both of due process and equal protection of the laws."

In a final opinion, the court upheld the federal old age insurance system in the case of *Helvering* v. *Davis*.[1] Justice Cardozo, again speaking for the majority, stated that it was now settled that Congress could spend money for the general welfare.[2] The benefits provided in Title II were intended to serve the general welfare, for "the hope behind this statute is to save men and women from the rigors of the poor house as well as from the haunting fear that such a lot awaits them when journey's end is near." After summarizing

---

[1] 301 U.S. 619.

[2] The precedents cited for this were not only the *Steward Machine Co.* v. *Davis* case but also *United States* v. *Butler*, 297 U.S. 1.

the economic difficulties which aged persons found in modern society, and which indicated that approximately three out of four persons of sixty-five years or over were probably dependent in whole or part on others for support, the court went on to say:

"The problem is plainly national in area and dimensions. Moreover, laws of the separate states cannot deal with it effectively. Congress, at least, had a basis for that belief. States and local governments are often lacking in the resources that are necessary to finance an adequate program of security for the aged. . . . Apart from the failure of resources, states and local governments are at times reluctant to increase so heavily the burden of taxation to be borne by their residents for fear of placing themselves in a position of economic disadvantage as compared with neighbors or competitors. . . . A system of old age pensions has special dangers of its own, if put in force in one state and rejected in another. The existence of such a system is a bait to the needy and dependent elsewhere, encouraging them to migrate and seek a haven of repose. Only a power that is national can serve the interests of all.

"Whether wisdom or unwisdom resides in the scheme of benefits set forth in Title II, it is not for us to say. The answer to such inquiries must come from Congress, not the courts. Our concern, here, as often, is with power, not with wisdom. Counsel for respondent has recalled to us the virtues of self-reliance and frugality. There is a possibility, he says, that aid from a paternal government may sap those sturdy virtues and breed a race of weaklings. If Massachusetts so believes and shapes her laws in that conviction, must her breed of sons be changed, he asks, because some other philosophy of government finds favor in the halls of Congress? But the answer is not doubtful. One might ask with equal reason whether the system of protective tariffs is to be set aside at will in one state or another whenever local policy prefers the rule of *laissez faire*. The issue is a closed one. It was fought out long ago. When money is spent to promote the general welfare, the concept of welfare or the opposite is shaped by Congress, not the states. So the concept be not arbitrary, the locality must yield."

Having approved of Title II, the court went on to say that the payroll tax under Title VIII was a valid exercise of congressional power for the reasons assigned in the case of *Steward Machine Co.* v. *Davis*. Justices McReynolds and Butler filed a dissent which stated that the provisions under consideration were "repugnant to the Tenth Amendment,"[1] which declared that powers not delegated or assigned to the federal government were presumed to reside in the states.[2]

[1] I.e., "The powers not delegated to the United States by the Constitution or prohibited by it to the States, are reserved to the States respectively, or to the people."

[2] It is obvious in these decisions that Justice Roberts cast, in reality, the deciding vote. In these cases, as in those involving the Wagner Labor Rela-

2. *Old Age Pensions or Assistance*

Every state and territory now has an old age pension or assistance law which has been approved by the Social Security Board;[1] and by the end of May, 1938, there were approximately 1,686,000 aged persons who were being aided in this manner. This was an increase of slightly over half a million as compared with the number who had been aided under forty-two approved plans in December, 1936. This meant that in practice 21.6 per cent of the persons in the country who were sixty-five years of age and over, or slightly over one in five, were in receipt of such a pension. This ratio, however, varied greatly from state to state, as will be seen from the following table, which gives the number per thousand of the population sixty-five years and over who were in receipt of such grants in December, 1937.

---

tions Act, 301 U.S. 1–148, and the Washington Minimum Wage Law, 300 U.S. 379, he voted to uphold the statutes.

These decisions were consistent with his 1934 decision upholding the state fixation of the price of milk (see *Nebbia* v. *New York* 291 U.S. 502) but seem to be inconsistent with those which he made in 1935 in the Railway Pension Act (*Railroad Retirement Board* v. *Alton R. R.* 295 U.S. 330), where a pooled fund was involved; and in 1936, in the New York Minimum Wage case (*Tipaldo* v. *Morehead* 298 U.S. 587).

It is generally both gratuitous and uncharitable to attempt to probe into men's motives, and I do not propose to do so in this case. It is at least possible, however, that Justice Roberts' shift of ground may have been affected by the manifestation of the public will in the fall of 1936 and by the President's subsequent proposal to alter the composition of the Supreme Court.

[1] Virginia did not pass such an act until March, 1938.

TABLE XV

TOTAL NUMBER OF THOSE RECEIVING OLD AGE PENSIONS OR ASSISTANCE,
AND RELATIVE NUMBER PER 1,000 POPULATION SIXTY-FIVE YEARS AND
OVER IN DECEMBER, 1937, BY STATES[1]

State	Total number receiving old age pensions or assistance	Relative number per 1,000 persons 65 years and over
Oklahoma	69,392	598
Utah	11,589	489
Colorado[2]	34,250	449
Texas	113,730	409
Montana	11,438	387
Minnesota	62,778	329
Idaho	8,123	323
South Dakota	13,261	317
Arizona	5,116	301
Louisiana	24,132	291
Washington	35,515	291
Wyoming	2,842	291
Nebraska	25,763	268
Missouri[3]	76,365	251
Florida	22,893	250
Illinois	121,897	248
Nevada	1,396	233
West Virginia	18,659	230
New Mexico	3,712	229
Michigan	63,318	222
Ohio	104,614	220
California	97,943	218
North Dakota	7,247	207
Iowa	44,414	206
Massachusetts	64,893	201
Kentucky	35,046	196
Mississippi	15,576	192
South Carolina	13,260	189
Wisconsin	37,816	176
Alaska	689	172
Georgia	22,287	164
Oregon[3]	12,963	160
Pennsylvania[3]	95,504	157

TABLE XV. (*Continued*)

State	Total number receiving old age pensions or as- sistance	Relative number per 1,000 persons 65 years and over
Maryland...............	16,250	151
Indiana³................	41,887	148
North Carolina..........	20,976	146
Hawaii.................	1,412	142
Delaware...............	2,888	138
Vermont................	5,214	137
New York...............	102,926	133
Alabama................	13,968	131
Connecticut.............	14,131	124
Rhode Island............	5,697	124
New Jersey..............	25,372	104
Kansas.................	13,554	93
Tennessee..............	13,393	90
District of Columbia.....	2,963	74
New Hampshire³........	3,592	71
Country as a whole	1,582,441	205

¹ Taken from *Public Assistance Statistics for the United States* (published by the Social Security Board), December, 1937, p. 14. The number of those sixty-five years and over are estimated for each state for July 1, 1937.

² In Colorado, pensions are paid under certain conditions to those of sixty and over, but the ratio is in terms of the total number of pensioners per thousand population of sixty-five years and over.

³ In these five states, pensions are paid only to those who are seventy years and over, but the computed relative ratios are based on those who are sixty-five years and over. The ratios to those in the eligible ages would, of course, be appreciably higher in these states.

It will be noted from the foregoing table that virtually 60 per cent of these in the eligible age group in Oklahoma were in receipt of pensions, as were 49 per cent in Utah, 45 per cent in Colorado, and 41 per cent of those in Texas. In Montana, the proportion was nearly 40 per cent, and in Minnesota about a third. The Missouri situation also exhibits the same tendencies. Under the law of that state, only those who are seventy years and over are entitled to receive old age pensions or assistance. And yet the 76,000 persons who received such aid formed 25.1 per cent of all those in the state who were sixty-five years and over. From computations which have been made, it seems probable that approximately 42 per cent of those in the eligible age group of seventy years and over were in receipt of such a pension.[1]

It will be seen that the states with the highest ratio of pensioners are in the southwest and the mountain ranges. Thus, Oklahoma, Missouri and Texas, which are three out of the five states with the highest ratios, are in the near southwest; while Colorado, Utah, Idaho and Montana, which are in the first nine, are in the mountain range. South Dakota and Minnesota are also in the first nine; and close behind come Washington, Louisiana and Wyoming.

There are numerous reasons for these high ratios. All of these states have a large volume of poverty. This is particularly true in the southwest, where the percentage of tenant farmers is high and where farm incomes are low. Secondly, the poverty-stricken tenant farmers have much more political influence in these states than they do in the deep south, where they are so frequently barred from voting by poll tax requirements. These groups, therefore, exert a great deal of pressure for relief,

---

[1] Computations based on Vol. III of the Population Census of 1930, p. 1320, and Vol. II, p. 566.

which naturally reflects itself in the ratios. Louisiana, which is tied for the tenth highest ratio in the country, is an added illustration of this tendency. That state is under the political control of the machine founded by the late Senator Huey Long, and a large part of its strength has always rested on the support of the poorer farmers and farm tenants.

The strength of the Townsend movement is a third factor in several of these states, and this is perhaps particularly the case in Colorado, Oklahoma, Montana and Washington.

A fourth cause in many of the southwestern and western states is the open-handed generosity of people who live in the open, and who keenly appreciate the difficulties which older men and women face. The public in these states, therefore, does not insist so rigidly on individual and family responsibility as do the people of many states in the north and east.

But these are not all the factors. There is a large volume of evidence to indicate that in some of these states the pension rolls have, in fact, been padded to build up the political power and prestige of the state administrations. This has been notably the case in Missouri[1] and Oklahoma.[2] In Missouri, the administration of the act has been transferred

---

[1] See the article by Geoffrey Parsons, Jr., in *The New York Herald Tribune* for January 2, 1938.

[2] See the releases of the Social Security Board on this situation, and the files of *Social Security*, as well as the article by Abraham Epstein, "Killing Old Age Security with Kindness," *Harpers Magazine*, July 1937.

from the horse trainer and livestock dealer who formerly conducted it, and a resurvey of those on the list is being conducted. In certain counties, the number of pensioners was found to be greater than the total number in the eligible age group. In one county for example, 40 per cent of the pension beneficiaries were dropped from the rolls on the ground that they were not in need.

In Oklahoma, *The Tulsa World* has charged that 39,000 pensioners were put on the state roles during Governor Marland's campaign in 1936 for the United States Senate and that more were added in anticipation of the November, 1937, elections.[1]

The Social Security Board has recently taken steps to reduce the abuses in Missouri and Oklahoma. In the latter state, a sample investigation in three counties indicated that about one-third of those receiving pensions were not in fact entitled to them. About three-eighths of the ineligibles were less than sixty-five years of age, and another three-eighths had outside incomes in excess of $30 a month. The remaining quarter either had excess property or had transferred it to relatives for the purpose of receiving pensions.[2] The recently appointed state director has admitted that there had previously been no investigations to determine the eligibility of the applicants. As a result of this situation, the Security Board in February of 1938 called a hearing on the question as to whether or

---

[1] *Social Security*, November, 1937, p. 8.
[2] *Ibid.*, March, 1938.

not the federal grants to Oklahoma should be withdrawn; and as a result of the evidence produced on this occasion, the board canceled the federal aid until such time as the abuses were corrected. In early May, the board refused to restore the grants. Later, however, it agreed to pay the federal share for those cases which, after being investigated by the state agencies, were certified as being entitled to benefits. Some pruning of the list was, however, being affected and by the end of May some 3,000 pensioners had been dropped. Pressure upon Missouri has also resulted in pruning the pension rolls of that state of several thousand ineligibles.

But abuses of administration have been by no means confined to the states mentioned above. In Ohio, for example, Governor Davey—who was a candidate for reelection in 1936—increased each pension in the summer of that year by $10 a month and then wrote each one of the 94,000 pensioners that he was doing so. Governor Davey then followed this up with another letter requesting each pensioner "to ask ten or fifteen of your relatives and friends to vote for me on November 3rd." In a third letter, he assured the pensioners that the increase would be maintained. But after his reelection, each pension was reduced.[1] Somewhat similar letters have recently been sent out in

---

[1] For the details of this affair, see Abraham Epstein, "Killing Old Age Security with Kindness," *Harpers Magazine*, Vol. 175 (July, 1937), pp. 186–187.

Georgia.[1] In the summer of 1937, the Social Security Board found it necessary to suspend federal aid to the state of Illinois because of defects in its administration of old age assistance. Substantial improvements were, however, made in that state, and federal aid was then resumed. As this edition goes to press, the board has taken cognizance of the Ohio situation and after preferring charges concerning the administration of the act in that state has summoned the Ohio authorities to a hearing on them.[2]

The evils of such abuses are obvious. The moneys which are given to those who are not entitled to receive pensions reduce the amounts which should be given to the genuinely dependent aged and also curtail the funds needed to finance other welfare activities. Thus, in Missouri, the average pension in December, 1937, was only $12.83; in Texas, $13.72; and in Oklahoma, $14.86. The legitimate features of the system are therefore being discredited by its being treated as a political slush fund, and the danger of the old people being ultimately thrown back upon the ordinary forms of relief is increased.

The Colorado situation is somewhat different. In 1936, the voters of that state passed, by popular referendum, a constitutional amendment which

---

[1] *Social Security*, March, 1938, p. 8.

[2] See a release of the Social Security Board on August 20. By order of Governor Davey, the Ohio authorities did not appear at this hearing and the governor defied the board to shut off the federal grants.

provided minimum monthly pensions of $45 a month to all citizens who were sixty years of age or over; and to finance these grants there was assigned 85 per cent of all the income derived from sales, excise and liquor taxes. It also provided that any sums left in the old age pension fund at the end of a calendar year should be distributed among the eligible claimants.[1]

The legislature attempted to reduce the liability of the state by passing an enabling act which made $45 the maximum pension and restricted payments for those between the ages of sixty and sixty-five to persons who had resided in the state for no less than thirty-five years, and who had been registered voters at the preceding election.[2] This last provision cut down the number under sixty-five years of age who were eligible, so that in May, 1938, only 2,800 of the approximate 36,000 of those who were receiving pensions were in this age group. While those in receipt of private incomes of over $45 a month were declared ineligible, and private income which a person possessed was also to be deducted from the amount of the pension, there was also a clause in both the amendment and the enabling act which provided that "no variation in the amount paid or other discrimination between persons eligible shall be permitted."

[1] See Constitutional Amendment No. 4, published by the Colorado State Department of Public Welfare.
[2] House Bill No. 1064. $45.00 Old Age Pension Act, published by the Colorado State Department of Public Welfare.

Since the average pension paid in December, 1937, amounted to $39.61,[1] and since there were in the next month 35,800 persons who were in receipt of such pensions, this meant that the state was spending slightly over $1,400,000 a month, or at the rate of between 14.5 and 14.0 millions of dollars a year for this purpose. The expenditure in a small state of such relatively large sums upon the aged compelled the state government to reduce its grants for the relief of the needy unemployed by about one-half and hence to grant grossly inadequate sums not only to those in the more active periods of life but to their children as well. Thus, families in Denver with several children, at the end of 1937, were receiving only $23 in relief as compared with the grant of nearly $40 a month paid to individual old people.

The reduction in relief was so severe that several social workers were actually shot and killed by relief clients. The funds for educational institutions and hospitals also had to be curtailed. In spite of these economies, it is estimated that the deficit for the current year will amount to nearly four million dollars. One extraordinary feature of the amendment was the so-called "jack-pot" clause, which provided for the distribution at the end of the year of all sums in the old age pension fund, regardless of the financial condition of the state. This provision was not contained in the act passed by the

---

[1] Owing to the shortage in funds, however, the average payment in April fell to a little less than $27 and remained on this level during May.

legislature, but it was ruled that it should be put into effect, and approximately one million dollars was distributed in this fashion, in per capita payments of approximately $28.

A great deal of opposition to the scale of the Colorado old age benefits is developing not only among the groups on relief but among those interested in schools, hospitals, etc., as well as among merchants and businessmen, and it is quite possible that the amounts may be reduced by another amendment to the constitution.

That the Townsend movement for universal old age pensions regardless has not spent its force is indicated not only by the Colorado developments but also by recent occurrences in Texas and California. In the former state, the candidate who won the Democratic nomination for governor by an overwhelming majority espoused a project for monthly pensions of $30 for everyone over sixty. In California a movement for a constitutional amendment granting *weekly* pensions of $30 to everyone over fifty and to be financed by a combination of sales tax and stamped scrip has already commanded great popular support and hundreds of thousands of voters have signed petitions asking that it be put on the ballot to be voted upon. In the recent Democratic primaries, the successful candidates for governor and senator were supporters of this proposal.

Along with the abuses which have unfortunately grown up, there is also a legitimate tendency to relax some of the rigorous eligibility requirements which were formerly imposed. Thus, the administrators of old age pensions tend in practice to free wage and salaried workers who have low incomes, and who are themselves hard-pressed, from the obligation of contributing heavily to the support of their aged parents. This tendency is seldom worked out in definite and published rules, but it is undoubtedly a growing administrative practice. There is also a drift in the laws to permit the aged to possess a larger amount of private property without being disqualified for benefits than was at first the case. This is evidenced by recent legislation broadening the exemption limits in California, Connecticut, Maryland, Missouri and Texas. The fact that Iowa, Michigan and Washington have repealed the sections of their acts which formerly confined benefits to citizens may indicate a slight movement in this direction, although the vast majority of states still retain this requirement.

Turning now to the amounts actually paid in the form of "pensions" or assistance, we find that they continue to be grossly inadequate in a large number of states. Average payments for December, 1937 are shown in Table XVI.

It will thus be seen that there are six states where the average pension was less than $10 a month, and ten more where the monthly average was between $10 and $15. These sums are, of course, grossly inadequate. It is worthy of notice

TABLE XVI

AVERAGE AMOUNT OF PENSIONS BY STATES IN DECEMBER, 1937[1]

State	Average grant per month	State	Average grant per month
Colorado	$39.61[1]	Rhode Island	$18.35
California	33.12	New Jersey	17.86
Alaska	28.55	Maryland	17.45
Massachusetts	27.94	Illinois	16.90
Nevada	27.70	North Dakota	16.79
Connecticut	26.30	Nebraska	16.67
Utah	25.60	Indiana	16.00
Arizona	25.20	Florida	15.92
District of Columbia	25.00	Oklahoma	15.02
New York	23.84	Vermont	14.05
Ohio	23.10	West Virginia	14.01
Washington	22.95	Hawaii	13.83
New Hampshire	22.44	Texas	13.70
Pennsylvania	21.79	Missouri	13.66
Idaho	21.68	Tennessee	13.33
Oregon	21.44	New Mexico	12.26
Wyoming	21.18	Alabama	11.06
Montana	20.45	South Carolina	11.04
Wisconsin	19.94	Delaware	10.82
Iowa	19.79	Louisiana	9.92
Minnesota	19.67	Kentucky	9.81
Michigan	18.96	Georgia	9.80
Kansas	18.52	North Carolina	9.28
South Dakota	18.36	Arkansas	9.15
		Mississippi	4.52
		Average for country as a whole	19.46

[1] *Public Assistance Statistics for December,* 1937 (Social Security Board), p. 14.
[2] The Colorado average had dropped by February, however, to $31.63.

that all of the states with average monthly pensions of less than $10 were in the south, namely, Mississippi, North Carolina, Arkansas, Louisiana, Kentucky and Georgia. Seven of the next ten lowest states were also either in the south or south-west, namely, South Carolina, Alabama, New Mexico, Missouri, Tennessee, Texas and West Virginia.

There are numerous reasons for the lowness of these pensions. (1) Most of these states are com-paratively poor and are somewhat lacking in re-sources with which to provide adequate pensions and at the same time maintain their other services. (2) The standard of living in the southern states tends to be appreciably lower for both farmers and industrial workers than it does for similar groups in the north and west, and this naturally leads the state authorities to make lower pension grants. (3) The presence of a racial minority with lower earnings and a lower standard of living than the native Anglo-Saxon stock also operates to lower the pension level. The whites in the south tend to believe that the Negroes can live on rather small sums and apply this policy to pensions as well as to other matters. In New Mexico, much the same policy is followed with respect to the Spanish-Mexican group. Similar influences are at work in Hawaii in connection with the oriental and na-tive Hawaiian stock. (4) Some of these states have undoubtedly given pensions to such an excessive number of persons that the amount paid to each legitimate pensioner has had to be reduced. This is certainly a primary cause for the lowness of the average pension in Missouri, Texas, Oklahoma and Louisiana. (5) It is also probable that in certain

[371]

cases, the full taxing powers of the states have not been levied upon those in the more prosperous income groups. This failure to act has necessarily curtailed the funds available to pay adequate pensions.

The two states with the most adequate pensions are Colorado and California, where minimum incomes of $45 and $35 a month must be guaranteed. In both of these states the Townsend movement has been strong, and this has undoubtedly played a part[1] in raising the pensions to their respective averages in January of approximately $40 and $33. Since then the average Colorado grant has declined to $26.75. Massachusetts is the state with the fourth highest average,[2] namely, over $27 a month. This is, in turn, largely caused by the law guaranteeing a minimum money income of $30 to aged pensioners without an eligible spouse. In general, the states with the highest average pensions tend to be those in the Rocky Mountains and the west. The generosity of the people and the strength of the Townsend movement are probably the chief causes.

On the whole, the case would seem strong for added federal aid to those states whose average pensions are low because of the poverty of their taxable resources. One way of effecting this would

---

[1] In California, the conservative governor, Merriam, found it desirable during the latter phases of his campaign against Upton Sinclair in the 1934 election, to support the Townsend plan, and consequently he has been more or less committed to a program of liberalizing old age pensions.

[2] If Alaska is omitted, it is the third.

be for the federal government to graduate the percentage of the pension which it would provide from its funds, according to the relative taxable assets per aged person of sixty-five years and over. Under such a plan the proportion of the total maximum cost which the federal government would furnish would not be invariably one-half but could vary from a minimum of one-third to a maximum of two-thirds. In the state with the highest comparable assessed value of property per aged person, the federal government would, for example, provide only one-third of the cost. In the state with the lowest comparable value, the federal government would bear two-thirds of the cost. A scale could then be devised for the intermediate states which would be graduated in such a way that the average percentage of cost borne by the national government would be approximately the same as now, namely, one-half. In this way, the most federal aid would be given to those states whose own resources were least, and the least federal aid would be given to those states whose own resources were greatest.

But while such a formula would be just, it would also be complicated. Because of this, and because of the inevitable opposition of the relatively richer states, it might be difficult to enact such a program. The method of making some "block" grants to all of the states which would not have to be matched might, therefore, have a better chance of enactment. Under this plan, a flat federal grant of $3 to $4 per month per pensioner could be made to the states, provided they did not decrease the average absolute per capita amounts which they were paying out of their own funds for old age assistance. In this way, added federal grants of from five to six and a half million dollars a month would be given to the states by the federal government to build up the sums received by the aged group. Any such plan would, however, have to be guarded carefully to prevent the states from flooding the federal government with large numbers of additional aged persons to whom the flat federal grants would be paid.

As was stated earlier in this book, it would also be desirable for the federal government to provide its full half of those individual pensions which, because of illness, high living costs in cities, etc., should be over $30 a month. Abraham Epstein has suggested a simple amendment to the Social Security Act which would permit this. According to this proposal, the federal government would meet half of the total cost for old age pensions in a state up to an *average* of $30 a month. Since there would be many who would receive less than this average, this would enable the government to share equally the cost of pensions in excess of this sum.

It is vital to an understanding of the American system of old age security to realize that the vast majority of the state laws have taken a very different form from that which was originally designed by the advocates of old age pensions. The pioneers in this movement, such as Rubinow, Epstein and Maurer, wanted legislation which would *guarantee* minimum incomes to aged persons, and under which public grants would build up private incomes to the minimum guaranteed amount. This differed in practice from the British system only in that it recognized the obligation of close relatives to contribute to the support of the aged person and hence made family income rather than individual income the primary criterion.

But the state laws, as they have been enacted, have, in the main, taken a very different turn. Except in three states,[1] the laws do not fix any minimum guaranteed income but instead generally provide that the combined private income and public grant *shall not exceed* a given amount. This is commonly, although not invariably, $30 a month. This permits the combined sums to be less than $30 a month at the discretion of the officials administering the act. This same opening of the way to administrative discretion is also permitted by the five laws[2] which fix neither maximum nor minimum limits to the size of the grants.

This abandonment of the idea of a guaranteed minimum income, and the substitution instead of the idea that the aged shall receive only what the administrative authorities think it best for them

[1] I.e., California, Colorado and Massachusetts.

[2] Namely, those in Arkansas, the District of Columbia, Louisiana, Montana, and New York.

to obtain, quite evidently transforms "pensions" into a type of aid which is perilously close to "relief." This shift of emphasis is recognized in the Social Security Act by the complete omission of the term "old age pensions" and the substitution instead of the phrase "old age assistance." Such a change of emphasis obviously creates a very different administrative system from that which was originally contemplated. Individual case work and the services of social workers are used to a far greater extent than was at first designed. It is said that if discretionary grants are to be made, it is highly important that they should be accurately apportioned to the specific and varying needs of individuals and that the aged person should receive the personal services of trained workers as well as cash assistance. In the majority of states, therefore, case workers are used to determine such matters as: (*a*) the personal income and property of the applicants; (*b*) the ability of relatives to support the applicant; (*c*) the general needs of the applicant; (*d*) subject to limitations of finance and the supervision of the central administration agencies, etc., the total amount of public aid to be given; and, finally, (*e*) the degree of medical aid and of hospitalization which the aged person needs, and arrangements for which are made by the social worker in charge of the "case."

However necessary all this may be, its effect is undoubtedly to blur the line between "pensions" and "relief" and to make those who thought they were going to receive the former come perilously close to receiving the latter. This is intensified by two other developments. (1) With the development of state and county public welfare departments, the administrative force in charge of "general relief" is in most cases that which is also in charge of "old age assistance." In a large percentage of the cases, including not only smaller cities and towns but also such a huge metropolis as New York, this means that the same case workers will handle both general relief cases and recipients of old age assistance, while the applications for both forms are often made in the same place or in closely adjoining offices. It is small wonder if, under such circumstances, it is difficult for recipients or administrators to distinguish between the two forms of aid. (2) This similarity is increased when the social workers begin to offer advice and exercise control over the ways in which the aged persons spend their grants. This is, of course, a common practice in cases handled by private charity, and it is also widely carried out in public relief. Despite frequent denials there is little doubt that some degree of oversight has been exercised by many social workers for those in receipt of old age assistance. When this happens, about the last distinguishing characteristics which might differentiate the old age grants from ordinary relief have disappeared. In fact, virtually the only remaining distinction is that since relief for the aged is federally aided, it is commonly on a somewhat

[377]

more generous scale than relief to other "unemployables" who are not covered by the federal Social Security Act. Disappointment with the way in which what were expected to be "pensions" have become "relief" has in turn been one of the forces behind the movement for universal old age pensions.

These tendencies have created two different sets of responses. One group, of which Miss Joanna Colcord of the Russell Sage Foundation is perhaps the leader, and which is largely recruited from the private welfare agencies, would frankly abandon any attempt to distinguish between the two methods and would indeed do away with all "categories" of special relief[1] and, instead, throw all cases into a general relief pool. The supporters of this point of view believe that the abolition of the categories would remove the residual stigma which now attaches itself to relief and that if adequate funds and trained supervision were provided, all groups could be adequately cared for in a self-respecting manner. They also stress the fact that all groups of the needy would thus be given equality of treatment.

The second group believes that progress in the field of social protection has largely been made by separating out specific groups from the undifferentiated mass of the needy and giving them

[1] Such as old age assistance, assistance to the blind and for dependent children. Some of this group even advocate abolishing unemployment insurance as such and putting this on a case work and relief basis!

special treatment and an opportunity to preserve and build up their self-respect. Thus, the poorhouse was an institution which gave congregate treatment to a wide variety of groups, such as the poverty-stricken but self-respecting old people, the sick, the depraved, the indolent, the feeble-minded, and the drunkards. But a worse institution than one which mixed such differing classes would be difficult to imagine. Similarly, outdoor relief, as distributed by local and county authorities, has also in the recent past drawn no distinction between the various forms of need.

The use of such a congregate relief pool has discouraged the needy aged from applying for admission to the poorhouse or for outdoor relief, because of the attendant personal humiliation. Old age pensions were originally advocated as a means of obtaining not only more adequate but more self-respecting forms of maintenance for the aged, so that they would receive allowances as a right and not as a charity. To abandon this principle and to return to a general distribution of undifferentiated relief seems to this group, and to the author himself, to be a return to the social dark ages, mitigated only by the fact that probably appreciably larger sums would be given than in the past.

If such practices are long-continued, the inevitable result will be to discredit the system in the eyes of the aged and lead to a reluctance on the part of many to apply for aid. Such prestige as the system enjoys at present in the minds of the aged is due more to the concept of pensions as a right than to the realities of the present situation.

This latter group, therefore, desires to give distinctly different treatment and status to the needy aged than to the general relief group, although there are naturally appreciable differences within it as to precisely how far we should go in this direction. (1) Virtually all of this group agree that social workers should not exercise control over the ways in which the aged spend these grants but that these sums should, on the contrary, be regarded as the property of the aged to do with as they wish. It is reassuring to note there is a growing tendency on the part of the leading officials administering old age assistance to recognize the desirability of this attitude and to restrict the activities of the social workers. But there is need for a still greater change. (2) There is also a growing desire to return to the original concept that the role of the state should be to supplement individual, and to some extent family, income in order to bring up the income of the aged person to a fixed amount. This would in itself do away with a great deal of the present investigating and case work. It would obviate the necessity of a case worker's deciding whether the maximum which an old person should receive should be $30, $25 or $15 a month. It would at once put the payments as between individuals on a more uniform basis, would decrease administrative costs, and would make the grants a legal right rather than an administrative gratuity. It would, in a sense, insure the old people against a grossly inadequate income and would constitute a real old age pension.

Evidences of this growing tendency can be seen in legislation recently passed in California, Colorado and Massachusetts. In California, the state grants are to build up the aged person's income to a total figure of $35 a month. In Colorado, as we have seen, the grants are to insure a total income of $45 a month. In Massachusetts, the state pensions are to be such that a single person will have an income of $30 a month, and an aged married couple a monthly income of $50. Suits have also been started in several states in behalf of aged persons to recover the difference between the amounts actually granted and the maximum sums stated in the legislation.

Another interesting development in this general direction is the central rating system adopted in Iowa by Byron J. Allen and Mrs. E. R. Meredith of the Old Age Assistance Commission. This deals objectively with four sets of factors in determining the total monthly grant to an aged person: (1) The income of the person in question. This is given a total importance of 77. (2) The condition of the individual, based on age and the degree of his ability. This is given a total importance of 15. (3) The condition of the community. This has a maximum total of 8 points. Then (4) the comparative ability of relatives to support the aged person, which is framed in terms of the income and dependents of these persons, is rated in terms of a maximum of minus 100.

Detailed information is gathered on each of these points by local investigators, who are under state control; and this is sent on prepared forms to the central office in Des Moines. Here the data for each person are gone over by a staff of specialists, each of whom gives a quantitative rating for the subject with which he deals, and these ratings are then combined into a final figure. The comparative ability of relatives to support, in terms of points, is subtracted from the sum of the other three criteria. If a person is given the maximum rating for need, he has a rating of 100 positive points, each of which entitles him to receive a monthly pension of twenty-five cents.[1] This gives him the maximum pension permissible under the state law of $25 per month. If his rating is less than this, his pension is proportionately scaled down. In this fashion, Iowa has been able to obviate discrepancies in grants due to differences in the judgments of case workers and to lessen the pressure upon a worker to discriminate between recipients. It has been able to obtain greater uniformity and to reduce the intrusions into the privacy of the recipients by case workers and has kept administrative costs to

---

[1] For a description of this method, see Knowles and Traugh, *Revision of Rating Scale in Use by the Old Age Assistance Commission* (1937), Iowa Old Age Assistance Commission, Des Moines, Iowa.

the very low ratio of about 5 per cent.[1] This gives every evidence of being a truly remarkable record and of deserving praise instead of the opposition which, unfortunately, it has aroused in certain quarters.

(3) A further way in which an effort is being made to differentiate "pensions" from "relief" is by separating the staffs which administer each. This calls, wherever possible, for separate offices at which applications are made and for a separate staff of investigators. Such a separation might be carried out within the framework of a state department of public welfare which would have jurisdiction over both relief and pensions, and this might also be done in most cities or counties of 100,000 population and over. In the smaller towns and counties, administrative economies would, however, probably be realized by having one staff handle the different types of cases. Unfortunately it is in these very regions where the psychological difference between "pensions" and "relief" is felt most keenly. But there are many who feel that if a state or local department of welfare is given general supervision over old age pensions, the predominance of "relief work" and of the case work concept will inevitably result in dragging down the old age pensions to the status of relief. This group, therefore, feels that in

[1] For the year 1934–1935, administrative costs were 6.7 per cent (*First Annual Report*, Old Age Assistance Commission, p. 29). For 1935–1936, the state and local administrative costs were only 4.03 per cent (*Second Annual Report*, p. 30).

order to protect the integrity of the pension ideal, it is necessary to have administrative autonomy all the way up the scale.

(4) Finally, as has been implicit in all of the preceding discussion, the advocates of a return to the "pension" idea would confine the amount of "social work" to be administered to the aged pensioners within somewhat restricted limits. The size of the grant and control over how it is to be spent would be taken from the social workers, and there would be left merely the investigation of the facts, together with such advice and aid concerning medical and hospital care as would either be solicited or could be offered incidentally. As long as the requirement that near relatives should contribute according to their ability is, however, retained, local investigations on this point will be necessary.

3. *Old Age Insurance*

The controversy over whether or not the reserve contemplated by the act will be excessive has, unfortunately, obscured the remarkable administrative achievements of the past year. Virtually everyone feared that the task of keeping central records for the millions of registrants would inevitably result in almost hopeless confusion and delay. It is a pleasure to record that this gigantic task has been handled with striking efficiency. The names of every one of the some 40,000,000 registrants have been indexed in such a fashion that they may be found in approximately three minutes, and individual earnings sheets have been prepared for each to which the earnings of the preceding quarter are being punctually posted. The work has been routinized with such skill that it is probably safe to say the expected difficulties have now been conquered. Too much credit cannot be given to the very efficient civil servants who have directed the work and to the International Business Machines Company, which has furnished and in some cases designed the amazingly efficient and automatic machines which are being used.[1]

With the administrative difficulties so efficiently handled and with the Clark amendment no longer being pushed, the most important ultimate issues are then, (*a*) the proper size and management of the reserve, (*b*) the coordination of the old age insurance and the old age assistance sections of the act. A less important but perhaps more immediately pressing question is (*c*) to what degree the coverage of the act should be extended and whether or not payments of annuities should be begun prior to the stipulated date of 1942.

Whether or not the reserve which will be created by the act is excessive is a question which has aroused wide discussion. In the first place, it is important to realize that the original estimate of an ultimate reserve of around forty-seven billion dollars was based on a large number of assumptions

---

[1] For a description of the methods used, see Fay and Wasserman, "Accounting Operations of the Bureau of Old Age Insurance," *Social Security Bulletin* (May, 1938).

and is in itself subject to a considerable margin of error. Secondly, the experience of the last year has shown that there will undoubtedly be many millions of workers who will be employed in the covered occupations for only relatively short periods of time,[1] but who under the present terms of the act will be entitled to receive large unearned annuities. The payments to these "drifters" will, therefore, appreciably reduce the maximum reserves which otherwise would be accumulated. Even with these qualifications, however, it is probable that the ultimate reserve will, under the present plan, still reach a very large figure.

The arguments advanced in support of such a reserve are approximately as follows: (1) Private insurance companies find it necessary to accumulate such reserves for their annuity business. It is only proper, therefore, that the government should follow their example. This defense is seldom explicitly stated, but there is little doubt that it was in the minds of many when the Morgenthau amendments were suggested and approved. This analogy is, however, a mistaken one. Private companies have to accumulate such reserves because—being voluntary institutions—they are not certain that they will be able to sell a sufficient volume of policies in the future to give them enough current revenue to meet the claims on past policies which will then mature. The national system is, however,

---

[1] And who will be in the excluded occupations, among the self-employed, or housewives, during the vast majority of their working years.

compulsory, and the government is certain to collect taxes, under Title VIII, from those who will be employed in the future. It can increase these taxes, if necessary, to meet the then current costs, and it can raise taxes from other sources. There is not, therefore, the same necessity for a reserve under the compulsory public system as there is under a private voluntary plan. Other things being equal, there would seem, however, to be a strong case for a contingency reserve with which to meet claims during depression periods. For, at such times, the current contributions will fall off because of unemployment and reduced earnings.[1]

(2) The second argument in favor of a reserve is stronger. It is that the reserve is necessary to reduce the taxes which would otherwise have to be paid in the future. As time goes on, the cost of the old age annuities will form an increasing proportion of the wages and salaries bill of the nation. This is both because the number of annuitants will increase as more persons move into the pensionable ages, and because the newer annuitants will, on the average, be receiving higher benefits than the former, since they will have been employed for successively longer periods of time. It is, therefore, estimated that if a strict pay-as-you-go policy is followed, a tax of 10 per cent will ultimately be required to pay the ultimate current benefits. It is feared that this would be an excessive burden,

---

[1] A reserve might also be designed to guard against a declining population, and a large increase in the proportion of aged persons of pensionable age.

particularly in view of the need for other forms of social insurance and assistance. The accumulation of a reserve compounded at 3 per cent is defended on the ground that it would yield a revenue equal to about 40 per cent of the final cost and hence permit the maximum tax rate under Title VIII to be kept at 6 per cent.[1] It is undeniable that this is what the reserve does. It confines the financing of the plan to payroll taxes which are distributed relatively evenly over a period of time. Whether it is wise to follow this policy or to have governmental contributions which will be financed otherwise is, of course, another issue. The importance of this issue is, however certainly obscured by the argument that higher payroll taxes during the next few decades will accumulate a reserve which, in turn, will reduce the payroll taxes which otherwise would have to be paid later.

Let us examine more closely the argument that the interest earned on the reserve will reduce the taxes that would otherwise have to be paid and ask where the interest is itself derived. Immediately, of course, the interest will in all probability be obtained from taxes.[2] Hence, on first thought, it would not seem necessary for the government to go through the solemn motions of accumulating a reserve in order that it might pay revenue to itself.

[1] See the able articles by A. W. Willcox, "The Old Age Reserve Account," *Quarterly Journal of Economics*, May, 1937 (Vol. 51), pp. 444–68; and E. E. Witte, "In Defense of the Federal Old Age Benefit Plan," read before the American Statistical Association, December 29, 1936.

[2] Except in a special case which I shall consider a little later.

For why might it not use the added taxes to pay old age benefits directly without resorting to the fiction of the old age fund?

This contention is powerful, but it does not fully meet the issue. If the accumulated reserves are used to buy up the national debt which is in the hands of private holders, and if these private holders then invest these sums in productive enterprise without decreasing the other investments which they would ordinarily make, then the national stock of capital goods is in fact increased. Since such capital instruments increase production, the total national income is also increased, and there is a correspondingly greater ability to pay taxes. The interest payments on the bonds held in the old age reserve may, therefore, be derived either directly or indirectly from this increased future income. There would be the same result if the government, instead of using the old age funds to retire the privately held public debt, should use them to construct publicly owned capital goods or to carry out services which would also increase the real income of the people. In both of these cases, therefore, the accumulation of a reserve invested in government bonds would have real economic meaning, since it would be drawn from an increase in national real income.

If, however, the private holders of bonds wasted in riotous living the money paid to them by the government, the community would be in no better position to pay taxes because of the mere piling up

[389]

of paper credits in the reserve. The higher cost of benefits to the aged would have to be met out of the same national income, and government aid could be given directly, instead of being disguised as a payment of interest. Or, what is more likely, if the government should itself waste the money on magnificent-appearing public works which neither (*a*) yielded a net revenue over operating costs nor (*b*) built up the productive power of the people themselves, the interest charges would have to be met out of a national income which would not have been increased by one iota through the creation of the government I.O.U.'s credited to the old age account.

The issue then partially turns on what may be expected to happen to the funds which will accumulate during the early years from payroll taxes. If these are invested either directly or indirectly in productive enterprises, then there is on this score at least a strong justification for such a reserve. If there is a stronger possibility, however, that they will be wasted on nonproductive purposes, this argument falls to the ground. What will have happened in such a case is that the standard of life of the workers and consumers will have been reduced during the intervening period by the amount of the reserve, without any greater ability being created to meet the heavier costs in the future. It must be confessed that unless careful safeguards are thrown around the actual use of the funds, there is great danger that precisely this may happen if the present plan is continued.

It is also important to consider the effect of this reserve upon business depressions. The annual excess of tax collections over benefit payments will, for a long period of time, be very large. For the year 1937, it was approximately 500 million dollars; while for 1940, it is estimated at around 750 millions. By 1943, this yearly excess will be nearly a billion dollars.

The accumulation of these balances is likely to exert a distinctly deflationary influence in periods of recession and depression. If the federal budget for other items is, for example, balanced, then the accumulation of such surpluses from tax collections reduces the effective demand and the consumption of the workers and general public by a corresponding amount. At the same time, the public debt in the hands of banks and private investors is retired. But the private investors, in a period of recession, reinvest or spend only a very small fraction of the amounts paid to them. They, instead, tend to leave the major portion idle in the banks, since at such times banks are afraid to lend, and businesses are afraid to borrow. The demand for consumers goods would therefore, be decreased, while there would be no corresponding increase in the demand for capital goods. The result would inevitably be to lower prices by reducing the volume of active purchasing power, to reduce production and to increase unemployment.

[391]

Let us assume, however, that the government budget is not balanced and that the old age funds are spent for other governmental purposes. The relative effect here turns on the question as to whether or not these other governmental expenditures would have been made irrespective of the old age funds. If they would, then these surplus taxes for the old age reserve would still exert a net deflationary influence, since they would reduce the steadying effect upon demand of the government's spending policy. If the government, however, increased its expenditures by the amount of the excess, then the decrease in the original demand for consumers goods on the part of the workers and the general public would be offset by the expenditure of these funds in other lines. Any possible deflationary effect would, therefore, be canceled. The moral would seem to be clear, namely, that the government should increase its expenditures during recessions and depressions to prevent this deflationary influence from making itself felt.[1] This might take the form of either: (1) increasing the scale of immediate benefits under the old age insurance act itself while decreasing the ultimate benefits or (2) using the funds for socially necessary and income-producing purposes, such as public housing. To make the latter program effective, however, the unit costs of building would have to

[1] For a more detailed statement of this point of view, see Douglas, *Controlling Depressions*, pp. 123–142; and a statement by the author before the Committee on Unemployment and Relief of the United States Senate, March 4, 1938.

be reduced through a lowering of the prices of materials, of contractors' charges and of the hourly wage rates of skilled labor as well.

Whether or not the old age funds are exercising a deflationary influence during the present recession depends, therefore, upon the question as to whether or not the administration has kept its expenditures at a correspondingly higher figure than it would have done had there been no excess collection of taxes under the old age provisions. I have seen no evidence to indicate this has been the case. I am forced to the conclusion, therefore, that the old age reserve has had an adverse effect upon business conditions during the last year. It would seem obvious that proper standards should be worked out for the management of such tax collections during depression periods so as to minimize these unfavorable effects.[1]

Another evident problem which is developing is that of the smaller payments under the old age insurance system than under the state old age assistance laws. The average payment per individual under old age assistance is, as we have seen, somewhere between $19 and $20 a month. For an aged couple, both of whom can qualify for aid, the average grant is between $33 and $34 a month.

---

[1] It follows from this that most of the criticism of the policy of the administration for using social security funds to meet current relief and other needs is ill-founded. Deprived of these funds, which would be accumulated in an idle reserve, the administration would have either to (1) reduce expenditures and hence deepen the depression or (2) tax or borrow additional sums. To tax more would reduce the purchasing power of those taxed.

Since these are averages, the amounts granted in many states are, naturally, greater. Now, the average monthly annuity for the country as a whole under old age insurance in 1942 will be from $17 to $18. This will be not only less than the average pension is now but probably still less than it will be then. In a great many states, the difference will be marked. The fact that an aged spouse can receive old age assistance but will not be entitled to benefits unless previously employed in insured employments will add to the disparity.

The fact that these workers who will have contributed toward the insurance system will in so many cases actually receive less than those outside the insurance system who will have paid in nothing directly will naturally arouse a great deal of discontent on the part of those receiving annuities. For in addition to contributing toward his own smaller benefit, as a taxpayer he may well have to contribute toward the larger amounts received by those under the old age assistance system.[1] If he is in need, as from 20 to 25 per cent of the old people seem to be, then in order to get the same amount as his neighbor under old age assistance, he will have to undergo a means test. He is then likely to inquire why he should have been compelled to pay added taxes on his wages or salary in order that in the end he may be in precisely the same position as his neighbors who were not compelled to do so.

[1] To the degree to which old age pensions are financed by sales taxes or taxes on such tangible property as the annuitant may own.

To meet this difficulty, some propose that the amounts paid to those who retire during the earlier years should be increased to an average of perhaps $25 a month, with the addition of a further benefit to the spouse.[1] An even wiser proposal is to increase the basic grants to the insured workers only slightly but to add further sums in behalf of wives and possibly widows. These are interesting suggestions. If such benefits were merely added to the existing scale, they might constitute such a great addition to the total costs as to make it impossible to extend social insurance to any further purpose such as health and hospital care. If they were adopted, it would, therefore, probably be necessary to reduce the maximum annuities payable in the more distant future from $85 a month to somewhere around $60. This would mean that the benefits would be determined much more according to standards of adequacy than according to the amounts specific individuals had earned or contributed under the insurance system. It would greatly increase the total paid out in so-called unearned annuities.

If any such plan were adopted, there would seem to be three further changes which would inevitably follow from it. (1) The insurance system should be extended to include not only those employed in the excluded industries but all of the self-employed as well. This universal coverage would reduce the amount of unearned annuities paid to those who

[1] Provided that the latter were not in receipt of an ordinary annuity.

are employed within the included occupations for short periods during their working lives, but who are engaged for most of their time in the groups which are at present not included in the system. If, as now seems probable, nearly everyone will come into the system so far as benefits are concerned, should they not also come into the system so as to pay contributions throughout their lifetimes? (2) The size of the reserve would be greatly reduced because of the larger payments which would be made during the earlier years. (3) Governmental contributions would be both necessary and desirable, since the costs to the government under old age assistance would be enormously reduced, and because the burden of the "unearned" annuities should not be allowed to rest on the insured alone.

The general outlines of such a plan would seem to be preferable to the present dual system with its manifest inadequacies and anomalies. The main difficulty with it is undoubtedly the fact that it would reduce the difference between the amounts which the long service and higher paid workers would receive, as compared with those who had been employed for short periods of time for low wages. It would also probably compel those with incomes under $3,000 a year to pay by far the major portion of the cost of protecting all the aged.

A variant of this plan, modeled upon the present Swedish system, might serve all the good purposes of such a method and at the same time remove some of its defects. Such an alternative plan would call first of all for the universal coverage of all gainfully employed persons. Those who were self-employed could pay their contributions in the form of a tax on their incomes.[1] Since they at least would have no employer, it is probable that in order to obtain uniformity, the present joint tax upon the employers and employees would have to be transformed into a tax resting solely upon the insured person. Such a change would, however, be more nominal than real, since the workers are already bearing the cost of most of the tax advanced by the employers. This tax should not, however, exceed 3 or 3½ per cent. Then, out of the sums thus paid by the employed and self-employed,[2] annuities could be granted on the three following bases: (1) A small flat sum irrespective of past earnings. This might be $10 a month, or $120 a year. (2) An annual sum at the age of sixty, which would be based directly on the total previous contributions paid by the claimant. This might be one-tenth or one-twelfth of the total amount. (3) Then, for those whose total incomes did not come up to certain minima (which would vary from section to section and from cities to the smaller towns), there would be a government grant to bring the total income up to these points. These

---

[1] The information about the earnings of the employed and the collection of their taxes could be obtained, as now, from the employers. It is possible that a stamp system could also be used for agricultural workers and domestics.

[2] The wives could be protected through the payments of their husbands.

grants would be largely, although not exclusively, financed by the national government and would be made according to objective standards of need, which would be nationally defined, even if locally administered.

Such a plan would establish horizontally tiered methods of protection for the entire population in place of the present vertical cleavage which is caused by our dual system. It would establish a rough proportionality between individual contributions and receipts, and it would permit the income groups above $3,000 a year to contribute toward the support of those whose private incomes did not come up to the fixed minimum. But such added sums would not be granted to all, as is virtually proposed under the former plan, but only to those who were in definite need.

4. *Unemployment Compensation*

Although there were only fifteen states on November 1, 1936, which had unemployment insurance laws, by July 1, 1937, or eight months afterward, every state and all of the territories had such legislation.[1] This movement came in two waves. No less than twenty-one states passed laws between November 20 and the end of 1936, since they believed they would not get their offsets for

[1] For convenient summaries of the existing legislation, see two valuable publications of the Social Security Board, namely: (1) *A Comparison of State Unemployment Compensation Laws as of October* 1, 1937, 65 pp. mimeographed; and (2) *An Analysis of State Unemployment Compensation Laws,* December 1, 1937, 33 pp.

1936 unless they put such legislation on the books before the end of the year.[1] Then, during the legislative sessions of 1937, the remaining states fell into line. Illinois and Missouri were the last states to act. In virtually all of these cases, the legislators worked either with model drafts prepared by the Social Security Board or with bills in the drafting of which the board had participated. This was an interesting example of "cooperative" action between the states and the federal government, and it largely accounts for the comparative uniformity between the state acts which were passed within any given period of time.

In general, the new legislation established the state-pooled fund as the predominant type. Nebraska, it is true, copied Wisconsin in setting up what was virtually a straight employers' reserve system; and Kentucky, South Dakota and Oregon passed laws on the Indiana model with one-sixth of the funds pooled and five-sixths kept in separate reserves. The Vermont law permits an employer to choose whether he wishes to come under the state pool or to set up his individual reserve. But aside from these seven laws, the remaining forty-four provide for the pooling of contributions into a state fund.

This development was not accomplished without a hard struggle, since large sections of the more

[1] These twenty-one states were Arizona, Colorado, Connecticut, Iowa, Kentucky, Maine, Maryland, Michigan, Minnesota, New Jersey, New Mexico, North Carolina, Ohio, Oklahoma, Pennsylvania, South Dakota, Tennessee, Texas, Vermont, Virginia and West Virginia.

conservative employers groups were insistent in demanding the individual reserve system and drew heavily upon the advocates of the Wisconsin plan for support.[1] The contest in Missouri and Illinois was especially close. Only the work of organized labor, the League of Women Voters, the Association for Social Security and certain well-informed legislators turned the tide in these states in favor of the pooled fund.

Of the forty-four laws providing for a pooled fund, thirty-three provide for merit rating[2] of one form or another; while eleven,[3] or the remainder, do not provide for this.

These new laws distinctly moved away from requiring the employees to make direct contributions. Whereas eight of the first fifteen state acts had such a provision, this was true of only two of the last thirty-six (i.e., Kentucky and New Jersey). In addition, Idaho and Indiana repealed their

[1] Thus, in Missouri, the director of the Wisconsin Unemployment Compensation Bureau addressed the joint committee of the legislature under the auspices of the Associated Industries in behalf of the bill sponsored by that group.

[2] There are twenty-seven states with automatic merit rating, i.e., Arizona, Arkansas, California, Colorado, Connecticut, Delaware, Florida, Idaho, Illinois, Iowa, Kansas, Louisiana, Michigan, Minnesota, Missouri, New Hampshire, New Jersey, New Mexico, North Dakota, Ohio, Oklahoma, South Carolina, Tennessee, Texas, Utah, West Virginia and Wyoming. Then there are six more with merit rating to be determined by the administrative agency, i.e., Alabama, Alaska, District of Columbia, Montana, Nevada and Washington. Most of the pooled funds with merit rating provide some safeguards which limit the reductions that individual employers can obtain if the reserve as a whole falls below a given ratio to past benefits, etc.

[3] The states without merit rating are Georgia, Hawaii, Maine, Maryland, Massachusetts, Mississippi, New York, North Carolina, Pennsylvania, Rhode Island and Virginia.

previous requirements for workers' contributions; although, in the case of the former state, this amendment was later invalidated by the state supreme court. This tendency away from workers' contributions was caused by several forces: (1) There was a recognition that the employers' contributions were, in the last analysis, largely borne by the workers through a shifting of the incidence backward in the form of lower wages and forward in the form of higher prices. (2) It was felt that the administrative difficulties involved in collecting such contributions outweighed the advantages that might be obtained from them. (3) The campaign on the part of the Republican party and some big employers during the campaign of 1936 to turn the workers against their contributions toward old age insurance rebounded into the field of unemployment insurance. Many were afraid to increase the direct burdens borne by the workers; while others felt that since so many employers had said they were opposed to workers' contributions for old age insurance, it was but poetic justice to free the latter from contributing toward unemployment insurance.

Another evident tendency in the state laws is to widen the coverage by lowering the minimum size of the firms included. While thirty-one laws cover only firms with eight or more employees, one state (Connecticut) includes concerns with five or more employees; six states,[1] those with four or more;

[1] I.e., Kentucky, New Mexico, New Hampshire, New York, Oregon and Rhode Island.

two states,[1] with two or more; and no less than ten states,[2] all concerns in the covered occupations which have even one employed worker.

Another change in the laws which began about the middle of December, 1936, and which was undoubtedly initiated by the security board, was the movement away from the "time" to the "wage" method of computing the amount, duration and qualifications for benefits. Formerly, the laws had (1) required a given number of weeks of prior employment to qualify for benefits; and (2) fixed the amount of the benefits at approximately 50 per cent of full-time wages, subject to minimum and maximum amounts; and (3) established the duration of benefits in terms of weeks. It was felt by the board that such a plan involved practical difficulties in determining the full-time weekly wages of the worker. The principle of "wage loss" was, therefore, substituted with the belief that it would do away with the necessity for a monthly and even possibly a weekly report by employers on the earnings and employment of individuals[3] and would merely require quarterly reporting. Under the new plan, the quarter becomes the accounting unit, and the amount of the weekly benefit is fixed within a given minimum and

[1] I.e., Arizona and Ohio.

[2] Arkansas, Delaware, District of Columbia, Hawaii, Idaho, Minnesota, Montana, Nevada, Pennsylvania and Wyoming.

[3] Personally, I have always believed that a statement of a worker's full-time weekly earnings made every year, or at the most every quarter, would be sufficient.

maximum at one-twenty-sixth of the total amounts actually earned during that quarter, out of the first eight during the preceding nine quarters in which the earnings of the worker were the highest. This amounts to (*a*) taking as the full-time weekly wage one-thirteenth of the best quarterly record of earnings which the worker made during the two years preceding the last completed calendar quarter and (*b*) making the weekly benefit one-half of this sum. Thus, if a worker became unemployed on April 2, 1939, for example, the highest earnings during the eight quarters from January 1, 1937, to December 31, 1938, would be taken as the quarter from which the computations were to be made. If the earnings in this quarter were $260, then the full-time weekly wage would be taken as one-thirteenth of this, or $20; while the weekly benefit would, in turn, be one-half of this, or $10. The worker is then credited with one-sixth of the amounts that he has earned during each of the quarters in this base period as the maximum amount that he can receive. In the quarter thus described, this would be $43.33 (i.e., $260 ÷ 6). If his earnings in a given quarter are in excess of $390, however, no more than $65 (or one-sixth of $390) will be credited to his account. This account is accumulated throughout the base period of the first eight out of the preceding nine calendar quarters, and against it are charged the total unemployment benefits paid out to the worker. The benefits in any year may not under any circumstances exceed the total credited to him, nor may they exceed a given number of times (generally fifteen) his weekly benefits. Thus, in the case stated, where the weekly benefit was to be $10, if the total past credits did not exceed $100, then the maximum period in the benefit year for which benefits would be paid would be ten weeks (i.e., $100 ÷ 10). If, however, the total past credits amounted to $200, the amounts paid out would only be fifteen times the weekly benefit, or $150. In other words, whichever is the smaller of these two sums is taken as the total that can be paid in a given benefit year.[1]

Such a plan obviously reduces the amounts that irregularly employed workers whose past earnings have been low can receive. To help compensate for this, the requirement for prior employment as a condition of eligibility is, however, also reduced; so that all that is necessary is for the worker to have earned during the first four out of the preceding five calendar quarters at least fifteen or sixteen times his weekly benefit. This would be approximately seven and a half to eight weeks of employment, instead of the requirement of thirteen to twenty-six weeks or so which characterized the laws passed prior to December, 1936.

It will be noticed from the preceding description that the last completed calendar quarter is not

---

[1] The benefit year, in turn, is a period of fifty-two weeks immediately following the period when benefits are first payable to an individual and the successive years that follow.

used in determining the worker's benefit rate or his eligibility or the duration of benefits. It is instead a "slide" quarter, during which the earnings for the previous quarter are entered on the worker's record sheet and his credits posted. This plan, by integrating the basis for computing benefits with the reports of individual earnings, was advocated on the ground that it would make the administration somewhat less complicated than it otherwise would be and would also introduce a greater degree of correspondence between a worker's past earnings and employment and his total benefits. For otherwise a worker could, as in Great Britain, be employed on only one day during each of the qualifying number of weeks, and yet draw the standard number of weeks of benefit.

Virtually all of the states provide benefits for part-time unemployment. These generally do not begin until the earnings on the job have fallen to a total that is either only $2 a week, or one-fifth, more than his weekly benefit amount. There will inevitably be a great deal of difficulty in administering these provisions. As we shall point out, employers in states with the employer reserve plan will tend to resort to part time in order to reduce the charges against their separate reserves. There will be much the same tendency under the merit rating system applied within pooled funds.[1] This tendency

---

[1] This will result in a smaller total disbursement of monetary purchasing power to the workers and, in the case of the reserve system, in a greater accumulation of idle reserves than would be the case were the available

will not, however, be present where there is a straight pooled fund without merit rating.

As we have stated, Wisconsin was the first state, up to 1938, that had paid benefits. Its system of benefits began in July, 1936, and it therefore had a year and a half of benefit experience before the other states started their payments. During the first year, the Wisconsin system, however, paid out only $964,000 in benefits,[1] although its credit in the federal unemployment trust fund was approximately $23,000,000 by the end of the fiscal year. There were several reasons why these payments were relatively low: (1) The year 1936–1937 was a year of rising prosperity and employment, during which the proportion of claims would naturally be low. (2) The Wisconsin law was so framed as to prevent the workers from acquiring any claims to benefits during the two preceding years during which contributions from the employers were collected. The workers, in other words, began to accumulate credit for benefit payments only *after* July, 1936, and this naturally reduced the amounts payable to them. (3) Under the Wisconsin law, the liability of any one employer for benefits is limited to one week for every four to six weeks of employment, and this liability is assumed in the inverse order of employment.[2] But

work concentrated upon fewer men and the remainder paid unemployment benefits.

[1] Matschek and Atkinson, *Unemployment Compensation Benefits in Wisconsin 1936–1937*, p. 64.

[2] *Wisconsin Statutes*, 1935–1936, Chapter 108.06 (1).

no employer is liable for any unemployment that occurs more than twenty-six weeks after a worker has terminated his employment with him.[1] Thus, if a worker were employed by A from July 1 to December 31 and, after working for B for the next half year, became unemployed on July 1 of the next year, he would have a claim upon B of four and one-half to six and one-half weeks of benefit, depending upon the size of the weekly benefit rate. But even though he continued to be unemployed, he would have no claim upon A. This would naturally result in a curtailment of benefits, and it is precisely this which has happened in Wisconsin. (4) The benefits for partial unemployment in Wisconsin do not begin until the worker's earnings are less than the weekly benefit. This benefit is only approximately 50 per cent of earnings. This means that an employer can avoid liability under the individual reserve system of Wisconsin by working his men part time instead of laying some of them off. He will have no liability at all as long as he gives them more than half time; and even when he gives them less, he is liable only for the difference between their actual earnings and half of their full-time wages. In this way, by "sharing the work," or "sharing the poverty," he can protect his funds and prevent the workers from receiving benefits. There is evidence that this method is being quite widely used in Wisconsin and that it is at least partially responsible for the low total

[1] *Ibid.*, Chapter 108.06 (3).

volume of payments. It is probably not too harsh a statement to say that Wisconsin was able to cut down benefits and accumulate large reserves by severe and drastic restrictions upon the degree of protection which the system afforded to the unemployed.

In spite of all this, there were seventeen funds which were individually insolvent at the end of the year 1936–1937.[1] The unemployed received full benefits in these cases only because of the change in the law which pooled the interest earnings of the funds and used them to pay benefits to claimants of funds that were exhausted. It is obvious, however, that these pooled sums are not sufficient to meet a strain of any large dimensions.

The total expenses of the Wisconsin Unemployment Compensation Department for the year (exclusive of the expenses of the employment service) were $455,000 or $418,000 after deducting the cost of equipment.[2] This latter figure amounted to slightly over 43 per cent of all benefits paid out. This, of course, is an extraordinarily high ratio of administrative expense. It is defended by the advocates of the Wisconsin system on the ground that benefits were limited in the first year because the workers had no previously accumulated rights and that as the benefits increase—as they will in subsequent years—this expense ratio will markedly

---

[1] Approximately eighty funds are now (May, 1938) insolvent.
[2] Matschek and Atkinson, *Unemployment Compensation Benefits in Wisconsin*, p. 70.

fall. There is solid merit to this defense, but it will be interesting to see by how much the percentage of administrative costs will be reduced.

An administrative problem which quickly developed and which was briefly commented upon in the preceding chapter was that of a choice between: (*a*) the current reporting of individual earnings on a quarterly basis to the state authorities so that a worker's benefit rights can be determined in advance of unemployment; and (*b*) severance or separations reporting, in which the employers would make these reports only when a worker had his employment terminated. Wisconsin uses the separations method, which is based on the precedent of accident compensation; but the vast majority of the other states use the method of current earnings.

The supporters of the separations system advance the following arguments: (1) It is urged that it would reduce the work both of the employers and of the state agencies. Information would not be furnished on wage earners who continued to be employed but would be given only when a worker lost his job and later applied for benefits. It is alleged that the majority of workers are employed steadily, and this would free the employers from the task of making out periodical reports for them. It is also said that this would free the state unemployment insurance authority from posting earnings periodically to each worker's account and let it deal merely with the cases that present themselves for benefits. (2) Since the employers will have to make some report under the current reporting system when the worker is separated from his job, it is urged that duplication will be avoided by their making their entire report on past employment and earnings at that time. (3) The analogy with accident compensation is stressed. (4) The Wisconsin experience is stated to have been favorable.

Against this, the advocates of current reporting urge: (1) Current reporting would give full details about each worker's past employment and earnings. This information will be ready when the worker applies for benefits and will enable his weekly benefits to be quickly computed and paid. (2) If, on the other hand, separations reporting is depended upon, no information will be obtained until after the worker files his claim for benefit. It will then be necessary to find out who his previous employers were and to obtain from them his past record of employment and earnings. This will involve a great deal of labor, and past experience has shown that it is difficult to get this material from employers. Thus, in California, where separations reporting was given up at the request of the employers, the administrator has estimated that 67 per cent of the employers never filed the required separations reports.[1]

---

[1] J. L. Mathews, *The Birth of Unemployment Service in California*, p. 6. Delivered before the Association Executives Trade Conference, Los Angeles (no date).

Long delays would inevitably occur while the unemployed were waiting for benefits, and the whole system would be discredited.

(3) The precedent of accident compensation does not apply, since the volume of work is very much less in this case than it would be under unemployment compensation. (4) The separations method would impose a far greater burden upon employers with a higher turnover rate than would current reporting. It is much more work to make out a separate and detailed report on the past earnings and employment of each man than to enter his name and earnings on a composite form which is already being prepared, since in the former case it is necessary to hunt back through an accumulation of past payrolls, etc., to get the record of the separated worker. (5) The system of requiring current quarterly reports on the earnings of individual employees will compel the employer to audit automatically the monthly reports on total payroll and the contributions that he makes on this basis. It will also furnish the state with an automatic check and largely eliminate the need for costly field audits.

On the whole, the case for current reporting seems to be much stronger, and it is reassuring that the vast majority of states have adopted it. It will save distinct expense, however, if the current earnings are posted by machine instead of by hand, as is practiced in some states. For the former method can be handled by less than one-fourth the number of employees that the latter requires. From estimates prepared by Dr. Peter Swanish, the Illinois administrator, it appears that one clerk operating a Hollerith machine can post earnings records for some 30,000 workers per quarter.

One of the great administrative needs is, however, to consolidate, simplify, and reduce the number of reports that employers have, under the security act, to make to national and state authorities. Thus, at present an employer must: (1) file with the Treasury Department a total earnings report for old age insurance for all wages and salaries, except amounts over $3,000, and accompany this with the taxes paid by him and his employees; (2) file quarterly with the Social Security Board a full list of his employees subject to old age insurance, with their account numbers and earnings during the given quarter; (3) file with the Treasury Department statements on the total earnings of employees who are subject to the unemployment insurance sections of the act and accompany this with the necessary tax payments; (4) file similar statements with the state authorities administering unemployment insurance and accompany this with the payment of the necessary state taxes; (5) file quarterly with the state authorities the individual earnings and account numbers of their employees.

It is obvious that this is an excessive load upon the employers. It can be greatly reduced by consolidating state and federal reporting and so integrating the scope of the unemployment insurance and old age insurance sections as to make one set of reports largely serve all purposes. One step would be to make the coverage of the two major insurance systems identical. This would involve: (1) Bringing into the unemployment insurance system all firms within the included occupations employing one or more workers, which it will be remembered is the coverage of the old age insurance sections. (2) Either taxing those portions of the wages and salaries over $3,000 a year for old age insurance (Title VIII) or exempting these sums from taxation under Title IX. In other words, the scope of the incomes covered should, if possible, be identical. (3) Providing that those who continue to be employed after the age of sixty-five will still fall under Title VIII. (4) Making the clauses governing casual labor identical.

If this were done, it would then be possible for an employer to fill out one detailed report quarterly on his covered employees and their individual earnings. Two copies of this could be sent to the treasury for the purpose of entering the earnings of individuals to their account numbers and for the payment of taxes for both old age and unemployment insurance. A triplicate of the same report could then be sent to the state unemployment insurance authorities for the purpose of posting the individual's earnings to his record; and this might also serve as the basis for the state tax report.

Even if all of this program could not be carried out, a much greater coordination of reporting could be effected by the states accepting duplicates of the present basic form for old age insurance (i.e., SS 1) for earnings reports under unemployment insurance. It is encouraging that some progress is being made in this direction.

On January 1 of 1938, the eligible unemployed in twenty-two additional states were entitled to ask for benefits. These were Alabama, Arizona, California, Connecticut, District of Columbia, Louisiana, Maine, Maryland, Massachusetts, Minnesota, New Hampshire, New York, North Carolina, Oregon, Pennsylvania, Rhode Island, Tennessee, Texas, Utah, Vermont, Virginia and West Virginia. It is estimated that there were approximately 11,500,000 workers in these states, or about half of the total number covered in the country as a whole. During the first month, about 2,000,000 of the unemployed registered and claimed benefits. 565,000 of these were in New York, and 442,000 in Pennsylvania, and the total for Massachusetts was reported to be nearly 200,000. In February, the number of new claimants was well over half a million. While the work of paying benefits was handled satisfactorily and speedily in smaller states such as New Hampshire, Rhode Island and Connecticut, in the three large industrial states which have been mentioned the services were virtually swamped. In many cases, an insufficient staff had been assembled without proper training. Inadequate facilities were provided for registration; and in some cases, including New York, registration by mail was permitted. The claims for benefit frequently did not contain sufficient information; and it was also discovered that a considerable percentage of the covered employers had not, in fact, been reported to the state departments and that in these cases information about the earnings and employment of the unemployed workers, upon which benefits could be paid, therefore was not ready. The computation of benefits was also found to be an extremely complicated and time-consuming process. The result was widespread delay. By February 12, only a total of 618,000 benefit checks had been sent out. Only 9 per cent of these, or 57,600, came from New York, although that state had nearly 30 per cent of the claimants.

Another complication was the fact that a considerable percentage of the claimants did not follow up their applications. One cause of this may have been that many were already receiving more in relief or from the WPA than they could get in unemployment benefits. The average unemployment benefit for the country as a whole was $10.16. The average for New York was $11.71; and for Arizona, $12.72. In North Carolina, however, the average was only $5.92; while in Alabama, Tennessee and Virginia, the averages were respectively $6.79, $7.01 and $7.76. Taking the seven months

[415]

from January to July inclusive, an approximate total of $216,000,000 was paid out in benefits.

The whole experience shows the absolute necessity of simplifying the methods of computing benefits and of making more adequate arrangements for their payment. The number of employment offices, for example, certainly needs to be increased for purposes of registration, and a staff trained in advance to handle applications. Unless this is done by the eight states[1] which will begin payments during 1938, and by the remainder which will start in January or July of 1939, still further delays will be experienced which will seriously handicap and discredit the system.

There is a further necessity for simplifying the methods of computing and paying the benefit amounts. As the present author predicted,[2] it is very cumbersome to compute benefits to exactly 50 per cent of the standard wage or, as provided by some laws, to the nearest figure of twenty cents. For this requires checks of an almost infinite series of amounts and, in turn, necessitates that the checks shall be paid out from only one place. This swamps the central agency in a period of mass unemployment and leads to prolonged and widespread delays. It would be better to have only five or six categories of benefits, let us say, of $5 per week for those receiving less than $10 a week;

[1] I.e., Indiana, Mississippi, Iowa, Michigan, South Carolina, Idaho, New Mexico and Oklahoma.

[2] I.e., in *Standards of Unemployment Insurance* (1933) and the early editions of this book.

[416]

$7.50 for those between $10 and $15; $10 for those between $15 and $20; $12.50 for the group between $20 and $25; and $15 for those getting over $25 a week. At the very least, if a 50 per cent basis were retained, benefits might be paid only to the nearest dollar,[1] since this would reduce the number of different denominations of benefits to a total of eleven. By thus reducing the number of different-sized checks to more manageable proportions, payments could be speeded up. Checks of these different denominations could be printed, and all that would be needed would be to write in the name of the recipient. After the initial determination by the central state office of the benefit amount for an individual claimant, the local offices could then fill in the blanks for the separate checks subject to state audit. Or if this would unduly open the way to fraud, the central office could continue to make out the individual checks but ship them in bundles to the local offices for distribution.

In either event, it would no longer be necessary to pay the benefits by mail. For obviously this is conducive to fraud. A man could, for example, get hold of the account numbers of several insured workers and make application in their names.[2] Then, if he did not have to appear personally for the checks, it would not be difficult for him to

---

[1] This would, however, excite the opposition of those who on a strict 50 per cent basis would be entitled to more than the amount paid.

[2] Thus, in Illinois it was found in an establishment employing 2,500 workers that 196 of them had from two to five social security account numbers.

obtain them through the mails without serious risk of detection. As a matter of fact, it should not be so difficult to manage the work of having the unemployed sign the register during hours of employment at the employment offices and receive their benefits in person. This could be done by having one section sign the register on Mondays, Wednesdays and Fridays, and the other on Tuesdays, Thursdays and Saturdays. The benefit payments could then be made on the last of each of these sets of days. To reduce the waiting time to a minimum, groups of the unemployed in alphabetical order could, therefore, be given blocks of half an hour during which they would sign the register to signify they were unemployed and on the last day receive their benefits. Such an orderly routine, combined with the setting up and maintenance of an adequate number of employment offices, should prevent the unemployed from waiting too long to report and should greatly lessen the danger of fraud.

A few further comments may also be in order. As the various state laws begin to move into active operation, officials are beginning to realize how many interstate migrants are being excluded. This was pointed out by the author and others when the Social Security Act was under consideration, but those in charge of the legislation made no provision for it. In all probability, a pooled federal fund will be needed adequately to take care of these persons. An attempt is being made, however, to handle this problem by reciprocal agreements which have now been concluded by the unemployment insurance agencies of thirty-six states.

There is also the very clear prospect that as long as seasonal unemployment is treated on the same basis as other types, after the present balances are used up it will be very difficult for reserves of any magnitude to be accumulated for any appreciable future depression. For those in the building, mining, clothing and other seasonal trades will draw out enormous sums in benefits even in the more prosperous years, despite the fact that their daily wages when employed will already have largely compensated them for the off seasons. They will thus be paid twice for regularly recurring unemployment. Most of the states, with the exception of Michigan and Illinois, have, however, been very slow to face this issue; and unless a widespread awareness of the problem develops, there is every prospect that a large proportion of the funds will be dissipated in this manner. The remedy is probably to fix certain periods of the year for each of the highly seasonal industries, corresponding to their off seasons, during which benefits will not be paid. This will probably be easier to administer than to require a longer waiting period for these industries, since it will remove the necessity for the unemployed to report during these periods.

The drain upon the funds during the current year of 1938 promises to be heavy for those states which are starting benefit payments. This is both

TABLE XVII
BALANCE CREDITED TO ACCOUNTS OF VARIOUS STATES IN UNEMPLOYMENT
TRUST FUND AS OF JANUARY 31, 1938
(In thousands of dollars)

State	Amount credited	State	Amount credited

A. States Paying Benefits on or before January 1, 1938

State	Amount credited	State	Amount credited
Alabama	8,338	New York	96,603
Arizona	1,761	North Carolina	9,153
California	63,257	Oregon	5,464
Connecticut	15,031	Pennsylvania	60,435
District of Columbia	6,058	Rhode Island	7,892
Idaho	1,933	Tennessee	7,459
Kentucky	9,539	Texas	19,594
Louisiana	7,593	Utah	2,401
Maine	3,595	Virginia	8,445
Maryland	8,346	West Virginia	8,145
Massachusetts	39,137	Wisconsin	30,435
Minnesota	10,623		
New Hampshire	4,064	Total	435,301

B. States Where Benefits Will Begin after January, 1938, but within the Year

State	Amount credited	State	Amount credited
Idaho	1,933	New Mexico	1,265
Indiana	23,948	Oklahoma	6,668
Iowa	7,318	South Carolina	4,408
Michigan	45,156		
Mississippi	2,350	Total	90,696

C. States Where Benefits Will Begin during 1939

State	Amount credited	State	Amount credited
Alaska	238	Montana	1,608
Arkansas	1,925	Nebraska	2,184
Colorado	4,923	Nevada	590
Florida	3,008	New Jersey	31,417
Georgia	4,514	North Dakota	604
Hawaii	957	Ohio	55,282
Illinois	4,000	South Dakota	1,053
Kansas	3,724	Washington	6,238
Kentucky	9,539	Wyoming	905
Missouri	5,700		
Grand total = 664,406[1]		Total	138,409

[1] The total advanced from the central fund to the respective state funds in January of 1938 was approximately 34 millions of dollars. By the end of February, the total reserve in the account was 741 millions of dollars and by the end of May the net balance was 838 millions.

because of the current business "recession" and because of the seasonal drain which I have mentioned. To meet this, the twenty-four states had the following total reserves credited to their accounts on January 31, 1938. These are given in terms of thousands of dollars.

Since the only benefits which were paid out during 1937 were the relatively small sums disbursed in Wisconsin; it follows that the unemployment compensation taxes, for the reasons previously described, exercised a net deflationary influence in that year and with the taxes for old age insurance helped to intensify the depression of that year. During the first part of 1938, this same deflationary influence was continued since only 140 millions of dollars were paid out in benefits while 350 millions of dollars were collected in taxes with a consequent swelling of the total reserve.

It is possible, and in my opinion probable, that the funds in some of these states will be drawn to a low figure by the end of 1938 and that unless there is a marked improvement in the business situation, some of them may be exhausted during 1939. Thus Rhode Island in the first six months of the year paid out 65 per cent more than it took in from contributions and used up 55 per cent of all the monies collected during two and a half years. In West Virginia the payments during the same period were 72 per cent greater than the current receipts and actually absorbed 57 per cent of the total collections. In Maine and Utah the state balances were drawn down to nearly an equal extent by the end of June. We shall, therefore, in all probability, shortly face two problems which were discussed in the original edition of this volume, namely, what should be done: (1) In the case of those states which have exhausted their reserves, and which are compelled to curtail the standard benefits to which the unemployed supposed themselves to be entitled, but who are still out of work and in need. (2) In the case of those who have exhausted their claims for benefit but are still in need.

There will undoubtedly be a need in the first case for federal funds to "bail out" and reinforce the exhausted state funds. In the second, there will be a need for a second-line trench to back up the insurance system.

The experience thus far has, indeed, shown the necessity of at least coordinating the various forms of social security. Thus, when the payment of unemployment benefits began, some of those eligible were, as stated, on relief or employed with the W.P.A. In the latter case, the amounts which they received were commonly appreciably above those to which they were entitled under unemployment insurance. Those on relief who had large families were also frequently receiving more. In these cases, therefore, the unemployed were not anxious to be transferred to the unemployment benefit rolls. This was intensified by the fact that they would (1) be compelled to go through a waiting period of two to four weeks and then (2) find that after thirteen to sixteen weeks, their benefit period would be exhausted and they might then have distinct difficulty in getting back on relief or with the W.P.A.

That the coming of unemployment benefits did, nevertheless, somewhat reduce the relief load from what it would otherwise have been may be seen from the fact that during the first five months, there were 39,800 relief cases in Pennsylvania which were "closed" because of such transfers.[1]

The fact that no benefits at all are paid during the waiting period is forcing a certain percentage of the unemployed to ask for and receive relief during those weeks. These cases in Milwaukee seem to range between 4 and 8 per cent of those receiving unemployment benefit, although in Baltimore this ratio was less than 1 per cent. It is also evident that supplementary relief will have to be given to many of the families where the benefits are inadequate to maintain them. This was true of about 1 per cent of those in receipt of unemployment benefits in Baltimore, Milwaukee and New York City during March and April. In Buffalo, however, this ratio ran as high as 5 per cent.[2]

Moreover, once the unemployment benefits are exhausted, a large percentage are forced to fall

---

[1] Ewan Clague, "The Relationship between Unemployment Compensation and Relief from a National Point of View," *Social Security Bulletin* (May, 1938), p. 9.
[2] *Ibid.*, p. 11.

back on relief or W.P.A. Thus, in Pennsylvania alone, no less than 31,000 persons were put on relief for such a cause during the first five months of 1938, and this number was rapidly increasing at the end of this period. It is obvious, therefore, that we must coordinate relief payments and W.P.A. practice with unemployment benefits much more closely than is now the case.

The experience with unemployment benefits has also furnished a further illustration of the need for health insurance. For if unemployed workers who are receiving benefits are once taken ill, they thereby lose their claim to benefits since they are no longer "able to work." This is manifestly unjust; and while these cases cannot be handled under unemployment insurance, which can cover only those "able to work, willing to work but unable to find suitable employment," there is need for a supplementary system which will protect them.[1] The Conference on public health called by the government during the summer showed a striking degree of agreement on the part of many groups that some form of pooled protection against sickness is needed and it is probably not unsafe to forecast developments in this field in the not distant future.

Finally mention should be made of the passage by Congress in June, 1938, of the Railway Unemployment Compensation Act. This takes the

[1] See Peter T. Swanish, "Unemployment Compensation Summons Health Insurance," *Oral Hygiene* (April, 1938), pp. 455-460.

[424]

railway workers out of the forty-eight state acts and puts them in one National system under the Railway Retirement Board. The benefits granted to the railway men under this act are appreciably more liberal than those provided by the state acts and probably can be administered much more effectively upon a national basis. The employer's contribution is 3 per cent or the same as under Table IX of the Security Act. One-tenth of this is to be used for administrative purposes. Benefits do not begin until July 1, 1939 and up to that time the unemployed railway workers are to be taken care of by the various state systems. The new benefits provided for the higher paid workers are as generous as those which they would receive under the state systems while those granted the lower paid workers are appreciably more generous. This is shown by the following scale of benefits which are to be paid after a waiting period of one week and which as will be seen are based upon the total earnings during the previous base year.[1]

By using days of unemployment as the basis of benefits instead of weeks of total or partial unemployment, the payment of benefits for partial unemployment was eliminated and administration was correspondingly simplified. Further simplification was also introduced by the abandonment of

[1] See Public No. 722, 75th Congress, 3d Session (H.R. 10127). See also an article by W. J. Couper in the *Social Security Bulletin*, August, 1938, pp. 12–16.

merit rating. The author believes merit rating to
be of dubious value for industry as a whole and it
is certainly peculiarly inappropriate for the railways, which have little individual control over the
volume of their traffic and hence over the amount of
employment which they can offer.

Total compensa-tion during base year	Daily benefit rate	Semi-monthly benefit rate	Maximum benefits during benefit years
$ 150–$199.99	$1.75	$14.00	$140
200– 474.99	2.00	16.00	160
475– 749.99	2.25	18.00	180
750–1024.99	2.50	20.00	200
1025–1299.99	2.75	22.00	220
$1300 and over	3.00	24.00	240

5. *The Welfare Services*

The act has led to a very appreciable increase in
the aid given for dependent children. By the end
of 1937, there were thirty-eight states, together
with Hawaii and the District of Columbia, which
had plans approved by the Social Security Board.
These provided grants in behalf of children who
were in need through having lost a parent by
death, desertion, or physical or mental incapacity.[1]
In these states, approximately 218,500 families
were receiving such aid in January, 1938, and this
was being paid in behalf of 542,000 children.[2]

[1] For an analysis of the state laws on this subject, see *Characteristics of
State Plans for Aid to Dependent Children*, December 1, 1937 (Social Security
Board), 19 pp.

[2] *Social Security Bulletin*, March, 1938 (Social Security Board), p. 50.

By May the total number of children who were thus aided had risen to 595,000. In other states such as Illinois, whose plans had not been approved as yet by the Social Security Board, there were additional numbers[1] being aided under the state plans. The number of children who were aided by the federal grants had increased to the foregoing total from 226,000 in June, 1936, and 425,000 in June, 1937.

Since the total amount paid out for this purpose in January was $7,004,000, this meant the average monthly grant per family was $32.06, while the average per child was $12.92. The average number of children aided per family was almost precisely two and a half.[2]

As in the case of old age pensions, there are wide variations between the states both in the proportion aided and in the average size of the grants. So far as the proportions aided was concerned, the average number per 1,000 children under sixteen years in the country as a whole was nineteen. But this varied from four in North Dakota to forty in Maryland and Oklahoma, as is shown by Table XVIII.[3]

It will be noticed that seven of the eight states with the highest ratios of aid for children were also among the twelve states with the highest ratios for old age pensions.

---

[1] Possibly reaching to nearly 40,000.
[2] Or, to be exact, 2.49.
[3] *Public Assistance Statistics* for December, 1937, pp. 16–17.

TABLE XVIII

PROPORTION OF DEPENDENT CHILDREN AIDED IN JANUARY, 1938, TO TOTAL
NUMBER UNDER SIXTEEN YEARS OF AGE, BY STATES

State	Proportion of aided children per 1,000 under 16 years of age	State	Proportion of aided children per 1,000 under 16 years of age
Maryland	40	Arkansas	19
Oklahoma	40	New York	18
Idaho	35	Hawaii	18
Utah	34	Delaware	16
Washington	34	Minnesota	16
Louisiana	33	Ohio	16
Arizona	32	Alabama	15
Colorado	29	Pennsylvania	15
District of Columbia	29	Maine	14
Indiana	27	Kansas	13
Wisconsin	27	Rhode Island	13
New Mexico	26	North Carolina	10
Montana	25	Oregon	10
Nebraska	24	Georgia	8
West Virginia	24	New Hampshire	8
New Jersey	22	South Carolina	7
Wyoming	22	Vermont	7
Tennessee	21	North Dakota	4
California	20	Average for all states	19
Michigan	20		

So far as the sizes of the grants were concerned,
these varied on a family basis from $10.40 in
Arkansas to $61.16 in Massachusetts. Six states,
Alabama, Arkansas, North Carolina, Oklahoma,
Tennessee and Vermont, paid family grants that
ranged between $10 and $20 per month. Ten
states[1] gave grants that were between $20 and $30;

[1] I.e., Georgia, Idaho, Indiana, Kansas, Louisiana, New Jersey, New
Mexico, South Carolina, Washington and West Virginia.

and seventeen,[1] between $30 and $40. Two jurisdictions, namely, the District of Columbia and
New York, paid between $40 and $50 a month;
while one, Rhode Island, paid between $50 and $60.
One only, Massachusetts, paid more than $60.

A study in 1937 by the Security Board of some
163,000 children receiving such aid showed that
only about one-sixth were living with both parents;
2½ per cent were living with their fathers alone,
and about 6 per cent with relatives other than
parents. Approximately 74 per cent were living
with their mothers alone. Of the mothers in this
last group, six-tenths were widowed, and a quarter
were deserted, divorced, or separated. In about a
twelfth of these cases, the husbands were in hospitals or in penal or correctional institutions. Sum-
ming up all of the cases, it appears that in slightly
more than half the cases the aid was given because
of the death of a parent, in about a quarter of the
cases because of a continuing absence from home on
the part of the parent, and in approximately a fifth
because of the mental or physical incapacity of the
parent.[2]

It is apparent that the average grants for such
children are still insufficient, since the cost of
maintenance is very appreciably in excess of the
amounts paid. It would seem wise, therefore,
(a) to raise the maximum limits of $18 and $12 a
month, respectively, for which the federal govern-

[1] I.e., Arizona, California, Colorado, Delaware, Hawaii, Maine, Maryland,
Michigan, Minnesota, New Hampshire, North Dakota, Ohio, Oregon, Pennsylvania, Utah, Wisconsin and Wyoming.

[2] *Second Annual Report* of the Social Security Board.

ment will share the expense; and (*b*) to raise the share of the federal government from one-third to an average of one-half. It is also desirable to construct a flexible apportionment formula which will enable a larger share of federal aid to go to the poorer than to the richer states.

Aid to the blind was also being given in January, 1938, to 44,800 persons, with total monthly grants of $1,145,000. This meant a monthly average of $25.54. There were thirty-nine jurisdictions with approved systems at that time, with the usual wide variations between states. Thus, the average monthly grant ranged from $9.11 in Arkansas to $48.06 in California. The average number thus aided per 100,000 population was 45 for the country as a whole, but the Florida rate was only 8, and the Michigan rate 11, as compared with a rate of 109 in Pennsylvania and 130 in Maine. In addition, it is estimated that there were an appreciable number of blind persons who were being aided in states whose plans had not yet received federal approval.

It will be remembered that the Children's Bureau of the Department of Labor was made responsible for (1) maternal and child health services, (2) services for crippled children, and (3) child welfare services. All of the states have now approved plans for carrying out the first of these programs; all but one (Louisiana) are operating under approved plans for the second, and all but two (Arizona and Wyoming) for the third. During the fiscal year of 1936–1937, the federal grants to the states for maternal and child health which had to be matched amounted to $2,380,000, while $745,000 was also given in unmatched grants. A wide range of work was conducted with these moneys. Thus, physicians were assigned to 205 counties, and nearly 2,800 public health nurses were also employed. Over 2,900 maternal welfare centers were established, and prenatal nursing service was made available in 1,100 counties. In addition, $2,150,000 of federal funds were provided for crippled children, while special federal grants for child welfare totaled $1,200,000.

Progress has also been made in the field of public health. The Surgeon-General apportioned 30.7 per cent of the $8,000,000 of federal grants to the states according to the ratio of their population, and 38.6 per cent according to special health problems. The states were asked at least to match those sums with grants of their money, and at least one-half of these sums were required to be newly appropriated so that they would constitute net additions to the amounts raised by the states themselves. Finally, another 30.7 per cent was distributed among the states according to their relative financial need. These sums did not have to be matched by the states.

In the field of vocational rehabilitation, all of the jurisdictions except Delaware and Kansas had not only accepted the provisions of the federal act by July 1, 1937, but had their programs in effect. Some 43,000 persons were receiving rehabilitation training and service at that time.

The following note suggests only a few of the more obvious works. It does not touch on references to European social insurance. For those who want a more adequate bibliography on unemployment insurance see my *Standards of Unemployment Insurance*, pp. 198–199; and a special bibliography compiled by the United States Bureau of Labor Statistics and published as Bulletin No. 611 of that organization. *Unemployment Insurance and Reserves in the United States* (1935).

I. General Books on Social Insurance

>BURNS, EVELINE M., *Toward Social Security*, Whittlesey House, 1936.

>RUBINOW, I. M., *The Quest for Security*, Holt, 1934.

>EPSTEIN, ABRAHAM, *Insecurity*, second edition, Random House, 1936.

>ARMSTRONG, BARBARA N., *Insuring the Essentials*, Macmillan, 1932.

II. Unemployment Insurance

>DOUGLAS, PAUL H., and DIRECTOR, AARON, *The Problem of Unemployment*, Macmillan, 1931.

>DOUGLAS, PAUL H., *Standards of Unemployment Insurance*, University of Chicago Press, 1933.

>HANSEN, A. H., and MURRAY, M. G., *Unemployment Reserves*, University of Minnesota Press, 1933.

>HANSEN, A. H., MURRAY, M, G., STEVENSON, R. A., and STEWART, BRYCE, *A Program for Unemployment Insurance*, University of Minnesota Press, 1934.

>ELBERT, R. G., *Unemployment and Relief*, 1934.

>*Report of Ohio Commission on Unemployment Insurance*, Columbus, 1932 and 1933, 2 vols.

>HOAR, R. S., *Unemployment Insurance in Wisconsin*, Stuart Press, Milwaukee, 1932.

III. Old Age Pensions

>EPSTEIN, ABRAHAM, *Facing Old Age*, Knopf, 1922.

>EPSTEIN, ABRAHAM, *The Challenge of the Aged*, Vanguard, 1928.

LATIMER, MURRAY W., *Industrial Pension Systems,* Industrial Relations Counsellors, 1933, 2 vols.

RUBINOW, I. M., (editor), *The Care of the Aged,* University of Chicago Press, 1931.

IV. The Federal Act

⌐ *Report to the President of the Committee on Economic Security,* January 15, 1935.

Supplement to the Report of the Committee on Economic Security.

Hearings before the Committee on Finance, U. S. Senate, 74th Congress, 1st Session, on S. 1130, 1935.

⌐ *Hearings before the Committee on Ways and Means,* House of Representatives, 74th Congress, 1st Session, on H. R. 4120, 1935.

Report of Senate Committee on Finance on H. R. 7260, 74th Congress, 1st Session, Report No. 628, Calendar 661 (1935).

Hearings before Sub-committee of the Ways and Means Committee, House of Representatives, 73rd Congress, 2nd Session, 1934 (on Wagner-Lewis bill).

Hearings before Sub-committee of the Committee of Labor, House of Representatives, 74th Congress, 1st Session, on H. R. 2827 (1935) (Lundeen bill).

V. Health Insurance

FALK, I. S., ROREM, C. R., and RING, M. D., *The Cost of Medical Care,* University of Chicago Press, 1933.

DAVIS, M. M., *Paying Your Sickness Bills,* University of Chicago Press, 1931.

SIMONS, A. M., and SINAI, NATHAN, *The Way of Health Insurance,* University of Chicago Press, 1932.

For additional material see the annual volumes on *Social Security,* 1928–1935, published by the American Association for Social Security; and also the monthly journal of that organization. See also the *American Labor Legislation Review* and *The Survey.*

Supplementary Bibliography for 1937–1938

I. Books

STEWART, MAXWELL S., *Social Security*, Norton, 1937.

NORTON, THOMAS L., *Old Age and the Social Security Act*, Foster and Stewart, Buffalo, 1937.

WYATT, R. E., and WANDELL, W. H., *The Social Security Act in Operation*, Graphic Arts Press, Washington, 1937.

Twentieth Century Fund, *More Security for Old Age*, 1937.

American Association for Social Security, *Social Security* 1937 (contains papers delivered at 1937 conference of this association).

American Association for Social Security, *Social Security* 1938.

Social Security Board, *Social Security in America*, U.S. Printing Office, 1937 (contains staff reports to the original Government Committee on Economic Security).

II. Administrative Studies

LANSDALE, R. T., and others, *The Administration of Old Age Assistance in Three States*, Public Administration Service, 1936.

MATSCHEK, WALTER, *Unemployment Compensation Administration in Wisconsin and New Hampshire*, Public Administration Service, 1936.

MATSCHEK, WALTER, and ATKINSON, R. C., *The Administration of Unemployment Compensation Benefits in Wisconsin, July 1, 1936–June 30, 1937*, Public Administration Service, 1937.

III. Legal Analyses and Current Statistics

GOLDY, D. L., *Trends in Unemployment Compensation*, 1937, American Public Welfare Association.

GOLDY, D. L., *Legislative Developments in Unemployment Compensation*, 1937, American Public Welfare Association.

[435]

Social Security Board, *An Analysis of State Unemployment Compensation Laws*, U.S. Printing Office, 1937.

Social Security Board, *A Comparison of State Unemployment Compensation Laws*, 1937.

Social Security Board, *Characteristics of State Plans for Old Age Assistance*, 1938.

Social Security Board, *Characteristics of State Plans for Aid to the Blind*, 1938.

Social Security Board, *Characteristics of State Plans for Aid to Dependent Children*.

Social Security Board, *Social Security Bulletin*, monthly. An invaluable current source.

Social Security Board, *Statistics of Public Assistance for the United States*, monthly.

U.S. Children's Bureau, *The Child*, monthly.

First and Second Annual Reports of the Social Security Board.

Appendix

THE TEXT OF THE FEDERAL SOCIAL SECURITY ACT

[PUBLIC—NO. 271—74TH CONGRESS]
[H. R. 7260]

AN ACT

To provide for the general welfare by establishing a system of Federal old-age benefits, and by enabling the several States to make more adequate provision for aged persons, blind persons, dependent and crippled children, maternal and child welfare, public health, and the administration of their unemployment compensation laws; to establish a Social Security Board; to raise revenue; and for other purposes.

Be it enacted by the Senate and House of Representatives of the United States of America in Congress assembled,

TITLE I—GRANTS TO STATES FOR OLD-AGE ASSISTANCE

APPROPRIATION

SECTION 1. For the purpose of enabling each State to furnish financial assistance, as far as practicable under the conditions in such State, to aged needy individuals, there is hereby authorized to be appropriated for the fiscal year ending June 30, 1936, the sum of $49,750,000, and there is hereby authorized to be appropriated for each fiscal year thereafter a sum sufficient to carry out the purposes of this title. The sums made available under this section shall be used for making payments to States which have submitted, and had approved by the Social Security Board established by Title VII (hereinafter referred to as the "Board"), State plans for old-age assistance.

[437]

STATE OLD-AGE ASSISTANCE PLANS

Sec. 2. (a) A State plan for old-age assistance must (1) provide that it shall be in effect in all political subdivisions of the State, and, if administered by them, be mandatory upon them; (2) provide for financial participation by the State; (3) either provide for the establishment or designation of a single State agency to administer the plan, or provide for the establishment or designation of a single State agency to supervise the administration of the plan; (4) provide for granting to any individual, whose claim for old-age assistance is denied, an opportunity for a fair hearing before such State agency; (5) provide such methods of administration (other than those relating to selection, tenure of office, and compensation of personnel) as are found by the Board to be necessary for the efficient operation of the plan; (6) provide that the State agency will make such reports, in such form and containing such information, as the Board may from time to time require, and comply with such provisions as the Board may from time to time find necessary to assure the correctness and verification of such reports; and (7) provide that, if the State or any of its political subdivisions collects from the estate of any recipient of old-age assistance any amount with respect to old-age assistance furnished him under the plan, one-half of the net amount so collected shall be promptly paid to the United States. Any payment so made shall be deposited in the Treasury to the credit of the appropriation for the purposes of this title.

(b) The Board shall approve any plan which fulfills the conditions specified in subsection (a), except that it shall not approve any plan which imposes, as a condition of eligibility for old-age assistance under the plan—

(1) An age requirement of more than sixty-five years, except that the plan may impose, effective until January 1, 1940, an age requirement of as much as seventy years; or

[438]

(2) Any residence requirement which excludes any resident of the State who has resided therein five years during the nine years immediately preceding the application for old-age assistance and has resided therein continuously for one year immediately preceding the application; or

(3) Any citizenship requirement which excludes any citizen of the United States.

PAYMENT TO STATES

SEC. 3. (a) From the sums appropriated therefor, the Secretary of the Treasury shall pay to each State which has an approved plan for old-age assistance, for each quarter, beginning with the quarter commencing July 1, 1935, (1) an amount, which shall be used exclusively as old-age assistance equal to one-half of the total of the sums expended during such quarter as old-age assistance under the State plan with respect to each individual who at the time of such expenditure is sixty-five years of age or older and is not an inmate of a public institution, not counting so much of such expenditure with respect to any individual for any month as exceeds $30, and (2) 5 per centum of such amount, which shall be used for paying the costs of administering the State plan or for old-age assistance, or both, and for no other purpose: *Provided,* That the State plan, in order to be approved by the Board, need not provide for financial participation before July 1, 1937 by the State, in the case of any State which the Board, upon application by the State and after reasonable notice and opportunity for hearing to the State, finds is prevented by its constitution from providing such financial participation.

(b) The method of computing and paying such amounts shall be as follows:

(1) The Board shall, prior to the beginning of each quarter, estimate the amount to be paid to the State for such quarter under the provisions of clause (1) of subsection (a), such estimate to be based on (A) a report filed by the State containing its estimate of the total sum to be ex-

[439]

pended in such quarter in accordance with the provisions of such clause, and stating the amount appropriated or made available by the State and its political subdivisions for such expenditures in such quarter, and if such amount is less than one-half of the total sum of such estimated expenditures, the source or sources from which the difference is expected to be derived, (B) records showing the number of aged individuals in the State, and (C) such other investigation as the Board may find necessary.

(2) The Board shall then certify to the Secretary of the Treasury the amount so estimated by the Board, reduced or increased, as the case may be, by any sum by which it finds that its estimate for any prior quarter was greater or less than the amount which should have been paid to the State under clause (1) of subsection (a) for such quarter, except to the extent that such sum has been applied to make the amount certified for any prior quarter greater or less than the amount estimated by the Board for such prior quarter.

(3) The Secretary of the Treasury shall thereupon, through the Division of Disbursement of the Treasury Department and prior to audit or settlement by the General Accounting Office, pay to the State, at the time or times fixed by the Board, the amount so certified, increased by 5 per centum.

OPERATION OF STATE PLANS

SEC. 4. In the case of any State plan for old-age assistance which has been approved by the Board, if the Board, after reasonable notice and opportunity for hearing to the State agency administering or supervising the administration of such plan, finds—

(1) that the plan has been so changed as to impose any age, residence, or citizenship requirement prohibited by section 2 (b), or that in the administration of the plan any such prohibited requirement is imposed, with the knowl-

edge of such State agency, in a substantial number of
cases; or

(2) that in the administration of the plan there is a
failure to comply substantially with any provision required
by section 2 (a) to be included in the plan;

the Board shall notify such State agency that further payments will not be made to the State until the Board is satisfied
that such prohibited requirement is no longer so imposed,
and that there is no longer any such failure to comply. Until
it is so satisfied it shall make no further certification to the
Secretary of the Treasury with respect to such State.

ADMINISTRATION

SEC. 5. There is hereby authorized to be appropriated for
the fiscal year ending June 30, 1936, the sum of $250,000, for
all necessary expenses of the Board in administering the
provisions of this title.

DEFINITION

SEC. 6. When used in this title the term "old-age assistance" means money payments to aged individuals.

TITLE II—FEDERAL OLD-AGE BENEFITS

OLD-AGE RESERVE ACCOUNT

SECTION 201. (a) There is hereby created an account in the
Treasury of the United States to be known as the "Old-Age
Reserve Account" hereinafter in this title called the "Account". There is hereby authorized to be appropriated to the
Account for each fiscal year, beginning with the fiscal year
ending June 30, 1937, an amount sufficient as an annual
premium to provide for the payments required under this
title, such amount to be determined on a reserve basis in
accordance with accepted actuarial principles, and based
upon such tables of mortality as the Secretary of the Treasury
shall from time to time adopt, and upon an interest rate of
3 per centum per annum compounded annually. The Secre-

tary of the Treasury shall submit annually to the Bureau of the Budget an estimate of the appropriations to be made to the Account.

(b) It shall be the duty of the Secretary of the Treasury to invest such portion of the amounts credited to the Account as is not, in his judgment, required to meet current withdrawals. Such investment may be made only in interest-bearing obligations of the United States or in obligations guaranteed as to both principal and interest by the United States. For such purpose such obligations may be acquired (1) on original issue at par, or (2) by purchase of outstanding obligations at the market price. The purposes for which obligations of the United States may be issued under the Second Liberty Bond Act, as amended, are hereby extended to authorize the issuance at par of special obligations exclusively to the Account. Such special obligations shall bear interest at the rate of 3 per centum per annum. Obligations other than such special obligations may be acquired for the Account only on such terms as to provide an investment yield of not less than 3 per centum per annum.

(c) Any obligations acquired by the Account (except special obligations issued exclusively to the Account) may be sold at the market price, and such special obligations may be redeemed at par plus accrued interest.

(d) The interest on, and the proceeds from the sale or redemption of, any obligations held in the Account shall be credited to and form a part of the Account.

(e) All amounts credited to the Account shall be available for making payments required under this title.

(f) The Secretary of the Treasury shall include in his annual report the actuarial status of the Account.

OLD-AGE BENEFIT PAYMENTS

SEC. 202. (a) Every qualified individual (as defined in section 210) shall be entitled to receive, with respect to the period beginning on the date he attains the age of sixty-five, or on January 1, 1942, whichever is the later, and ending on the date of his death, an old-age benefit (payable as nearly as practicable in equal monthly installments) as follows:

(1) If the total wages (as defined in section 210) determined by the Board to have been paid to him, with respect to employment (as defined in section 210) after December 31, 1936, and before he attained the age of sixty-five, were not more than $3,000, the old-age benefit shall be at a monthly rate of one-half of 1 per centum of such total wages;

(2) If such total wages were more than $3,000, the old-age benefit shall be at a monthly rate equal to the sum of the following:

(A) One-half of 1 per centum of $3,000; plus

(B) One-twelfth of 1 per centum of the amount by which such total wages exceeded $3,000 and did not exceed $45,000; plus

(C) One-twenty-fourth of 1 per centum of the amount by which such total wages exceeded $45,000.

(b) In no case shall the monthly rate computed under subsection (a) exceed $85.

(c) If the Board finds at any time that more or less than the correct amount has theretofore been paid to any individual under this section, then, under regulations made by the Board, proper adjustments shall be made in connection with subsequent payments under this section to the same individual.

(d) Whenever the Board finds that any qualified individual has received wages with respect to regular employment after he attained the age of sixty-five, the old-age benefit payable to such individual shall be reduced, for each calendar month in any part of which such regular employment occurred, by an amount equal to one month's benefit. Such reduction shall be made, under regulations prescribed by the Board, by deductions from one or more payments of old-age benefit to such individual.

PAYMENTS UPON DEATH

Sec. 203. (a) If any individual dies before attaining the age of sixty-five, there shall be paid to his estate an amount equal to 3½ per centum of the total wages determined by the Board to have been paid to him, with respect to employment after December 31, 1936.

(b) If the Board finds that the correct amount of the old-age benefit payable to a qualified individual during his life under section 202 was less than 3½ per centum of the total wages by which such old-age benefit was measurable, then there shall be paid to his estate a sum equal to the amount, if any, by which such 3½ per centum exceeds the amount (whether more or less than the correct amount) paid to him during his life as old-age benefit.

(c) If the Board finds that the total amount paid to a qualified individual under an old-age benefit during his life was less than the correct amount to which he was entitled under section 202, and that the correct amount of such old-age benefit was 3½ per centum or more of the total wages by which such old-age benefit was measurable, then there shall be paid to his estate a sum equal to the amount, if any, by which the correct amount of the old-age benefit exceeds the amount which was so paid to him during his life.

PAYMENTS TO AGED INDIVIDUALS NOT QUALIFIED FOR BENEFITS

Sec. 204. (a) There shall be paid in a lump sum to any individual who, upon attaining the age of sixty-five, is not a qualified individual, an amount equal to 3½ per centum of the total wages determined by the Board to have been paid to him, with respect to employment after December 31, 1936, and before he attained the age of sixty-five.

(b) After any individual becomes entitled to any payment under subsection (a), no other payment shall be made under this title in any manner measured by wages paid to him, except that any part of any payment under subsection (a)

[444]

which is not paid to him before his death shall be paid to his estate.

AMOUNTS OF $500 OR LESS PAYABLE TO ESTATES

SEC. 205. If any amount payable to an estate under section 203 or 204 is $500 or less, such amount may, under regulations prescribed by the Board, be paid to the persons found by the Board to be entitled thereto under the law of the State in which the deceased was domiciled, without the necessity of compliance with the requirements of law with respect to the administration of such estate.

OVERPAYMENTS DURING LIFE

SEC. 206. If the Board finds that the total amount paid to a qualified individual under an old-age benefit during his life was more than the correct amount to which he was entitled under section 202, and was 3½ per centum or more of the total wages by which such old-age benefit was measurable, then upon his death there shall be repaid to the United States by his estate the amount, if any, by which such total amount paid to him during his life exceeds whichever of the following is the greater: (1) Such 3½ per centum, or (2) the correct amount to which he was entitled under section 202.

METHOD OF MAKING PAYMENTS

SEC. 207. The Board shall from time to time certify to the Secretary of the Treasury the name and address of each person entitled to receive a payment under this title, the amount of such payment, and the time at which it should be made, and the Secretary of the Treasury through the Division of Disbursement of the Treasury Department, and prior to audit or settlement by the General Accounting Office, shall make payment in accordance with the certification by the Board.

APPENDIX

ASSIGNMENT

SEC. 208. The right of any person to any future payment under this title shall not be transferable or assignable, at law or in equity, and none of the moneys paid or payable or rights existing under this title shall be subject to execution, levy, attachment, garnishment, or other legal process, or to the operation of any bankruptcy or insolvency law.

PENALTIES

SEC. 209. Whoever in any application for any payment under this title makes any false statement as to any material fact, knowing such statement to be false, shall be fined not more than $1,000 or imprisoned for not more than one year or both.

DEFINITIONS

SEC. 210. When used in this title—

(a) The term "wages" means all remuneration for employment, including the cash value of all remuneration paid in any medium other than cash; except that such term shall not include that part of the remuneration which, after remuneration equal to $3,000 has been paid to an individual by an employer with respect to employment during any calendar year, is paid to such individual by such employer with respect to employment during such calendar year.

(b) The term "employment" means any service, of whatever nature, performed within the United States by an employee for his employer, except—

(1) Agricultural labor;

(2) Domestic service in a private home;

(3) Casual labor not in the course of the employer's trade or business;

(4) Service performed as an officer or member of the crew of a vessel documented under the laws of the United States or of any foreign country;

[446]

(5) Service performed in the employ of the United States Government or of an instrumentality of the United States;

(6) Service performed in the employ of a State, a political subdivision thereof, or an instrumentality of one or more States or political subdivisions;

(7) Service performed in the employ of a corporation, community chest, fund, or foundation, organized and operated exclusively for religious, charitable, scientific, literary, or educational purposes, or for the prevention of cruelty to children or animals, no part of the net earnings of which inures to the benefit of any private shareholder or individual.

(c) The term "qualified individual" means any individual with respect to whom it appears to the satisfaction of the Board that—

(1) He is at least sixty-five years of age; and

(2) The total amount of wages paid to him, with respect to employment after December 31, 1936, and before he attained the age of sixty-five, was not less than $2,000; and

(3) Wages were paid to him, with respect to employment on some five days after December 31, 1936, and before he attained the age of sixty-five, each day being in a different calendar year.

Title III—Grants to States for Unemployment Compensation Administration

APPROPRIATION

SEC. 301. For the purpose of assisting the States in the administration of their unemployment compensation laws, there is hereby authorized to be appropriated, for the fiscal year ending June 30, 1936, the sum of $4,000,000, and for each fiscal year thereafter the sum of $49,000,000, to be used as hereinafter provided.

PAYMENTS TO STATES

SEC. 302. (a) The Board shall from time to time certify to the Secretary of the Treasury for payment to each State which has an unemployment compensation law approved by the Board under Title IX, such amounts as the Board determines to be necessary for the proper administration of such law during the fiscal year in which such payment is to be made. The Board's determination shall be based on (1) the population of the State; (2) an estimate of the number of persons covered by the State law and of the cost of proper administration of such law; and (3) such other factors as the Board finds relevant. The Board shall not certify for payment under this section in any fiscal year a total amount in excess of the amount appropriated therefor for such fiscal year.

(b) Out of the sums appropriated therefor, the Secretary of the Treasury shall, upon receiving a certification under subsection (a), pay, through the Division of Disbursement of the Treasury Department and prior to audit or settlement by the General Accounting Office, to the State agency charged with the administration of such law the amount so certified.

PROVISIONS OF STATE LAWS

SEC. 303. (a) The Board shall make no certification for payment to any State unless it finds that the law of such State, approved by the Board under Title IX, includes provisions for—

(1) Such methods of administration (other than those relating to selection, tenure of office, and compensation of personnel) as are found by the Board to be reasonably calculated to insure full payment of unemployment compensation when due; and

(2) Payment of unemployment compensation solely through public employment offices in the State or such other agencies as the Board may approve; and

(3) Opportunity for a fair hearing, before an impartial tribunal, for all individuals whose claims for unemployment compensation are denied; and

[448]

(4) The payment of all money received in the unemployment fund of such State, immediately upon such receipt, to the Secretary of the Treasury to the credit of the Unemployment Trust Fund established by section 904; and

(5) Expenditure of all money requisitioned by the State agency from the Unemployment Trust Fund, in the payment of unemployment compensation, exclusive of expenses of administration; and

(6) The making of such reports, in such form and containing such information, as the Board may from time to time require, and compliance with such provisions as the Board may from time to time find necessary to assure the correctness and verification of such reports; and

(7) Making available upon request to any agency of the United States charged with the administration of public works or assistance through public employment, the name, address, ordinary occupation and employment status of each recipient of unemployment compensation, and a statement of such recipient's rights to further compensation under such law.

(b) Whenever the Board, after reasonable notice and opportunity for hearing to the State agency charged with the administration of the State law, finds that in the administration of the law there is—

(1) a denial, in a substantial number of cases, of unemployment compensation to individuals entitled thereto under such law; or

(2) a failure to comply substantially with any provision specified in subsection (a);

the Board shall notify such State agency that further payments will not be made to the State until the Board is satisfied that there is no longer any such denial or failure to comply. Until it is so satisfied it shall make no further certification to the Secretary of the Treasury with respect to such State.

APPENDIX

Title IV—Grants to States for Aid to Dependent Children

APPROPRIATION

Section 401. For the purpose of enabling each State to furnish financial assistance, as far as practicable under the conditions in such State, to needy dependent children, there is hereby authorized to be appropriated for the fiscal year ending June 30, 1936, the sum of $24,750,000, and there is hereby authorized to be appropriated for each fiscal year thereafter a sum sufficient to carry out the purposes of this title. The sums made available under this section shall be used for making payments to States which have submitted, and had approved by the Board, State plans for aid to dependent children.

STATE PLANS FOR AID TO DEPENDENT CHILDREN

Sec. 402. (a) A State plan for aid to dependent children must (1) provide that it shall be in effect in all political subdivisions of the State, and, if administered by them, be mandatory upon them; (2) provide for financial participation by the State; (3) either provide for the establishment or designation of a single State agency to administer the plan, or provide for the establishment or designation of a single State agency to supervise the administration of the plan; (4) provide for granting to any individual, whose claim with respect to aid to a dependent child is denied, an opportunity for a fair hearing before such State agency; (5) provide such methods of administration (other than those relating to selection, tenure of office, and compensation of personnel) as are found by the Board to be necessary for the efficient operation of the plan; and (6) provide that the State agency will make such reports, in such form and containing such information, as the Board may from time to time require, and comply with such provisions as the Board may from time to time find necessary to assure the correctness and verification of such reports.

(b) The Board shall approve any plan which fulfills the conditions specified in subsection (a), except that it shall not approve any plan which imposes as a condition of eligibility for aid to dependent children, a residence requirement which denies aid with respect to any child residing in the State (1) who has resided in the State for one year immediately preceding the application for such aid, or (2) who was born within the State within one year immediately preceding the application, if its mother has resided in the State for one year immediately preceding the birth.

PAYMENT TO STATES

Sec. 403. (a) From the sums appropriated therefor, the Secretary of the Treasury shall pay to each State which has an approved plan for aid to dependent children, for each quarter, beginning with the quarter commencing July 1, 1935, an amount, which shall be used exclusively for carrying out the State plan, equal to one-third of the total of the sums expended during such quarter under such plan, not counting so much of such expenditure with respect to any dependent child for any month as exceeds $18, or if there is more than one dependent child in the same home, as exceeds $18 for any month with respect to one such dependent child and $12 for such month with respect to each of the other dependent children.

(b) The method of computing and paying such amounts shall be as follows:

(1) The Board shall, prior to the beginning of each quarter, estimate the amount to be paid to the State for such quarter under the provisions of subsection (a), such estimate to be based on (A) a report filed by the State containing its estimate of the total sum to be expended in such quarter in accordance with the provisions of such subsection and stating the amount appropriated or made

[451]

available by the State and its political subdivisions for such expenditures in such quarter, and if such amount is less than two-thirds of the total sum of such estimated expenditures, the source or sources from which the difference is expected to be derived, (B) records showing the number of dependent children in the State, and (C) such other investigation as the Board may find necessary.

(2) The Board shall then certify to the Secretary of the Treasury the amount so estimated by the Board, reduced or increased, as the case may be, by any sum by which it finds that its estimate for any prior quarter was greater or less than the amount which should have been paid to the State for such quarter, except to the extent that such sum has been applied to make the amount certified for any prior quarter greater or less than the amount estimated by the Board for such prior quarter.

(3) The Secretary of the Treasury shall thereupon, through the Division of Disbursement of the Treasury Department and prior to audit or settlement by the General Accounting Office, pay to the State, at the time or times fixed by the Board, the amount so certified.

OPERATION OF STATE PLANS

SEC. 404. In the case of any State plan for aid to dependent children which has been approved by the Board, if the Board, after reasonable notice and opportunity for hearing to the State agency administering or supervising the administration of such plan, finds—

(1) that the plan has been so changed as to impose any residence requirement prohibited by section 402 (b), or that in the administration of the plan any such prohibited requirement is imposed, with the knowledge of such State agency, in a substantial number of cases; or

(2) that in the administration of the plan there is a failure to comply substantially with any provision required by section 402 (a) to be included in the plan;

[452]

the Board shall notify such State agency that further payments will not be made to the State until the Board is satisfied that such prohibited requirement is no longer so imposed, and that there is no longer any such failure to comply. Until it is so satisfied it shall make no further certification to the Secretary of the Treasury with respect to such State.

ADMINISTRATION

SEC. 405. There is hereby authorized to be appropriated for the fiscal year ending June 30, 1936, the sum of $250,000 for all necessary expenses of the Board in administering the provisions of this title.

DEFINITIONS

SEC. 406. When used in this title—

(a) The term "dependent child" means a child under the age of sixteen who has been deprived of parental support or care by reason of the death, continued absence from the home, or physical or mental incapacity of a parent, and who is living with his father, mother, grandfather, grandmother, brother, sister, stepfather, stepmother, stepbrother, stepsister, uncle, or aunt, in a place of residence maintained by one or more of such relatives as his or their own home;

(b) The term "aid to dependent children" means money payments with respect to a dependent child or dependent children.

TITLE V—GRANTS TO STATES FOR MATERNAL AND CHILD WELFARE

Part 1—Maternal and Child Health Services

APPROPRIATION

SECTION 501. For the purpose of enabling each State to extend and improve, as far as practicable under the conditions in such State, services for promoting the health of mothers and children, especially in rural areas and in areas suffering from severe economic distress, there is hereby

authorized to be appropriated for each fiscal year, beginning
with the fiscal year ending June 30, 1936, the sum of $3,800,-
000. The sums made available under this section shall be
used for making payments to States which have submitted,
and had approved by the Chief of the Children's Bureau,
State plans for such services.

SEC. 502. (a) Out of the sums appropriated pursuant to
section 501 for each fiscal year the Secretary of Labor shall
allot to each State $20,000, and such part of $1,800,000 as
he finds that the number of live births in such State bore to
the total number of live births in the United States, in the
latest calendar year for which the Bureau of the Census has
available statistics.

(b) Out of the sums appropriated pursuant to section 501
for each fiscal year the Secretary of Labor shall allot to the
States $980,000 (in addition to the allotments made under
subsection (a)), according to the financial need of each State
for assistance in carrying out its State plan, as determined
by him after taking into consideration the number of live
births in such State.

(c) The amount of any allotment to a State under subsection (a) for any fiscal year remaining unpaid to such
State at the end of such fiscal year shall be available for
payment to such State under section 504 until the end of
the second succeeding fiscal year. No payment to a State
under section 504 shall be made out of its allotment for any
fiscal year until its allotment for the preceding fiscal year
has been exhausted or has ceased to be available.

SEC. 503. (a) A State plan for maternal and child-health
services must (1) provide for financial participation by the
State; (2) provide for the administration of the plan by the
State health agency or the supervision of the administration

of the plan by the State health agency; (3) provide such methods of administration (other than those relating to selection, tenure of office, and compensation of personnel) as are necessary for the efficient operation of the plan; (4) provide that the State health agency will make such reports, in such form and containing such information, as the Secretary of Labor may from time to time require, and comply with such provisions as he may from time to time find necessary to assure the correctness and verification of such reports; (5) provide for the extension and improvement of local maternal and child-health services administered by local child-health units; (6) provide for cooperation with medical, nursing, and welfare groups and organizations; and (7) provide for the development of demonstration services in needy areas and among groups in special need.

(b) The Chief of the Children's Bureau shall approve any plan which fulfills the conditions specified in subsection (a) and shall thereupon notify the Secretary of Labor and the State health agency of his approval.

PAYMENT OF STATES

SEC. 504. (a) From the sums appropriated therefor and the allotments available under section 502 (a), the Secretary of the Treasury shall pay to each State which has an approved plan for maternal and child-health services, for each quarter, beginning with the quarter commencing July 1, 1935, an amount, which shall be used exclusively for carrying out the State plan, equal to one-half of the total sum expended during such quarter for carrying out such plan.

(b) The method of computing and paying such amounts shall be as follows:

(1) The Secretary of Labor shall, prior to the beginning of each quarter, estimate the amount to be paid to the State for such quarter under the provisions of subsection (a), such estimate to be based on (A) a report filed by the State containing its estimate of the total sum to

[455]

be expended in such quarter in accordance with the provisions of such subsection and stating the amount appropriated or made available by the State and its political subdivisions for such expenditures in such quarter, and if such amount is less than one-half of the total sum of such estimated expenditures, the source or sources from which the difference is expected to be derived, and (B) such investigation as he may find necessary.

(2) The Secretary of Labor shall then certify the amount so estimated by him to the Secretary of the Treasury, reduced or increased, as the case may be, by any sum by which the Secretary of Labor finds that his estimate for any prior quarter was greater or less than the amount which should have been paid to the State for such quarter, except to the extent that such sum has been applied to make the amount certified for any prior quarter greater or less than the amount estimated by the Secretary of Labor for such prior quarter.

(3) The Secretary of the Treasury shall thereupon, through the Division of Disbursement of the Treasury Department and prior to audit or settlement by the General Accounting Office, pay to the State, at the time or times fixed by the Secretary of Labor, the amount so certified.

(c) The Secretary of Labor shall from time to time certify to the Secretary of the Treasury the amounts to be paid to the States from the allotments available under section 502 (b), and the Secretary of the Treasury shall, through the Division of Disbursement of the Treasury Department and prior to audit or settlement by the General Accounting Office, make payments of such amounts from such allotments at the time or times specified by the Secretary of Labor.

OPERATION OF STATE PLANS

Sec. 505. In the case of any State plan for maternal and child-health services which has been approved by the Chief of the Children's Bureau, if the Secretary of Labor, after reasonable notice and opportunity for hearing to the State agency administering or supervising the administration of such plan, finds that in the administration of the plan there is a failure to comply substantially with any provision required by section 503 to be included in the plan, he shall notify such State agency that further payments will not be made to the State until he is satisfied that there is no longer any such failure to comply. Until he is so satisfied he shall make no further certification to the Secretary of the Treasury with respect to such State.

Part 2—Services for Crippled Children

APPROPRIATION

SEC. 511. For the purpose of enabling each State to extend and improve (especially in rural areas and in areas suffering from severe economic distress), as far as practicable under the conditions in such State, services for locating crippled children, and for providing medical, surgical, corrective, and other services and care, and facilities for diagnosis, hospitalization, and aftercare, for children who are crippled or who are suffering from conditions which lead to crippling, there is hereby authorized to be appropriated for each fiscal year, beginning with the fiscal year ending June 30, 1936, the sum of $2,850,000. The sums made available under this section shall be used for making payments to States which have submitted, and had approved by the Chief of the Children's Bureau, State plans for such services.

ALLOTMENTS TO STATES

SEC. 512. (a) Out of the sums appropriated pursuant to section 511 for each fiscal year the Secretary of Labor shall allot to each State $20,000, and the remainder to the States according to the need of each State as determined by him after taking into consideration the number of crippled children in such State in need of the services referred to in section 511 and the cost of furnishing such services to them.

(b) The amount of any allotment to a State under subsection (a) for any fiscal year remaining unpaid to such State at the end of such fiscal year shall be available for payment to such State under section 514 until the end of the second succeeding fiscal year. No payment to a State under section 514 shall be made out of its allotment for any fiscal year until its allotment for the preceding fiscal year has been exhausted or has ceased to be available.

APPROVAL OF STATE PLANS

SEC. 513. (a) A State plan for services for crippled children must (1) provide for financial participation by the State; (2) provide for the administration of the plan by a State agency or the supervision of the administration of the plan by a State agency; (3) provide such methods of administration (other than those relating to selection, tenure of office, and compensation of personnel) as are necessary for the efficient operation of the plan; (4) provide that the State agency will make such reports, in such form and containing such information, as the Secretary of Labor may from time to time require, and comply with such provisions as he may from time to time find necessary to assure the correctness and verification of such reports; (5) provide for carrying out the purposes specified in section 511; and (6) provide for cooperation with medical, health, nursing, and welfare groups and organizations and with any agency in such State charged with administering State laws providing for vocational rehabilitation of physically handicapped children.

(b) The Chief of the Children's Bureau shall approve any plan which fulfills the conditions specified in subsection (a) and shall thereupon notify the Secretary of Labor and the State agency of his approval.

PAYMENT TO STATES

SEC. 514. (a) From the sums appropriated therefor and the allotments available under section 512, the Secretary of the Treasury shall pay to each State which has an approved plan for services for crippled children, for each quarter, beginning with the quarter commencing July 1, 1935, an amount, which shall be used exclusively for carrying out the State plan, equal to one-half of the total sum expended during such quarter for carrying out such plan.

(b) The method of computing and paying such amounts shall be as follows:

(1) The Secretary of Labor shall, prior to the beginning of each quarter, estimate the amount to be paid to the State for such quarter under the provisions of subsection (a), such estimate to be based on (A) a report filed by the State containing its estimate of the total sum to be expended in such quarter in accordance with the provisions of such subsection and stating the amount appropriated or made available by the State and its political subdivisions for such expenditures in such quarter, and if such amount is less than one-half of the total sum of such estimated expenditures, the source or sources from which the difference is expected to be derived, and (B) such investigation as he may find necessary.

(2) The Secretary of Labor shall then certify the amount so estimated by him to the Secretary of the Treasury, reduced or increased, as the case may be, by any sum by which the Secretary of Labor finds that his estimate for any prior quarter was greater or less than the amount which should have been paid to the State for such quarter, except to the extent that such sum has been applied to make the amount certified for any prior quarter greater or less than the amount estimated by the Secretary of Labor for such prior quarter.

(3) The Secretary of the Treasury shall thereupon, through the Division of Disbursement of the Treasury Department and prior to audit or settlement by the General Accounting Office, pay to the State, at the time or times fixed by the Secretary of Labor, the amount so certified.

OPERATION OF STATE PLANS

SEC. 515. In the case of any State plan for services for crippled children which has been approved by the Chief of the Children's Bureau, if the Secretary of Labor, after reasonable notice and opportunity for hearing to the State agency administering or supervising the administration of such plan, finds that in the administration of the plan there is a failure to comply substantially with any provision required by section 513 to be included in the plan, he shall notify such State agency that further payments will not be made to the State until he is satisfied that there is no longer any such failure to comply. Until he is so satisfied he shall make no further certification to the Secretary of the Treasury with respect to such State.

Part 3—Child-Welfare Services

SEC. 521. (a) For the purpose of enabling the United States, through the Children's Bureau, to cooperate with State public-welfare agencies in establishing, extending, and strengthening, especially in predominantly rural areas, public-welfare services (hereinafter in this section referred to as "child-welfare services") for the protection and care of homeless, dependent, and neglected children, and children in danger of becoming delinquent, there is hereby authorized to be appropriated for each fiscal year, beginning with the fiscal year ending June 30, 1936, the sum of $1,500,000. Such amount shall be allotted by the Secretary of Labor for use by cooperating State public-welfare agencies on the basis of plans developed jointly by the State agency and the Children's Bureau, to each State, $10,000, and the remainder to each State on the basis of such plans, not to exceed such part of the remainder as the rural population of such State bears to the total rural population of the United States. The amount so allotted shall be expended for payment of part of the cost of district, county or other local child-welfare services in areas predominantly rural, and for developing State services for the encouragement and assistance of adequate methods of community child-welfare organization in areas predominantly rural and other areas of special need. The amount of any allotment to a State under this section for any fiscal year remaining unpaid to such State at the end of such fiscal year shall be available for payment to such State under this section until the end of the second succeeding fiscal year. No payment to a State under this section shall be made out of its allotment for any fiscal year until its allotment for the preceding fiscal year has been exhausted cr has ceased to be available.

(b) From the sums appropriated therefor and the allotments available under subsection (a) the Secretary of Labor shall from time to time certify to the Secretary of the Treasury the amounts to be paid to the States, and the Secretary of the Treasury shall, through the Division of Disbursement of the Treasury Department and prior to audit cr settlement by the General Accounting Office, make payments of such amounts from such allotments at the time or times specified by the Secretary of Labor.

Part 4—Vocational Rehabilitation

SEC. 531. (a) In order to enable the United States to cooperate with the States and Hawaii in extending and strengthening their programs of vocational rehabilitation of the physically disabled, and to continue to carry out the provisions and purposes of the Act entitled "An Act to provide for the promotion of vocational rehabilitation of persons disabled in industry or otherwise and their return to civil employment," approved June 2, 1920, as amended (U. S. C., title 29, ch. 4; U. S. C., Supp. VII, title 29, secs. 31, 32, 34, 35, 37, 39, and 40), there is hereby authorized to be appropriated for the fiscal years ending June 30, 1936, and June 30, 1937, the sum of $841,000 for each such fiscal year in addition to the amount of the existing authorization, and for each fiscal year

[461]

thereafter the sum of $1,938,000. Of the sums appropriated pursuant to such authorization for each fiscal year, $5,000 shall be apportioned to the Territory of Hawaii and the remainder shall be apportioned among the several States in the manner provided in such Act of June 2, 1920, as amended.

(b) For the administration of such Act of June 2, 1920, as amended, by the Federal agency authorized to administer it, there is hereby authorized to be appropriated for the fiscal years ending June 30, 1936, and June 30, 1937, the sum of $22,000 for each such fiscal year in addition to the amount of the existing authorization, and for each fiscal year thereafter the sum of $102,000.

Part 5—Administration

SEC. 541. (a) There is hereby authorized to be appropriated for the fiscal year ending June 30, 1936, the sum of $425,000, for all necessary expenses of the Children's Bureau in administering the provisions of this title, except section 531.

(b) The Children's Bureau shall make such studies and investigations as will promote the efficient administration of this title, except section 531.

(c) The Secretary of Labor shall include in his annual report to Congress a full account of the administration of this title, except section 531.

TITLE VI—PUBLIC HEALTH WORK

APPROPRIATION

SECTION 601. For the purpose of assisting States, counties, health districts, and other political subdivisions of the States in establishing and maintaining adequate public-health services, including the training of personnel for State and local health work, there is hereby authorized to be appropriated for each fiscal year, beginning with the fiscal year ending June 30, 1936, the sum of $8,000,000 to be used as hereinafter provided.

APPENDIX

STATE AND LOCAL PUBLIC HEALTH SERVICES

SEC. 602. (a) The Surgeon General of the Public Health Service, with the approval of the Secretary of the Treasury, shall, at the beginning of each fiscal year, allot to the States the total of (1) the amount appropriated for such year pursuant to section 601; and (2) the amounts of the allotments under this section for the preceding fiscal year remaining unpaid to the States at the end of such fiscal year. The amounts of such allotments shall be determined on the basis of (1) the population; (2) the special health problems; and (3) the financial needs; of the respective States. Upon making such allotments the Surgeon General of the Public Health Service shall certify the amounts thereof to the Secretary of the Treasury.

(b) The amount of an allotment to any State under subsection (a) for any fiscal year, remaining unpaid at the end of such fiscal year, shall be available for allotment to States under subsection (a) for the succeeding fiscal year, in addition to the amount appropriated for such year.

(c) Prior to the beginning of each quarter of the fiscal year, the Surgeon General of the Public Health Service shall, with the approval of the Secretary of the Treasury, determine in accordance with rules and regulations previously prescribed by such Surgeon General after consultation with a conference of the State and Territorial health authorities, the amount to be paid to each State for such quarter from the allotment to such State, and shall certify the amount so determined to the Secretary of the Treasury. Upon receipt of such certification, the Secretary of the Treasury shall, through the Division of Disbursement of the Treasury Department and prior to audit or settlement by the General Accounting Office, pay in accordance with such certification.

(d) The moneys so paid to any State shall be expended solely in carrying out the purposes specified in section 601, and in accordance with plans presented by the health author-

[463]

ity of such State and approved by the Surgeon General of the Public Health Service.

SEC. 603. (a) There is hereby authorized to be appropriated for each fiscal year, beginning with the fiscal year ending June 30, 1936, the sum of $2,000,000 for expenditure by the Public Health Service for investigation of disease and problems of sanitation (including the printing and binding of the findings of such investigations), and for the pay and allowances and traveling expenses of personnel of the Public Health Service, including commissioned officers, engaged in such investigations or detailed to cooperate with the health authorities of any State in carrying out the purposes specified in section 601: *Provided,* That no personnel of the Public Health Service shall be detailed to cooperate with the health authorities of any State except at the request of the proper authorities of such State.

(b) The personnel of the Public Health Service paid from any appropriation not made pursuant to subsection (a) may be detailed to assist in carrying out the purposes of this title. The appropriation from which they are paid shall be reimbursed from the appropriation made pursuant to subsection (a) to the extent of their salaries and allowances for services performed while so detailed.

(c) The Secretary of the Treasury shall include in his annual report to Congress a full account of the administration of this title.

TITLE VII—SOCIAL SECURITY BOARD

ESTABLISHMENT

SECTION 701. There is hereby established a Social Security Board (in this Act referred to as the "Board") to be composed of three members to be appointed by the President, by and with the advice and consent of the Senate. During his term of membership on the Board, no member shall engage

[464]

in any other business, vocation, or employment. Not more than two of the members of the Board shall be members of the same political party. Each member shall receive a salary at he rate of $10,000 a year and shall hold office for a term of six years, except that (1.) any member appointed to fill a vacancy occurring prior to the expiration of the term for which his predecessor was appointed, shall be appointed for the remainder of such term; and (2) the terms of office of the members first taking office after the date of the enactment of this Act shall expire, as designated by the President at the time of appointment, one at the end of two years, one at the end of four years, and one at the end of six years, after the date of the enactment of this Act. The President shall designate one of the members as the chairman of the Board.

DUTIES OF SOCIAL SECURITY BOARD

SEC. 702. The Board shall perform the duties imposed upon it by this Act and shall also have the duty of studying and making recommendations as to the most effective methods of providing economic security through social insurance, and as to legislation and matters of administrative policy concerning old-age pensions, unemployment compensation, accident compensation, and related subjects.

EXPENSES OF THE BOARD

SEC. 703. The Board is authorized to appoint and fix the compensation of such officers and employees, and to make such expenditures, as may be necessary for carrying out its functions under this Act. Appointments of attorneys and experts may be made without regard to the civil-service laws.

REPORTS

SEC. 704. The Board shall make a full report to Congress, at the beginning of each regular session, of the administration of the functions with which it is charged.

Title VIII—Taxes with Respect to Employment

INCOME TAX ON EMPLOYEES

Section 801. In addition to other taxes, there shall be levied, collected, and paid upon the income of every individual a tax equal to the following percentages of the wages (as defined in section 811) received by him after December 31, 1936, with respect to employment (as defined in section 811) after such date:

(1) With respect to employment during the calendar years 1937, 1938, and 1939, the rate shall be 1 per centum.

(2) With respect to employment during the calendar years 1940, 1941, and 1942, the rate shall be 1½ per centum.

(3) With respect to employment during the calendar years 1943, 1944, and 1945, the rate shall be 2 per centum.

(4) With respect to employment during the calendar years 1946, 1947, and 1948, the rate shall be 2½ per centum.

(5) With respect to employment after December 31, 1948, the rate shall be 3 per centum.

DEDUCTION OF TAX FROM WAGES

Sec. 802. (a) The tax imposed by section 801 shall be collected by the employer of the taxpayer, by deducting the amount of the tax from the wages as and when paid. Every employer required so to deduct the tax is hereby made liable for the payment of such tax, and is hereby indemnified against the claims and demands of any person for the amount of any such payment made by such employer.

(b) If more or less than the correct amount of tax imposed by section 801 is paid with respect to any wage payment, then, under regulations made under this title, proper adjustments, with respect both to the tax and the amount to be deducted, shall be made, without interest, in connection with subsequent wage payments to the same individual by the same employer.

[466]

DEDUCTIBILITY FROM INCOME TAX

SEC. 803. For the purposes of the income tax imposed by Title I of the Revenue Act of 1934 or by any Act of Congress in substitution therefor, the tax imposed by section 801 shall not be allowed as a deduction to the taxpayer in computing his net income for the year in which such tax is deducted from his wages.

EXCISE TAX ON EMPLOYERS

SEC. 804. In addition to other taxes, every employer shall pay an excise tax, with respect to having individuals in his employ, equal to the following percentages of the wages (as defined in section 811) paid by him after December 31, 1936, with respect to employment (as defined in section 811) after such date:

(1) With respect to employment during the calendar years 1937, 1938, and 1939, the rate shall be 1 per centum.

(2) With respect to employment during the calendar years 1940, 1941, and 1942, the rate shall be 1½ per centum.

(3) With respect to employment during the calendar years 1943, 1944, and 1945, the rate shall be 2 per centum.

(4) With respect to employment during the calendar years 1946, 1947, and 1948, the rate shall be 2½ per centum.

(5) With respect to employment after December 31, 1948, the rate shall be 3 per centum.

ADJUSTMENT OF EMPLOYERS' TAX

SEC. 805. If more or less than the correct amount of tax imposed by section 804 is paid with respect to any wage payment, then, under regulations made under this title, proper adjustments with respect to the tax shall be made, without interest, in connection with subsequent wage payments to the same individual by the same employer.

APPENDIX

REFUNDS AND DEFICIENCIES

Sec. 806. If more or less than the correct amount of tax imposed by section 801 or 804 is paid or deducted with respect to any wage payment and the overpayment or underpayment of tax cannot be adjusted under section 802 (b) or 805 the amount of the overpayment shall be refunded and the amount of the underpayment shall be collected, in such manner and at such times (subject to the statutes of limitations properly applicable thereto) as may be prescribed by regulations made under this title.

COLLECTION AND PAYMENT OF TAXES

Sec. 807. (a) The taxes imposed by this title shall be collected by the Bureau of Internal Revenue under the direction of the Secretary of the Treasury and shall be paid into the Treasury of the United States as internal-revenue collections. If the tax is not paid when due, there shall be added as part of the tax interest (except in the case of adjustments made in accordance with the provisions of sections 802 (b) and 805) at the rate of one-half of 1 per centum per month from the date the tax became due until paid.

(b) Such taxes shall be collected and paid in such manner, at such times, and under such conditions, not inconsistent with this title (either by making and filing returns, or by stamps, coupons, tickets, books, or other reasonable devices or methods necessary or helpful in securing a complete and proper collection and payment of the tax or in securing proper identification of the taxpayer), as may be prescribed by the Commissioner of Internal Revenue, with the approval of the Secretary of the Treasury.

(c) All provisions of law, including penalties, applicable with respect to any tax imposed by section 600 or section 800 of the Revenue Act of 1926, and the provisions of section 607 of the Revenue Act of 1934, shall, insofar as applicable and

[468]

not inconsistent with the provisions of this title, be applicable with respect to the taxes imposed by this title.

(d) In the payment of any tax under this title a fractional part of a cent shall be disregarded unless it amounts to one-half cent or more, in which case it shall be increased to 1 cent.

RULES AND REGULATIONS

SEC. 808. The Commissioner of Internal Revenue, with the approval of the Secretary of the Treasury, shall make and publish rules and regulations for the enforcement of this title.

SALE OF STAMPS BY POSTMASTERS

SEC. 809. The Commissioner of Internal Revenue shall furnish to the Postmaster General without prepayment a suitable quantity of stamps, coupons, tickets, books, or other devices prescribed by the Commissioner under section 807 for the collection or payment of any tax imposed by this title to be distributed to, and kept on sale by, all post offices of the first and second classes, and such post offices of the third and fourth classes as (1) are located in county seats, or (2) are certified by the Secretary of the Treasury to the Post-master General as necessary to the proper administration of this title. The Postmaster General may require each such postmaster to furnish bond in such increased amount as he may from time to time determine, and each such postmaster shall deposit the receipts from the sale of such stamps, coupons, tickets, books, or other devices, to the credit of, and render accounts to, the Postmaster General at such times and in such form as the Postmaster General may by regulations prescribe. The Postmaster General shall at least once a month transfer to the Treasury as internal-revenue collections all receipts so deposited together with a statement of the additional expenditures in the District of Columbia and elsewhere incurred by the Post Office Department in perform-ing the duties imposed upon said Department by this Act, and the Secretary of the Treasury is hereby authorized and directed to advance from time to time to the credit of the Post Office Department from appropriations made for the collection of the taxes imposed by this title, such sums as may be required for such additional expenditures incurred by the Post Office Department.

PENALTIES

SEC. 810. (a) Whoever buys, sells, offers for sale, uses, transfers, takes or gives in exchange, or pledges or gives in pledge, except as authorized in this title or in regulations made pursuant thereto, any stamp, coupon, ticket, book, or other device, prescribed by the Commissioner of Internal Revenue under section 807 for the collection or payment of any tax imposed by this title, shall be fined not more than $1,000 or imprisoned for not more than six months, or both.

(b) Whoever, with intent to defraud, alters, forges, makes, or counterfeits any stamp, coupon, ticket, book, or other device prescribed by the Commissioner of Internal Revenue under section 807 for the collection or payment of any tax imposed by this title, or uses, sells, lends, or has in his possession any such altered, forged, or counterfeited stamp, coupon, ticket, book, or other device, or makes, uses, sells, or has in his possession any material in imitation of the material used in the manufacture of such stamp, coupon, ticket, book, or other device, shall be fined not more than $5,000 or imprisoned not more than five years, or both.

DEFINITIONS

SEC. 811. When used in this title—

(a) The term "wages" means all remuneration for employment, including the cash value of all remuneration paid in any medium other than cash; except that such term shall not include that part of the remuneration which, after remuneration equal to $3,000 has been paid to an individual by an employer with respect to employment during any calendar year, is paid to such individual by such employer with respect to employment during such calendar year.

(b) The term "employment" means any service, of whatever nature, performed within the United States by an employee for his employer, except—

(1) Agricultural labor;

(2) Domestic service in a private home;

(3) Casual labor not in the course of the employer's trade or business;

(4) Service performed by an individual who has attained the age of sixty-five;

(5) Service performed as an officer or member of the crew of a vessel documented under the laws of the United States or of any foreign country;

(6) Service performed in the employ of the United States Government or of an instrumentality of the United States;

(7) Service performed in the employ of a State, a political subdivision thereof, or an instrumentality of one or more States or political subdivisions;

(8) Service performed in the employ of a corporation, community chest, fund, or foundation, organized and operated exclusively for religious, charitable, scientific, literary, or educational purposes, or for the prevention of cruelty to children or animals, no part of the net earnings of which inures to the benefit of any private shareholder or individual.

Title IX—Tax on Employers of Eight or More

imposition of tax

Section 901. On and after January 1, 1936, every employer (as defined in section 907) shall pay for each calendar year an excise tax, with respect to having individuals in his employ, equal to the following percentages of the total wages (as defined in section 907) payable by him (regardless of the time of payment) with respect to employment (as defined in section 907) during such calendar year:

(1) With respect to employment during the calendar year 1936 the rate shall be 1 per centum;

(2) With respect to employment during the calendar year 1937 the rate shall be 2 per centum;

(3) With respect to employment after December 31, 1937, the rate shall be 3 per centum.

CREDIT AGAINST TAX

SEC. 902. The taxpayer may credit against the tax imposed by section 901 the amount of contributions, with respect to employment during the taxable year, paid by him (before the date of filing his return for the taxable year) into an unemployment fund under a State law. The total credit allowed to a taxpayer under this section for all contributions paid into unemployment funds with respect to employment during such taxable year shall not exceed 90 per centum of the tax against which it is credited, and credit shall be allowed only for contributions made under the laws of States certified for the taxable year as provided in section 903.

CERTIFICATION OF STATE LAWS

SEC. 903. (a) The Social Security Board shall approve any State law submitted to it, within thirty days of such submission, which it finds provides that—

(1) All compensation is to be paid through public employment offices in the State or such other agencies as the Board may approve;

(2) No compensation shall be payable with respect to any day of unemployment occurring within two years after the first day of the first period with respect to which contributions are required;

(3) All money received in the unemployment fund shall immediately upon such receipt be paid over to the Secretary of the Treasury to the credit of the Unemployment Trust Fund established by section 904;

(4) All money withdrawn from the Unemployment Trust Fund by the State agency shall be used solely in the

[472]

payment of compensation, exclusive of expenses of administration;

(5) Compensation shall not be denied in such State to any otherwise eligible individual for refusing to accept new work under any of the following conditions: (A) If the position offered is vacant due directly to a strike, lockout, or other labor dispute; (B) if the wages, hours, or other conditions of the work offered are substantially less favorable to the individual than those prevailing for similar work in the locality; (C) if as a condition of being employed the individual would be required to join a company union or to resign from or refrain from joining any bona fide labor organization;

(6) All the rights, privileges, or immunities conferred by such law or by acts done pursuant thereto shall exist subject to the power of the legislature to amend or repeal such law at any time.

The Board shall, upon approving such law, notify the Governor of the State of its approval.

(b) On December 31 in each taxable year the Board shall certify to the Secretary of the Treasury each State whose law it has previously approved, except that it shall not certify any State which, after reasonable notice and opportunity for hearing to the State agency, the Board finds has changed its law so that it no longer contains the provisions specified in subsection (a) or has with respect to such taxable year failed to comply substantially with any such provision.

(c) If, at any time during the taxable year, the Board has reason to believe that a State whose law it has previously approved, may not be certified under subsection (b), it shall promptly so notify the Governor of such State.

UNEMPLOYMENT TRUST FUND

SEC. 904. (a) There is hereby established in the Treasury of the United States a trust fund to be known as the "Unemployment Trust Fund," hereinafter in this title called the

"Fund." The Secretary of the Treasury is authorized and directed to receive and hold in the Fund all moneys deposited therein by a State agency from a State unemployment fund. Such deposit may be made directly with the Secretary of the Treasury or with any Federal reserve bank or member bank of the Federal Reserve System designated by him for such purpose.

(b) It shall be the duty of the Secretary of the Treasury to invest such portion of the Fund as is not, in his judgment, required to meet current withdrawals. Such investment may be made only in interest bearing obligations of the United States or in obligations guaranteed as to both principal and interest by the United States. For such purpose such obligations may be acquired (1) on original issue at par, or (2) by purchase of outstanding obligations at the market price. The purposes for which obligations of the United States may be issued under the Second Liberty Bond Act, as amended, are hereby extended to authorize the issuance at par of special obligations exclusively to the Fund. Such special obligations shall bear interest at a rate equal to the average rate of interest, computed as of the end of the calendar month next preceding the date of such issue, borne by all interest-bearing obligations of the United States then forming part of the public debt; except that where such average rate is not a multiple of one-eighth of 1 per centum, the rate of interest of such special obligations shall be the multiple of one-eighth of 1 per centum next lower than such average rate. Obligations other than such special obligations may be acquired for the Fund only on such terms as to provide an investment yield not less than the yield which would be required in the case of special obligations if issued to the Fund upon the date of such acquisition.

(c) Any obligations acquired by the Fund (except special obligations issued exclusively to the Fund) may be sold at the market price, and such special obligations may be redeemed at par plus accrued interest.

(d) The interest on, and the proceeds from the sale or re-demption of, any obligations held in the Fund shall be credited to and form a part of the Fund.

(e) The Fund shall be invested as a single fund, but the Secretary of the Treasury shall maintain a separate book account for each State agency and shall credit quarterly on March 31, June 30, September 30, and December 31, of each year, to each account, on the basis of the average daily balance of such account, a proportionate part of the earnings of the Fund for the quarter ending on such date.

(f) The Secretary of the Treasury is authorized and directed to pay out of the Fund to any State agency such amount as it may duly requisition, not exceeding the amount standing to the account of such State agency at the time of such payment.

ADMINISTRATION, REFUNDS, AND PENALTIES

SEC. 905. (a) The tax imposed by this title shall be col-lected by the Bureau of Internal Revenue under the direction of the Secretary of the Treasury and shall be paid into the Treasury of the United States as internal-revenue collections. If the tax is not paid when due, there shall be added as part of the tax interest at the rate of one-half of 1 per centum per month from the date the tax became due until paid.

(b) Not later than January 31, next following the close of the taxable year, each employer shall make a return of the tax under this title for such taxable year. Each such return shall be made under oath, shall be filed with the collector of internal revenue for the district in which is located the principal place of business of the employer, or, if he has no principal place of business in the United States, then with the collector at Baltimore, Maryland, and shall contain such information and be made in such manner as the Commissioner of Internal Revenue, with the approval of the Secretary of the Treasury, may by regulations prescribe. All provisions of law (including penalties) applicable in respect to the taxes imposed by section 600 of the Revenue Act of 1926, shall, insofar as not inconsistent with this title, be applicable in respect of the tax imposed by this title. The Commissioner may extend the time for filing the return of the tax imposed by this title, under such rules and regulations as he may prescribe with the approval of the Secretary of the Treasury, but no such extension shall be for more than sixty days.

(c) Returns filed under this title shall be open to inspection in the same manner, to the same extent, and subject to the same provisions of law, including penalties, as returns made under Title II of the Revenue Act of 1926.

(d) The taxpayer may elect to pay the tax in four equal installments instead of in a single payment, in which case the first installment shall be paid not later than the last day prescribed for the filing of returns, the second installment shall be paid on or before the last day of the third month, the third installment on or before the last day of the sixth month, and the fourth installment on or before the last day of the ninth month, after such last day. If the tax or any installment thereof is not paid on or before the last day of the period fixed for its payment, the whole amount of the tax unpaid shall be paid upon notice and demand from the collector.

(e) At the request of the taxpayer the time for payment of the tax or any installment thereof may be extended under regulations prescribed by the Commissioner with the approval of the Secretary of the Treasury, for a period not to exceed six months from the last day of the period prescribed for the payment of the tax or any installment thereof. The amount of the tax in respect of which any extension is granted shall be paid (with interest at the rate of one-half of 1 per centum per month) on or before the date of the expiration of the period of the extension.

(f) In the payment of any tax under this title a fractional part of a cent shall be disregarded unless it amounts to one-half cent or more, in which case it shall be increased to 1 cent.

APPENDIX

INTERSTATE COMMERCE

Sᴇᴄ. 906. No person required under a State law to make payments to an unemployment fund shall be relieved from compliance therewith on the ground that he is engaged in interstate commerce, or that the State law does not distinguish between employees engaged in interstate commerce and those engaged in intrastate commerce.

DEFINITIONS

Sᴇᴄ. 907. When used in this title—

(a) The term "employer" does not include any person unless on each of some twenty days during the taxable year, each day being in a different calendar week, the total number of individuals who were in his employ for some portion of the day (whether or not at the same moment of time) was eight or more.

(b) The term "wages" means all remuneration for employment, including the cash value of all remuneration paid in any medium other than cash.

(c) The term "employment" means any service, of whatever nature, performed within the United States by an employee for his employer, except—

(1) Agricultural labor;

(2) Domestic service in a private home;

(3) Service performed as an officer or member of the crew of a vessel on the navigable waters of the United States;

(4) Service performed by an individual in the employ of his son, daughter, or spouse, and service performed by a child under the age of twenty-one in the employ of his father or mother;

(5) Service performed in the employ of the United States Government or of an instrumentality of the United States;

(6) Service performed in the employ of a State, a political subdivision thereof, or an instrumentality of one or more States or political subdivisions;

[477]

(7) Service performed in the employ of a corporation, community chest, fund, or foundation, organized and operated exclusively for religious, charitable, scientific, literary, or educational purposes, or for the prevention of cruelty to children or animals, no part of the net earnings of which inures to the benefit of any private shareholder or individual.

(d) The term "State agency" means any State officer, board, or other authority, designated under a State law to administer the unemployment fund in such State.

(e) The term "unemployment fund" means a special fund, established under a State law and administered by a State agency, for the payment of compensation.

(f) The term "contributions" means payments required by a State law to be made by an employer into an unemployment fund, to the extent that such payments are made by him without any part thereof being deducted or deductible from the wages of individuals in his employ.

(g) The term "compensation" means cash benefits payable to individuals with respect to their unemployment.

RULES AND REGULATIONS

SEC. 908. The Commissioner of Internal Revenue, with the approval of the Secretary of the Treasury, shall make and publish rules and regulations for the enforcement of this title, except sections 903, 904, and 910.

ALLOWANCE OF ADDITIONAL CREDIT

SEC. 909. (a) In addition to the credit allowed under section 902, a taxpayer may, subject to the conditions imposed by section 910, credit against the tax imposed by section 901 for any taxable year after the taxable year 1937, an amount, with respect to each State law, equal to the amount, if any, by which the contributions, with respect to employment in such taxable year, actually paid by the taxpayer under such law before the date of filing his return for such taxable year, is exceeded by whichever of the following is the lesser—

(1) The amount of contributions which he would have been required to pay under such law for such taxable year if he had been subject to the highest rate applicable from time to time throughout such year to any employer under such law; or

(2) Two and seven-tenths per centum of the wages payable by him with respect to employment with respect to which contributions for such year were required under such law.

(b) If the amount of the contributions actually so paid by the taxpayer is less than the amount which he should have paid under the State law, the additional credit under subsection (a) shall be reduced proportionately.

(c) The total credits allowed to a taxpayer under this title shall not exceed 90 per centum of the tax against which such credits are taken.

CONDITIONS OF ADDITIONAL CREDIT ALLOWANCE

SEC. 910. (a) A taxpayer shall be allowed the additional credit under section 909, with respect to his contribution rate under a State law being lower, for any taxable year, than that of another employer subject to such law, only if the Board finds that under such law—

(1) Such lower rate, with respect to contributions to a pooled fund, is permitted on the basis of not less than three years of compensation experience;

(2) Such lower rate, with respect to contributions to a guaranteed employment account, is permitted only when his guaranty of employment was fulfilled in the preceding calendar year, and such guaranteed employment account amounts to not less than $7\frac{1}{2}$ per centum of the total wages payable by him, in accordance with such guaranty, with respect to employment in such State in the preceding calendar year;

[479]

(3) Such lower rate, with respect to contributions to a separate reserve account, is permitted only when (A) compensation has been payable from such account throughout the preceding calendar year, and (B) such account amounts to not less than five times the largest amount of compensation paid from such account within any one of the three preceding calendar years, and (C) such account amounts to not less than 7½ per centum of the total wages payable by him (plus the total wages payable by any other employers who may be contributing to such account) with respect to employment in such State in the preceding calendar year.

(b) Such additional credit shall be reduced, if any contributions under such law are made by such taxpayer at a lower rate under conditions not fulfilling the requirements of subsection (a), by the amount bearing the same ratio to such additional credit as the amount of contributions made at such lower rate bears to the total of his contributions paid for such year under such law.

(c) As used in this section—

(1) The term "reserve account" means a separate account in an unemployment fund, with respect to an employer or group of employers, from which compensation is payable only with respect to the unemployment of individuals who were in the employ of such employer, or of one of the employers comprising the group.

(2) The term "pooled fund" means an unemployment fund or any part thereof in which all contributions are mingled and undivided, and from which compensation is payable to all eligible individuals, except that to individuals last employed by employers with respect to whom reserve accounts are maintained by the State agency, it is payable only when such accounts are exhausted.

(3) The term "guaranteed employment account" means a separate account, in an unemployment fund, of contributions paid by an employer (or group of employers) who

(A) guarantees in advance thirty hours of wages for each of forty calendar weeks (or more, with one weekly hour deducted for each added week guaranteed) in twelve months, to all the individuals in his employ in one or more distinct establishments, except that any such individual's guaranty may commence after a probationary period (included within twelve or less consecutive calendar weeks), and

(B) gives security or assurance, satisfactory to the State agency, for the fulfillment of such guaranties, from which account compensation shall be payable with respect to the unemployment of any such individual whose guaranty is not fulfilled or renewed and who is otherwise eligible for compensation under the State law.

(4) The term "year of compensation experience," as applied to an employer, means any calendar year throughout which compensation was payable with respect to any individual in his employ who became unemployed and was eligible for compensation.

Title X—Grants to States for Aid to the Blind

APPROPRIATION

Section 1001. For the purpose of enabling each State to furnish financial assistance, as far as practicable under the conditions in such State, to needy individuals who are blind, there is hereby authorized to be appropriated for the fiscal year ending June 30, 1936, the sum of $3,000,000, and there is hereby authorized to be appropriated for each fiscal year thereafter a sum sufficient to carry out the purposes of this title. The sums made available under this section shall be used for making payment to States which have submitted, and had approved by the Social Security Board, State plans for aid to the blind.

STATE PLANS FOR AID TO THE BLIND

Sec. 1002. (a) A State plan for aid to the blind must (1) provide that it shall be in effect in all political subdivisions

[481]

of the State, and, if administered by them, be mandatory upon them; (2) provide for financial participation by the State; (3) either provide for the establishment or designation of a single State agency to administer the plan, or provide for the establishment or designation of a single State agency to supervise the administration of the plan; (4) provide for granting to any individual, whose claim for aid is denied, an opportunity for a fair hearing before such State agency; (5) provide such methods of administration (other than those relating to selection, tenure of office, and compensation of personnel) as are found by the Board to be necessary for the efficient operation of the plan; (6) provide that the State agency will make such reports, in such form and containing such information, as the Board may from time to time require, and comply with such provisions as the Board may from time to time find necessary to assure the correctness and verification of such reports; and (7) provide that no aid will be furnished any individual under the plan with respect to any period with respect to which he is receiving old-age assistance under the State plan approved under section 2 of this Act.

(b) The Board shall approve any plan which fulfills the conditions specified in subsection (a), except that it shall not approve any plan which imposes, as a condition of eligibility for aid to the blind under the plan—

(1) Any residence requirement which excludes any resident of the State who has resided therein five years during the nine years immediately preceding the application for aid and has resided therein continuously for one year immediately preceding the application; or

(2) Any citizenship requirement which excludes any citizen of the United States.

PAYMENT TO STATES

SEC. 1003. (a) From the sums appropriated therefor, the Secretary of the Treasury shall pay to each State which has an approved plan for aid to the blind, for each quarter, beginning with the quarter commencing July 1, 1935, (1) an amount, which shall be used exclusively as aid to the blind, equal to one-half of the total of the sums expended during such quarter as aid to the blind under the State plan with respect to each individual who is blind and is not an inmate of a public institution, not counting so much of such expenditure with respect to any individual for any month as exceeds $30, and (2) 5 per centum of such amount, which shall be used for paying the costs of administering the State plan or for aid to the blind, or both, and for no other purpose.

(b) The method of computing and paying such amounts shall be as follows:

(1) The Board shall, prior to the beginning of each quarter, estimate the amount to be paid to the State for such quarter under the provisions of clause (1) of subsection (a), such estimate to be based on (A) a report filed by the State containing its estimate of the total sum to be expended in such quarter in accordance with the provisions of such clause, and stating the amount appropriated or made available by the State and its political subdivisions for such expenditures in such quarter, and if such amount is less than one-half of the total sum of such estimated expenditures, the source or sources from which the difference is expected to be derived, (B) records showing the number of blind individuals in the State, and (C) such other investigation as the Board may find necessary.

(2) The Board shall then certify to the Secretary of the Treasury the amount so estimated by the Board, reduced or increased, as the case may be, by any sum by which it finds that its estimate for any prior quarter was greater or less than the amount which should have been paid to the State under clause (1) of subsection (a) for such quarter, except to the extent that such sum has been applied to make the amount certified for any prior quarter greater

[483]

or less than the amount estimated by the Board for such prior quarter.

(3) The Secretary of the Treasury shall thereupon, through the Division of Disbursement of the Treasury Department and prior to audit or settlement by the General Accounting Office, pay to the State, at the time or times fixed by the Board, the amount so certified, increased by 5 per centum.

OPERATION OF STATE PLANS

SEC. 1004. In the case of any State plan for aid to the blind which has been approved by the Board, if the Board, after reasonable notice and opportunity for hearing to the State agency administering or supervising the administration of such plan, finds—

(1) that the plan has been so changed as to impose any residence or citizenship requirement prohibited by section 1002 (b), or that in the administration of the plan any such prohibited requirement is imposed, with the knowledge of such State agency, in a substantial number of cases; or

(2) that in the administration of the plan there is a failure to comply substantially with any provision required by section 1002 (a) to be included in the plan;

the Board shall notify such State agency that further payments will not be made to the State until the Board is satisfied that such prohibited requirement is no longer so imposed, and that there is no longer any such failure to comply. Until it is so satisfied it shall make no further certification to the Secretary of the Treasury with respect to such State.

ADMINISTRATION

SEC. 1005. There is hereby authorized to be appropriated for the fiscal year ending June 30, 1936, the sum of $30,000, for all necessary expenses of the Board in administering the provisions of this title.

APPENDIX

DEFINITION

Sec. 1006. When used in this title the term "aid to the blind" means money payments to blind individuals.

Title XI—General Provisions

DEFINITIONS

Section 1101. (a) When used in this Act—

(1) The term "State" (except when used in section 531) includes Alaska, Hawaii, and the District of Columbia.

(2) The term "United States" when used in a geographical sense means the States, Alaska, Hawaii, and the District of Columbia.

(3) The term "person" means an individual, a trust or estate, a partnership, or a corporation.

(4) The term "corporation" includes associations, joint-stock companies, and insurance companies.

(5) The term "shareholder" includes a member in an association, joint-stock company, or insurance company.

(6) The term "employee" includes an officer of a corporation.

(b) The terms "includes" and "including" when used in a definition contained in this Act shall not be deemed to exclude other things otherwise within the meaning of the term defined.

(c) Whenever under this Act or any Act of Congress, or under the law of any State, an employer is required or permitted to deduct any amount from the remuneration of an employee and to pay the amount deducted to the United States, a State, or any political subdivision thereof, then for the purposes of this Act the amount so deducted shall be considered to have been paid to the employee at the time of such deduction.

(d) Nothing in this Act shall be construed as authorizing any Federal official, agent, or representative, in carrying out any of the provisions of this Act, to take charge of any child over the objection of either of the parents of such child, or of the person standing in loco parentis to such child.

RULES AND REGULATIONS

SEC. 1102. The Secretary of the Treasury, the Secretary of Labor, and the Social Security Board, respectively, shall make and publish such rules and regulations, not inconsistent with this Act, as may be necessary to the efficient administration of the functions with which each is charged under this Act.

SEPARABILITY

SEC. 1103. If any provision of this Act, or the application thereof to any person or circumstance, is held invalid, the remainder of the Act, and the application of such provision to other persons or circumstances shall not be affected thereby.

RESERVATION OF POWER

SEC. 1104. The right to alter, amend, or repeal any provision of this Act is hereby reserved to the Congress.

SHORT TITLE

SEC. 1105. This Act may be cited as the "Social Security Act."

Approved, August 14, 1935.

INDEX

[487]

W

Wagner Industrial Disputes Act, 94, 138, 256

Wagner-Lewis Bill, 1934, 11, 21*ff*., 37, 48, 49
1935, 49–51, 84*ff*.
hearings on, 95–99
House debate on, 108*ff*.
House report on, 100–108
Senate Debate on, 116*ff*.
Senate report on, 110*ff*.

Wagner-Peyser Act, 32, 210–211, 325

Wagner, Senator Robert, 21, 84, 95

Welfare grants, 92–94

Willcox, A. W., 388*n*.

Winant, John G., 227

Wisconsin Act, 15, 16, 113

Witte, Edwin E., 26, 27, 95, 155, 388*n*.

Wolman, Leo, 13*n*.

Y

Yoder, Dale, 15*n*., 63*n*.

ᗺ

DATE DUE